The Sacred & the Digital

The Sacred & the Digital: Critical Depictions of Religions in Video Games

Special Issue Editor

Frank G. Bosman

MDPI • Basel • Beijing • Wuhan • Barcelona • Belgrade

Special Issue Editor
Frank G. Bosman
Tilburg University
The Netherlands

Editorial Office
MDPI
St. Alban-Anlage 66
4052 Basel, Switzerland

This is a reprint of articles from the Special Issue published online in the open access journal *Religions* (ISSN 2077-1444) from 2018 to 2019 (available at: https://www.mdpi.com/journal/religions/special_issues/video_games)

For citation purposes, cite each article independently as indicated on the article page online and as indicated below:

LastName, A.A.; LastName, B.B.; LastName, C.C. Article Title. *Journal Name* **Year**, *Article Number*, Page Range.

ISBN 978-3-03897-830-5 (Pbk)
ISBN 978-3-03897-831-2 (PDF)

Cover image courtesy of pexels.com user Jamie McInal.

Contents

About the Special Issue Editor

Frank G. Bosman, Dr., senior researcher at Tilburg Cobbenhagen Center, Tilburg University, The Netherlands. Bosman is specialized in cultural theology in general and in religion and digital games in particular. His latest book on this subject is: *Gaming and the Divine. A New Systematic Theology of Video Games* (Routledge: London, 2019).

Editorial

The Sacred and the Digital. Critical Depictions of Religions in Digital Games

Frank G. Bosman

Department of Systematic Theology and Philosophy, Tilburg University, 5037 AB Tilburg, The Netherlands; f.g.bosman@tilburguniversity.edu

Received: 17 January 2019; Accepted: 21 February 2019; Published: 22 February 2019

Abstract: In this editorial, guest editor Frank Bosman introduces the theme of the special issue on critical depictions of religion in video games. He does so by giving a tentative oversight of the academic field of religion and video game research up until present day, and by presenting different ways in which game developers critically approach (institutionalized, fictional and non-fictional) religions in-game, of which many are discussed by individual authors later in the special issue. In this editorial, Bosman will also introduce all articles of the special issue at hand.

Keywords: game studies; religion studies; games and religion studies; religion criticism

---

1. Introduction

Video game studies are a relative young but flourishing academic discipline. But within game studies, however, the perspective of religion and spirituality is rather neglected, both by game scholars and religion scholars. Although some fine studies have appeared, like *Halos & Avatars* (Detweiler 2010), *Godwired. Religion, ritual, and virtual reality* (Wagner 2012), *eGods. Faith versus fantasy in computer gaming* (Bainbridge 2013), *Of Games and God* (Schut 2013), *Playing with Religion in digital games* (Campbell and Grieve 2014), *Methods for Studying Video Games and Religion* (Sisler et al. 2018), and *Gaming and the Divine* (Bosman 2019), still little attention has been given to the depiction of religion, both institutionalized and privatized, both fantasy and non-fictional, deployed by game developers for their games' stories, aesthetics, and lore.

Video games have used religion as a source of inspiration since decades, while on very different levels and through different modes (Bosman 2016). Games have used religious themes, languages, images, symbolisms and the like to construct instant recognizable lores, characters and/or narratives (for example *DMC. Devil May Cry* or *Diablo III*), but also to stimulate the player to contemplate existential notions (for example *The Turing Test* or *The Talos Principle*) or invite them (sometimes even force them) to behave in a way traditionally associated with religion (for example *Bioshock Infinite*). In some instances, it has been argued that the act of gaming itself could be regarded a religious act in itself (Wagner 2012, Bosman 2019).

Two dedicated academic journals on religion and video games exist: *Gamenvironments* (since 2014), hosted by the universities of Bremen (Germany) and edited by Kerstin Radde-Antweiler (Bremen) and Zenia Zeiler (Helsinki); and *Online—Heidelberg Journal of Religions on the Internet* (from 2004 to 2010 and 2014 to present), hosted by the University of Heidelberg (Germany) and edited by Gregor Ahn and Tobias Knoll (both from Heidelberg as well). While *Online*'s scope is broader than just video games, they have published three dedicated issues on the subject: *Religion in digital games. Multiperspective and interdisciplinary approaches* (Heidbrink and Knoll 2014), *Religion in digital games reloaded. Immersion into the field* (Heidbrink et al. 2015) and *Religion in digital games respawned* (Heidbrink and Knoll 2016).

While religion can take different shapes in digital games (Bosman 2016), ranging from material and referential to reflexive and ritual, it is not necessarily true that game developers depict their in-game religions in a positive, confirming way, but ever so often games approach the topic critically and disavowingly, like for example *Far Cry 4* and *Bioshock Infinite*. The first depicts a clearly Christian-inspired violent doomsday sect, issuing a reign of religious terror on their environment, while the second criticizes the Christian roots of American exceptionalism (both games are discussed in this issue). The developers do not operate in a cultural void, but are tapping into a larger cultural criticism on the religion phenomenon in general. Richard Dawkins, the godfather of battle-ready New Atheism, for example, ends the preface of his famous *The God delusion* (Dawkins 2006, p. 5) as follows:

> If this book works as I intend, religious readers who open it will be atheists when they put it down. What presumptuous optimism! Of course, dyed-in-the-wool faith-heads are immune to argument, their resistance built up over years of childhood indoctrination using methods that took centuries to mature (whether by evolution or design).

And Dawkins isn't the only prominent thinker to link religion with violence. Atheist authors like Hitchens (2007), Harris (2004), and Stenger (2008) have suggested the same. They echo the chorus, made famous by John Lennon's song *Imagine*, that the world would definitely be a better place if there was "no religion too". And some developers seem to echo the same idea in their digital games.

The religion criticisms found in video games can be categorized as follows (Bosman 2019): religion as (1) fraud, aimed to manipulate the uneducated masses (for example *The Rise of the Tomb Raider*); as (2) blind obedience towards an invisible but ultimately non-existing deity/ies (for example *The Binding of Isaac*); as (3) violence against those who do not share the same set of religious rules (for example *Far Cry 5*); as (4) madness, a deranged alternative for logical reasoning (for example *Nier: Automata*); and as (5) suppression in the hands of the powerful elite to dominate and subdue the masses into submission and obedience (for example *Dishonored* and *Dishonored 2*).

The critical depictions of religion in video games by their developers is the focus of this special issue.

2. Contributions

The articles in this special edition of *Religions* are dedicated to the analysis of video games and religion, most of them concerning the critical use of (institutionalized) religion in video games. Many contributors opted to discuss individual games and game series, that feature religion critical content.

Jarell Paulissen focusses in his article 'The Dark Covenant' on *Halo: Combat Evolved*, *Halo 2*, and *Halo: Reach*, arguing that "the apparent dichotomy between humans portrayed as rational thinkers and the aliens presented as religious fanatics is too simplistic". Using Barbour (1989) idea of 'non-overlapping magisteria', he opts for the 'dialogue' model of interaction between religion and science as being present in the *Halo* series.

Heidi Rautalahti concentrated, in her article 'Disenchanting faith', on the three *Dishonored* installments (1, 2, and *The Death of Outsider*), and especially on the religious fractions featuring in the games: the Outsider, the order of The Abbey of the Everyman, and witch Delilah Copperspoon with her witch coven. Using Weber's (Weber [1922] 1978) three ideals of authority—charismatic, traditional, and legal—she demonstrates that all religious authorities in the game series are contested ones.

Jan Wysocki, in his 'Critique with limits', makes a stock-taking of all religious motives and themes in the game *Bioshock Infinite*, especially concerning the 'Church of Comstock'. *Infinite*, as the author judges, is "strangely vacillating between a biting liberal caricature of religiously fueled nationalism and a nod to widespread moderate mainstream values in which unusual religious movements are negatively portrayed".

Archibald van Wieringen and Frank Bosman analyse the intertextual relationship (Kristeva 1980) between the game *The Binding of Isaac* and the Biblical story by the same name. In their article 'I have faith in Thee, Lord', the demonstrate that McMillen's game starts as a rathe dull and obvious criticism on religion and/as child abuse, but is gradually developed into a rather neutral depiction of religion as a copying mechanism, cumulating in a surprising critique on the effects on children of their parents' (violent) divorce.

Other authors chose a more broader approach to the over-arching theme of games and religion criticism. Tobias Knoll, in his article 'Instant Karma', discusses the use of the original religious notion of 'karma' in modern video games, especially with regard to so-called 'morality systems' in digital games: systems that—implicitly or explicitly—judge the moral actions of the gamer, influencing the outcome of certain quests (missions) and/or the game's ending(s). Knoll used the game *Mass Effect 2* to show that such systems usually feature "strong elements of moral duality", as well as a "a strong notion of cause and effect".

Pavel Nosachev concentrates on the different ways "occult bricolage", a "play with themes and images from the sphere of Western esotericism", is conceived in the game *Gray Matter*. He differentiates between the three in-game answers, all incarnated in an in-game character. And Javier Gil-Gimeno, Celso Sánchez-Capdequí, and Josetxo Beriain argue that digital football games, like *FIFA 17* and *FIFA 18*, "creates meaning, and succeeded throughout two main processes such as the sportification and progressive rationalization of violence". In their article 'Play, game, and videogame', the authors compare two ideal types, the Dionysian-Messi versus the Apollonian-Ronaldo.

In 'Thing greater than thou' argue Lars De Wildt, Stef Aupers, Cindy Krassen, and Iulia Coanda that "modern technology (computers, AI, VR, androids) itself is becoming a sacred object of veneration in fiction, specifically post-apocalyptic games that imagine man-made annihilation," and showcase such with the help of the game *Fallout 3* and *Horizon: Zero Dawn*. Such game stories, as the authors suggest, "reflect developments in real life, in which technology such as artificial intelligence is feared as an increasingly powerful, opaque force."

A last category of authors concentrated on the idea of religion and world-building. Mark Wolf argues in his 'Contemplation, subcreation, and video games' that "religious and theological ideas can be made manifest in video games, including the appearance of religion and religious iconography within video games and through the playing of video games as a potentially religious activity, especially contemplative ones that vicariously place the player in a different environment". As examples he uses games like *Cyan's Myst, Riven, Journey,* and *Everything*.

And Connie Veugen, in her article 'Stay your blade' introduces Klastrup and Tosca's elements of transmedial worlds (Klastrup and Tosca 2004): "Mythos, the lore of the world, the central knowledge necessary to interpret and successfully interact with events in the world; Topos, the setting and detailed geography of the world; and Ethos, the explicit and implicit ethics and (moral) codex of behaviour." With the help of the *Assassin's Creed* series, it becomes clear that "the transmedial world uses different media to expand the Mythos of the series, while, on the other hand, the Ethos of the storyworld influences player decisions in the game world."

I want to express my gratitude towards all the contributors to this special issue, as well to Mildred Chen and Jie Gu from the *Religions* Editorial Office, who were so helpful in the whole realization of the issue.

Funding. This research received no external funding.

Conflicts of Interest: The author declares no conflict of interest.

Digital Games:
Arkane Studios. 2012. *Dishonored*. Bethesda Softworks.
Arkane Studios. 2016. *Dishonored 2*. Bethesda Softworks.
Arkane Studios. 2017. *Dishonored. Death of the Outsider*. Bethesda Softworks.
Bethesda Game Studios. 2008. *Fallout 3*. Bethesda Softworks.
BioWare. 2010. *Mass Effect 2*. Electronic Arts.
Blizzard Entertainment. 2012. *Diablo III*. Blizzard Entertainment.
Bulkhead Interactive. 2016. *The Turing Test*. Square Enix.
Bungie. 2001. *Halo: Combat Evolved*. Microsoft Game Studios.

Bungie. 2004. *Halo 2*. Microsoft Game Studios.
Bungie. 2010. *Halo: Reach*. Microsoft Game Studios.
Croteam. 2014. *The Talos Principle*. Devolver Digital.
Crystal Dynamics. 2015. *Rise of the Tomb Raider*. Square Enix.
Cyan. 1993. *Myst*. Brøderbund.
Cyan. 1997. *Riven*. Brøderbund.
David OReilly. 2017. *Everything*. Double Fine Productions.
EA Vancouver. 2016. *FIFA 17*. EA Sports.
EA Vancouver. 2017. *FIFA 18*. EA Sports.
Guerilla Games. 2017. *Horizon Zero Dawn*. Sony Interactive Entertainment.
id Software. 1992. Wolfenstein 3D. Spear of Destiny. FormGen.
id Software. 1992. *Wolfenstein 3D*. Apogee Software.
Irrational Games. 2013. *Bioshock Infinite*. 2K Games.
Nicalis. 2014. *The Binding of Isaac. Rebirth* edition. Nicalis.
Ninja Theory. 2013. *DmC. Devil May Cry*. Capcom.
PlatinumGames. 2017. *Nier: Automata*. Square Enix.
ThatGameCompany. 2015. *Journey*. Sony Computer Entertainment.
Ubisoft Montreal. 2007. *Assassin's Creed*. Rennes: Ubisoft Montreal.
Ubisoft Montreal. 2008. *Far Cry 2*. Ubisoft Montreal.
Ubisoft Montreal. 2009. *Assassin's Creed II*. Rennes: Ubisoft Montreal.
Ubisoft Montreal. 2010. *Assassin's Creed: Brotherhood*. Rennes: Ubisoft Montreal.
Ubisoft Montreal. 2011. *Assassin's Creed: Revelations*. Rennes: Ubisoft Montreal.
Ubisoft Montreal. 2012. *Assassin's Creed III*. Rennes: Ubisoft Montreal.
Ubisoft Montreal. 2013. *Assassin's Creed IV: Black Flag*. Rennes: Ubisoft Montreal.
Ubisoft Montreal. 2013. *Assassin's Creed Rogue*. Rennes: Ubisoft Sopfia.
Ubisoft Montreal. 2014. *Assassin's Creed Unity*. Rennes: Ubisoft Montreal.
Ubisoft Montreal. 2014. *Far Cry 4*. Ubisoft Montreal.
Ubisoft Montreal. 2015. *Assassin's Creed Syndicate*. Rennes: Ubisoft Quebec.
Ubisoft Montreal. 2017. *Assassin's Creed Origins*. Rennes: Ubisoft Montreal.
Ubisoft Montreal. 2018. *Far Cry 5*. Ubisoft Montreal.
Wizard Box. 2010. *Gray Matter*. dtp entertainment.

References

Bainbridge, William. 2013. *eGod. Faith versus Fantasy in Computer Gaming*. New York: Oxford University Press.
Barbour, Ian G. 1989. *Religion in an Age of Science*. London: SCM.
Bosman, Frank. 2016. The Word Has Become Game: Researching Religion in Digital Games. *Online—Heidelberg Journal of Religions on the Internet* 11: 28–45.
Bosman, Frank. 2019. *Gaming and the Divine. A New Systematic Theology of Video Games*. London: Routledge.
Campbell, Heidi, and Gregory Grieve, eds. 2014. *Playing with Religion in Digital Games*. Bloomington: Indiana University.
Dawkins, Richard. 2006. *The God Delusion*. London: Black Swan.
Detweiler, Craig, ed. 2010. *Halos and Avatars. Playing Video Games with God*. Louisville: Westminster John Knox Press.
Harris, Sam. 2004. *The End of Faith. Religion, Terror, and the Future of Reason*. New York: W.W. Norton & Company.
Heidbrink, Simone, and Tobia Knoll, eds. 2014. Religion in Digital Games. Multiperspective and Interdisciplinary Approaches [=Online. Heidelberg Journal of Religion on the Internet 5]. Available online: https://heiup.uni-heidelberg.de/journals/index.php/religions/issue/view/1449 (accessed on 12 February 2019).
Heidbrink, Simone, and Tobias Knoll, eds. 2016. Religion in Digital Games Respawned [=Online. Heidelberg Journal of Religion on the Internet 10]. Available online: https://heiup.uni-heidelberg.de/journals/index.php/religions/issue/view/2354 (accessed on 12 February 2019).

Heidbrink, Simone, Tobias Knoll, and Jan Wysocki, eds. 2015. Religion in Digital Games Reloaded. Immersion into the Field [=Online. Heidelberg Journal of Religion on the Internet 7]. Available online: https://heiup. uni-heidelberg.de/journals/index.php/religions/issue/view/1937 (accessed on 12 February 2019).

Hitchens, Christopher. 2007. *God is not Great. How Religion Poisons Everything*. New York: Twelve.

Klastrup, Lisbeth, and Susana Tosca. 2004. Transmedial Worlds—Rethinking Cyberworld Design. Paper Presented at the 2004 International Conference on Cyberworlds, Tokyo, Japan, November 18–20; pp. 409–16.

Kristeva, Julia. 1980. *Desire in Language: A Semiotic Approach to Literature and Art*. Edited by Leon Roudiez. New York: Columbia University Press.

Schut, Kevin. 2013. *Of Games and God. A Christian Exploration of Video Games*. Grand Rapids: Brazos Press.

Sisler, Vit, Kerstin Radde-Antweiler, and Xenia Zeiler, eds. 2018. *Methods for Studying Video Games and Religion*. New York: Routledge.

Stenger, Victor. 2008. *God. The Failed Hypothesis. How Science Shows that God Does Not Exist*. Amherst: Prometheus Books.

Wagner, Rachel. 2012. *Godwired. Religion, Ritual and Virtual Reality*. London: Routledge.

Weber, Max. 1978. *Economy and Society*, 4th ed. Berkeley: University of California Press, pp. 241–44. First published 1922.

Article

Stay Your Blade

Connie Veugen

Faculty of Humanities, Vrije Universiteit Amsterdam, De Boelelaan 1105,
1081 HV Amsterdam, The Netherlands; jil.veugen@vu.nl

Received: 14 June 2018; Accepted: 28 June 2018; Published: 3 July 2018

Abstract: In their article 'Transmedial worlds: Rethinking cyberworld design', Klastrup and Tosca show that the core elements of a Transmedial World are: Mythos, the lore of the world, the central knowledge necessary to interpret and successfully interact with events in the world; Topos, the setting and detailed geography of the world; and Ethos, the explicit and implicit ethics and (moral) codex of behaviour. Though other terms are used, in essence similar distinctions are made in game worlds and storyworlds. In this article, I will first discuss the game world and the storyworld and show that the storyworld in games is different from that in non-interactive narrative media. I then focus on the Mythos and Ethos elements in the world of the *Assassin's Creed* series as both govern the moral choices in the series and, by doing so, subtly direct the behaviour of the player.

Keywords: transmediality; transmedia storytelling; game worlds; storyworlds; transmedial worlds; Mythos; Ethos; *Assassin's Creed*

1. Introduction

In 2003, Henry Jenkins wrote "A good character can sustain multiple narratives and thus lead to a successful movie franchise. A good 'world' can sustain multiple characters (and their stories) and thus successfully launch a transmedia franchise" (Jenkins 2003a, §13). Jenkins' observation was made in the context of convergence culture and transmedia storytelling. However, storyworlds are also an important part of games, especially MMORPG's (Massively Multiplayer Online Role-Playing Games), such as *World of Warcraft*. According to Klastrup and Tosca (2004, p. 410), "the exploration activity that cyberworlds [games] allow for is a very substantial advantage over other media when trying to bring a world to life". In the same article 'Transmedial Worlds: Rethinking cyberworld design', Klastrup and Tosca show that the core elements of a Transmedial World are: Mythos, the lore of the world, the central knowledge necessary to interpret and successfully interact with events in the world; Topos, the setting and detailed geography of the world; and Ethos, the explicit and implicit ethics and (moral) codex of behaviour. In this article, I want to specifically look into the Mythos and Ethos of the transmedial world of the *Assassin's Creed* series as both govern the moral choices in the series. Before I do so, I will first explain the concepts transmedia storytelling and transmediality. Next, I will explain game worlds and storyworlds and argue that games of progression,[1] or story-structured games (Veugen 2011), are a sort of amalgam of the two. This part will frame Klastrup and Tosca's transmedial world and its main parts of Mythos, Topos, and Ethos. Finally, I will show how the *Assassin's Creed* series uses both Mythos and, especially, Ethos to influence the player's (moral) choices.

---

[1] In his 2005 book *Half-real: Video Games between Real Rules and Fictional Worlds*, Jesper Juul distinguishes between Games of Emergence, i.e., games where the outcome is determined by the built-in rules, and Games of Progression, where the designer determines the sequence of events.

2. Transmedia Storytelling and Transmediality

Any text that addresses narrativity has to acknowledge that narratives are medium-dependent. As (Hutcheon 2013) showed, a written narrative operates in a different mode (telling) than an audio-visual narrative (showing) or a participatory narrative (interacting).[2] This is also called medium specificity. In the telling mode (books), the reader has to create the visual world herself; in the showing mode (film, television), the visual world is already presented; and in the participatory mode, the player moves through the already imagined visual world (games). The medium that is used limits the kinds of stories that can be told and the way they are told. According to Marie-Laure Ryan, the choice of medium even influences why a story is told (Ryan and Thon 2014). With the rise of convergence culture[3] (Jenkins 2006) in the last decade of the 20th Century, narratives began to defy classical Aristotelian linearity and closure and to challenge the limits of the book, film, and game, resulting in new formal patterns and new aesthetics that surpass the individual medium (Ndalianis 2005). Or, as Jenkins puts it: More and more, storytelling has become the art of world building, as artists create compelling environments that cannot be fully explored or exhausted within a single work or even a single medium (Jenkins 2006, p. 114). Such a polycentric open structure that employs different media demands an audience that is not only willing but also capable of piecing together the different storylines which are dispersed over different media texts. In Jenkins' words, modern audiences have become: "hunters and gatherers moving back across the various narratives trying to stitch together a coherent picture from the dispersed information" (Jenkins 2007, 8). Purposefully dispersing a narrative over different media was dubbed transmedia storytelling by (Jenkins 2006). However, as the term transmedia storytelling is still emerging, it is currently being defined differently for diverse purposes. In the context of the narratives discussed here, transmedia storytelling:

> […] represents a process where integral elements of a fiction get dispersed systematically across multiple delivery channels for the purpose of creating a unified and coordinated entertainment experience. Ideally, each medium makes its own unique contribution to the unfolding of the story.

> (Jenkins 2007, p. 1)

Transmedia storytelling and transmediality are often confused, but it should be pointed out that transmediality is a broader term than transmedia storytelling. Strictly speaking, transmedia just means 'across media'. In the theoretical context of narratology, intertextuality, and intermediality, transmedial concepts and transmedial phenomena usually denote concepts/phenomena that are not media-specific, such as a specific motif, discourse, or aesthetic (Rajewski 2005). In the context of storyworlds, transmedia denotes "the representation of a single storyworld through multiple media" (Ryan and Thon 2014, p. 14); for instance, the world of *The Lord of the Rings* or *Harry Potter*. It should be noted that although both these examples are transmedial, i.e., there are books, films, games, and, in the case of *Harry Potter*, even a theme park, these examples are not transmedia storytelling as each distinct medium basically tells the same story.

3. Game World, Storyworld, and Transmedial World

As Henry Jenkins observed, "most often, transmedia stories are based not on individual characters or specific plots but rather complex fictional worlds which can sustain multiple interrelated characters and their stories" (Jenkins 2007, p. 3). This holds true both for transmedial narratives, regardless

---

2   This does not mean that the first two modes (telling and showing) are not interactive, but as Hutcheon says "the move to participatory modes in which we also engage physically with the story and its world—whether it be in a violent action game or a role-playing or puzzle/skill testing one—is not more active but certainly active in a different way" (Hutcheon 2013, p. 23).

3   By the end of the 20th century, most media corporations have become global with interests in multiple media, e.g., books, films, comic books, games, theme parks, etc. cf. *Harry Potter*.

of whether these narratives stem from books (*A Song of Ice and Fire*), films (*Star Wars*), or games (*Tomb Raider*), and for transmedia storytelling (*Assassin's Creed*). It also holds true for single media franchises,[4] especially for games, as exploring the virtual world of the game and trying to unravel its rules is an integral part of gameplay, especially in adventure and action adventure games.

According to the *Encyclopaedia of Video Games*, many games "can be said to have a diegetic world, that is, the imaginary or fictional world in which the world's characters live and where events take place" (Wolf 2012, p. 692). This is the world of the computer game, in short, the game world. As the *Encyclopaedia* further points out, this world is usually created to back a narrative, but this does not necessarily have to be the case. Many games of emergence, such as *The Sims*, are also supported by a world. The game world consists at least of the following elements: some kind of space, inhabitants consisting of the player's character or avatar and program-controlled nonplayer characters (NPCs), and finally 'rules' that 'define' the consequences in the game world following actions either instigated by the player or emanating from the game world (Wolf 2012). These consequences are usually consistent so that the player can learn to anticipate the outcome, especially when consequences affect herself. According to Jesper Juul, this educational aspect is a fundamental aspect of games, as a player approaches every game with whatever repertoire of game skills he or she has, and then improves these skills in the course of playing the game (Juul 2005, p. 5). Game worlds are particularly important to (action) adventure games, as the exploration of the game world and the secrets it holds is an integral part of pursuing the critical path or accomplishing the critical goal the player has to achieve (Samsel and Wimberley 1998, p. 22).

Storyworlds derive from narrative theory. Marie-Laure Ryan (Ryan 1991) describes storyworlds as "mental models of who did what to and with whom, when, where, why, and in what fashion in the world to which the interpreters relocate" (in Herman et al. 2005, p. 270). The reader uses these mental models to comprehend the narrative in question by attempting to reconstruct the world, its occupants, objects, actions, and events. In that sense, storyworlds are quite immersive: "more than reconstructed timelines and inventories of existents [see below], then, storyworlds are mentally and emotionally projected environments in which interpreters are called upon to live out complex blends of cognitive and imaginative response" (ibid.). In 2014, Ryan adapted this concept of storyworlds into a media-conscious form that covers multimodal and transmedial texts. The rules of such a storyworld are contained within the separate media texts, whether these consist of a single medium or of multiple media, and it is the task of the reader/viewer/player to unravel them, or as Marie-Laure Ryan puts it: "The reader [...] of a narrative fiction has consequently no choice but to construct a world image in which the text is true" (Ryan and Thon 2014, p. 34).

According to Ryan (Ryan and Thon 2014), storyworlds consist of at least six components:

1. *Existents*, i.e., the characters and the objects that have special significance for the plot.
2. *Settings*, i.e., the space in which the existents are located.
3. *Physical laws*, i.e., the principles that determine what can and cannot happen in the world.
4. *Special rules and values*, i.e., principles that determine the obligations of the characters.
5. *Events*, i.e., the causes of the changes that happen in the time span of the narrative.
6. *Mental events*, i.e., how the individual characters react to both actual and perceived events.

For the reading and viewing mode, this set of six components makes sense. However, as I already pointed out, games convey their stories interactively. To do this, I would like to argue, they use both the game world as well as the storyworld, where the game world is not just a mental model, but also a represented world with its own modalities. For the above-mentioned components, this implies that at least one if the *existents* is the player character or the player's avatar. This is not the only way in which

---

4   Although in light of our present convergence culture it is only a matter of time before such franchises will also expand their storyworld into other media.

the existents in games differ from those in other, non-interactive, media. Where in books and films[5] other existents serve the plot, in games, some are significant for the plot and others are there for the gameplay. Using (Egenfeldt-Nielsen et al. 2013)'s four categories of in-game characters, I would say that, apart from the obvious role of the player character(s), the cast characters are there specifically for the plot, the functional characters for the gameplay, and the stage characters for ambience. As far as the 'special objects' are concerned, where in films these are usually highlighted and receive camera focus, in games, they are often hidden and the player has to actively locate them (Veugen 2011).

As for the space in which the existents are located, as I have pointed out elsewhere (Veugen 2011) space in games is different from space in other media because games are the only medium where we can 'move through' the digital environment, and, equally important, can interact with it.[6] Consequently, the settings and physical laws of the storyworld are not just a given, as in books or films; the game world is explored actively. That is to say, in games, the player's choices are always confined by the (physical) laws (rules) of the game that dictate how the world functions. Sometimes these rules can be baffling, e.g., that you can always whistle for a new horse in *Red Dead Redemption* even though your own faithful companion has just been mauled by a couple of mountain lions. However, in the context of *Red Dead Redemption's* game world, it is important that the player is always able to flee a dangerous situation; consequently, she can always whistle for a horse. Designers employ several techniques to help the player navigate the game world; for instance, by using literary repertoire, a term coined by (Iser 1980) to represent anything that the reader/viewer/player already may know from other media texts, social norms, or historical events. Examples are, for instance, using familiar architecture (Adams 2003) or evocative game spaces (Jenkins 2003b).[7] Despite the fact that these techniques are not medium-specific (we find them in books and films as well), for the player they are more relevant as her success or failure depends on them.

The special rules and values again are different because they influence the player's choices. In narrative games, actions should be meaningful (Murray 1999) and as interactors we not only should *see* the results of our decisions and choices, but we should also understand their consequences. Therefore, it can be argued that the special rules and values of the storyworld are more important for a player than for a reader or viewer because they can affect gameplay. For instance, in the 1993 *Legend of Zelda* game *Link's Awakening*, the player can steal a weapon from a shop instead of paying for it. At first, the consequences seem minor (the NPCs will call the player "Thief"). However, when the player returns to the same shop, the shop owner now has gained the ability to kill her. I will return to the special rules and values when discussing the Ethos of the *Assassin's Creed* storyworld.

Events in games are also different in the sense that player characters may have no choice but to undergo the event itself, but, once the event is triggered, the player will then choose how to react. In *Gabriel Knight: Sins of the Fathers*, the protagonist Gabriel (the player character) cannot prevent the scripted event in which his love interest Malia falls into a pit of molten lava. However, the player's next action determines how the game ends. She either rescues Malia and Gabriel lives, or she decides to sacrifice Malia in order to put an end to Malia's evil ancestor spirit Tetelo. When the player chooses the latter option, Gabriel also dies. As many story-structured games follow Joseph Campbell's classic mono-myth, they usually start with a major event (the "call to adventure") that not only prompts the player into action but also motivates her (initial) choices. For instance, in the second *Assassin's Creed* game, the main motivation is revenge. It is triggered by the hanging of the protagonist's father and brothers despite a promise that their arrests were an error that would be righted in time. As the main structure of the game is quite linear,[8] the player has no other choice

---

5 I use the terms books and films as placeholders for respectively the reading mode and the viewing mode. Of course, these modes represent different types of media.
6 Of course, theme parks are also interactive, but I would argue that their narratives are emergent.
7 For instance, real world places that evoke a particular atmosphere, such as New Orleans or Transylvania.
8 See Veugen 2011.

but to kill the betrayer. This is different in *Red Dead Redemption*, where the trigger event has taken place before the start of the game (the kidnapping of the protagonist's wife and children) and where the underlying structure allows for many different actions (Veugen 2011). In fact, when the player does not read the back story or has not seen the game's introductory trailer, there is nothing in the opening sequence, 'Exodus in America', a fifteen-minute cutscene, that informs the player about the protagonist's motivation. The first part of the sequence introduces the storyworld in word and image in which stage characters talk about religion and how the native Americans (the "savages") have been 'saved'. In the next part, the protagonist is taken to an old fort and although his guide (a functional character) asks a lot of questions, the protagonist is not very forthcoming, which prompts the comment "You are not very talkative, are you". Even when he has reached his destination, the player can only deduce from the conversation that the protagonist is there to get the bandit Bill Williamson (a cast character) to accompany him to town (allegedly to save him).

Finally, mental events, i.e., how the individual characters react to the events, are, of course, also different in that they should be separated into the mental events of the player, which are not visible but which can affect gameplay, the mental events of the player character as shown through cutscenes, which can influence the player as she identifies with the character, and the mental events of cast characters that may also influence the choices the player makes.

4. Mythos, Ethos, and Topos

The storyworld, as proposed by Klastrup and Tosca, is a transmedial world, i.e., an abstract content system that is medium-independent and from which "a repertoire of fictional stories and characters can be actualized or derived across a variety of media forms" (Klastrup and Tosca 2004, p. 409). The world has a number of distinguishing traits that both users and designers recognize as part of its 'worldness'. These traits usually stem from the first initiation of the storyworld, which Klastrup and Tosca refer to as the 'ur-world'. Not all originating worlds become transmedial worlds; only worlds that attract a following can expand either through the designers of the 'ur-world' or through the fan community. Klastrup and Tosca compare the transmedial world to another medium-independent system, that of genre as described in literary and film theory.[9] Genre is also a system of traits that came into being interchangeably and involved both the production as well as the reception context of the media texts (Bordwell and Thompson 2001). Genre is part of the repertoire of the community needed to decode texts. The same goes for the transmedial world. It is both the task of the designers and of the fans to ensure that a new expansion to or actualisation of the world adheres to the abstract content system which both parties agree on. Of course, for games this content system has long since existed and is referred to as *the lore* of the game world. As the many online discussions of, especially, online game worlds, e.g., *World of Warcraft*, show, fans take the 'correctness' of the world very seriously. In *Assassin's Creed*, for instance, the fans for a long time did not recognize the graphic novels as part of the transmedial world set out by the games, despite the fact that they were referred to in official game trailers and adhere to the Mythos, Topos, and Ethos of the world. As the transmedial world expands, it is critical that the consistency of the world is maintained. In games, this is often achieved by the so-called Game Bible. Before the release of *Assassin's Creed III* in 2011, Ubisoft had to call on the fan community to help them 'reconstruct' the transmedial world of the franchise. This resulted in the first version of the *Assassin's Creed Encyclopaedia*.

---

[9] It should be noted that while the concept of genre may be seen as being medium-agnostic, its interpretation/application is medium-specific.

Mythos, Topos, and Ethos[10] are, according to Klastrup and Tosca, the core elements that every transmedial world contains. They call the Mythos "the backstory of all backstories: the central knowledge one needs to have in order *to interact with or interpret events in the world* successfully" (Klastrup and Tosca 2004, p. 412). The characters, founding conflicts, and battles originate from the Mythos as well as lore items and creatures that are unique to the world. The Topos is the world's setting, in which both the rendering of the space as well as a sense of history are important. Finally, the Ethos tells the reader/viewer/player how to behave in the world. What is accepted and what is not? What is considered in character and what not? Ethos is both explicit and implicit, and the more familiar the reader/viewer/player is with the transmedial world the easier it will be to adhere to its moral codex. Klastrup and Tosca use several transmedial worlds to explain the three core elements. The first and most obvious one is *The Lord of the Rings*. However, the transmedial world Tolkien created did not originate in the trilogy as Klastrup and Tosca suggest. Middle Earth's Mythos, its characters, races, creatures, history etc., stems from Tolkien's longing for England's own myths and legends, its own cosmology which England lost after the Norman Conquest (Shippey 1982). Middle Earth as Topos is clearly recognizable as Tolkien's England with Hobbiton as the ideal rural version that is under threat, just as Tolkien and his vision of England lost their pastoral innocence in the first World War. Additionally, although Tolkien's Ethos is based on the myths and legends of the Norse Edda and early Germanic and Welsh legends, his Ragnarök is profoundly Christian: the sacrificing of the one for the good of the all. It is a world that appeals to us all, but also a world that can be expanded in different media texts for different audiences in different times (Veugen 2005).

5. The Transmedial World of *Assassin's Creed*

As Klastrup and Tosca argue, the source of the transmedial world lies in the 'ur-text'. In the case of *Assassin's Creed*, this is the first game that was launched in 2007.[11] As we will see, all the core elements of the transmedial world were already in place as the game's designer Patrice Désilets saw the game as the start of a new game franchise (North 2015), where each game would centre around a different assassin from a different time period. As (Jenkins 2003a) explains, game worlds are spatial in nature and thus have an inherent 'worldness'. The authors in (Mulligan and Patrovsky 2003) show that, in order for games to work, they need some background to provide the player with a motivation to play; consequently, it can be determined that every game world starts with a Topos and Mythos. In the first *Assassin's Creed* game, the overall Topoi of the game series are introduced: a present-day game world (2012 in the first game) and a historic time period (1191 in the first game). The Mythos introduces us to the centuries-old conflict between the Templars and the Assassins, where the Assassins believe in free will, while the Templars believe in order. The Mythos also introduces us to special artefacts, the so-called Pieces of Eden, that have hidden properties. The main piece of Eden in the first game is an Apple of Eden with which the wielder can manipulate the will of others. These Pieces of Eden were created by the so-called First Civilization, the Isu or 'Those who came before', a super human race that once lived on earth. Another core element in the Mythos of *Assassin's Creed* is 'the Animus', a piece of equipment with which a modern-day member of the Assassins can access the genetic memories of his Ancestor Assassins. The Animus in question belongs to Abstergo Industries, the modern-day front for the Templars. They use the Animus to locate Pieces of Eden in

---

[10] Klastrup and Tosca explain that their concept of transmedial worlds is based on genre and adaptation theory. In a later article 'MMOGs and the Ecology of Fiction: Understanding LOTRO as Transmedial World' (Klastrup and Tosca 2009), they explain that their methodology follows the traditional humanistic aesthetic approach. The terms Mythos and Ethos stem from Aristotle's *Poetics* (Aristotle 1996), where Ethos is the moral or ethical character of the agent, an interpretation that in modern narrative theory more or less has the same meaning but now also denotes the values of a people, group, nation, etc. Mythos in Aristotle's view denoted the plot as a logical sequence of events, focusing on the actions of the characters rather than on the characters themselves and their myths as modern narrative theory does.

[11] In this article I will only discuss the *Assassin's Creed* texts (various media) that were launched between 2007 and 2017, up to the game *Assassin's Creed Origins*. The data stem from a close reading of the various media texts.

history to retrieve them in the present-day. The first game does not reveal why the Templars pursue the Pieces of Eden so relentlessly; the player only knows that it has something to do with the date 21 December 2012. The Mythos also introduces the two main protagonists, 25-year-old Desmond Miles, who has been kidnapped by Abstergo to get access to the genetic memories of his Assassin Ancestors, and 25-year-old Altaïr-Ibn-La'Ahad, the Ancestor Assassin whose memories are being accessed.

As the game is the first in a new franchise, initially conceived as six games centering around Desmond Miles and his Ancestor Assassins, the game not only introduces the player to the Mythos and Topos of the game world but also to the Ethos of the Assassins: The Creed. As in other games, the player has to identify with her game alter ego. In this case it is Altaïr, as 90% of the game takes place in the Animus. Despite his youth, at 25 Altaïr already is a master Assassin (of Arab descent[12]). As I have argued elsewhere (2014), Altaïr is not a true player character but an avatar. Consequently, he is more of an open book for the player to inhabit than a character the player has to identify with (as is the case with the later Assassins). Despite being an avatar, Altaïr's path is certainly recognizable as it is based on Joseph Campbell's Monomyth: *The Hero's Journey*. Consequently, the player, be it perhaps subconsciously, is already familiar with the basic premises. The 'call to adventure' takes place at the very beginning of the game when we find Altaïr in Solomon's Temple in Jerusalem, where he is send by his mentor to retrieve the Apple of Eden. Altaïr fails this mission and consequently is demoted to the lowest rank, an ideal situation for the player as she can now learn the Creed alongside Altaïr. To regain his status as master Assassin, Altaïr has to kill nine individuals who, as far as is known at this moment in the game, stand in the way of peace (the game takes place during the Third Crusade). As the hero of the game, the player expects that the adversaries she has to kill are enemies that deserve no better; after all, her mentor has ordered their deaths. In a sense, Altaïr is a foot soldier: he himself does not give the orders, he obeys them. Killing for the greater good. As long as he obeys the Creed, his actions are justifiable.

In 2018, it is hard to grasp the innovative concept that was realized in *Assassin's Creed*. At first, the game was planned as a spin-off game for the already successful game franchise *Prince of Persia* and to be called *Prince of Peria Assassins* (Machinima 2010). However, Ubisoft did not like the idea that a *Prince of Persia* title would not centre on the Prince but on his bodyguard. So, Désilets decided to create a totally new game. One of his ambitions was to create a game with believable crowds; however, the memory of the two popular consoles at the time, the PS2 and Xbox, only allowed for eight characters at a time (DidYouKnowGaming 2014). Therefore, the decision was made to design the game exclusively for the upcoming PS3. To realise their ambitious plans, the team developed a new game engine called Anvil, which ultimately meant that the game could not be released at the launch of the PS3 as originally planned (Machinima 2010). Still, Ubisoft used the delay to their advantage by preceding the launch with a clever and at times stunning marketing campaign that not only started to build the Mythos of *Assassin's Creed* but that also discussed the new gameplay. In the promotional video *Assassin's Creed Developer Diary #3: Freedom* (2007), Patrice Désilets talks about the fact that the game world of *Assassin's Creed* was designed to be completely interactive: "It was really important that the player could go anywhere and interact with everything" (Désilets 2007). The concept is referred to as a 'Flower Box' design:[13] "In which everything is well-placed in a narrative structure" (ibid.). This also means that the game world and the storyworld are interwoven, as Désilets emphasizes: "So everything that you can do with your freedom is basically driving the story forward" (ibid.). The interaction with the stage characters in the game world was designed to be intuitive, which was referred to as organic design or social stealth: "So if you start bumping people around in real life, you will probably have some cops after you. It is the same thing in our game, if you are running and

---

[12] In the game itself it is not clear; only later in the book *The Secret Crusade* (2011) we learn that Altaïr's mother was Christian and his father Muslim. As his mother died in childbirth, Altaïr effectively grew up with his father in the order of the Assassins (Veugen 2014).

[13] Instead of the usual Sandbox design of other open world games.

use your 'tackle move' after a while some soldiers will come and they will try to arrest you, but you have some blades and we will see what happens after that" (ibid.).

The apparently complete freedom of the game is not as free as Désilets' words suggest. Basically, the player has three choices to overcome barriers in the game world, which often take the form of opponents that block certain areas the player needs to access. The player can fight the opponents, she can use the surrounding architecture to try and enter another way, or she can use a group of 'scholars' to hide amongst and thus enter the area. To leave an area (especially after an assassination), she can fight her way out, again use the architecture, or she can hide amongst the scholars/crowd or in certain places until the alert has passed. Thus, she not only determines her gameplay and the skills she needs but she also creates her own version of Altaïr, his moral choices, and his path through the narrative. Strictly speaking, the choice is hers, but this is where the Ethos of the transmedial world steps in: The Creed of the Assassins, which consists of the following three tenets:

1. Stay your blade from the flesh of an innocent
2. Hide in plain sight
3. Never compromise the Brotherhood

If we apply these to the gameplay, we see that according to the Ethos the player only has one correct way to tackle these situations: do not fight (tenet 1), do not cause any commotion (tenet 3), but use the scholars to enter an area and the scholars/crowd/special places[14] to 'leave' (tenet 2), otherwise there will be consequences. These tenets and their consequences are built into the design of the game. When you kill an innocent bystander, the game warns the player and once you have killed too many, you get desynced from the animus and have to start again from your last save-point. In side missions, you can actively help people and be awarded with the protection of their fathers/husbands/brothers from the guards. The scholars you help offer you a human shield and thus you can pass unnoticed through guarded places. Additionally, by killing through stealth rather than brute force, the assassinations do not attract unnecessary attention to yourself and to the Brotherhood. In fact, when Altaïr fails to remain undetected he cannot enter an Assassin's bureau to obtain his next mission.[15]

In the first failed mission, Altaïr, who should know better as he was trained as an Assassin from an early age, breaks all three tenets. First, he kills an old man who he fears might alert others to his presence. Secondly, he does not hide, but pursues his adversary in plain sight, as a result of which he leads the enemy to the stronghold of the Assassins, thus jeopardizing the Brotherhood. Of course, this is a deliberate design choice so that the player along with Altaïr can start from scratch. As Altaïr is punished for his disobedience, the player learns the Creed:

Altaïr: I did as I was asked.

Mentor: No, you did as you pleased. Malik has told me of the arrogance you displayed, your disregard of our ways.

Altaïr: What are you doing [he is being held back by two fellow Assassins].

Mentor: There are rules, we are nothing if we do not abide by the Assassin's Creed. Three simple tenets which you seem to forget. I will remind you. First and foremost, stay your blade . . .

Altaïr: from the flesh of an innocent. I know [the mentor slaps him].

Mentor: And stay your tongue unless I give you leave to use it. If you are so familiar with this tenet then why did you kill the old man inside the temple? He was innocent, he did not need to

---

14 There are certain places in the gameworld, such as wells and haystacks, that the Assassin can use to hide. After a certain amount of time, the player character becomes anonymous and can leave the place safely.

15 An exception to the first tenet are bombs. In *Assassin's Creed Altaïr's Chronicles*, Altaïr has to use a bomb. In *Assassin's Creed Revelations*, lethal bombs are introduced to help the player overcome opponents in the game world, a gameplay device that became a standard element in the games. Obviously, a bomb is indiscriminate and will kill innocent bystanders as well.

die. Your insolence knows no bounds. Make humble your heart child or I swear I'll tear it from you with my own hands. The second tenet is that which gives us strength. Hide in plain sight. Let the people mask you such that you become one with the crowd. Do you remember? Because, as I hear it, you chose to expose yourself drawing attention before you struck. Third, and final tenet, the worst of all your betrayals. Never compromise the Brotherhood. Its meaning should be obvious. Your actions must never bring harm upon us, direct or indirect. Yet your selfish act beneath Jerusalem placed us all in danger. Worse still, you brought our enemy to our home. Every man we have lost today was lost because of you. I'm sorry, truly I am [he draws a dagger].

Altaïr: What?

Mentor: But I cannot abide a traitor.

Altaïr: I am NOT a traitor.

Mentor: Your actions indicate otherwise and so you leave me no choice. Peace be upon you Altaïr. [The Mentor stabs Altaïr with the dagger, fade to black]

In the next scene, it becomes clear that the stabbing was an illusion. Now that Altaïr (and the player) has been reminded of the Creed, the rules can be followed.

There is one other element in the Ethos of *Assassin's Creed* which is introduced in the first game: pickpocketing. In certain missions, Altaïr must intercept secret messages. To be able to do this, the player must follow the messenger closely and keep a button on the controller pressed while the messenger is still moving. If successful, the player will see Altaïr 'brush' the messenger, then the player should react quickly and move into the crowd. If the messenger stands still, he will detect Altaïr and shout, which alerts the guards. In the first *Assassin's Creed* game, pickpocketing is a specific game skill needed to fulfil these missions, and although pickpocketing in the later games can be used to steal money, it is also needed for successful gameplay, for instance to steal keys to gain access to restricted areas.

6. *Assassin's Creed* and Transmedia Storytelling

Assassin's Creed started off as a transmedial world. At first, the world was created to accommodate six games centering around Desmond Miles and six of his Ancestor Assassins. In accordance with Jenkins' explanation that "A good character can sustain multiple narratives and thus lead to a successful movie franchise. A good 'world' can sustain multiple characters (and their stories) and thus successfully launch a transmedia franchise" (Jenkins 2003a, §13), the world in *Assassin's Creed* was created to sustain the stories of multiple characters (six Assassins) instead of just being the backdrop to Desmond's story. It can be debated if this premise still holds true for the next games—*Altaïr's Chronicles*, which was published in 2008 for the Nintendo DS, and *Assassin's Creed Bloodlines* (2009) for the PSP—that do not include the modern-day Desmond part. As both are solely about Altaïr (the first a prequel and the latter a sequel to the first game), they are rather part of a game franchise than a transmedial world. This was soon amended when Ubisoft decided on a book series to accompany the main games so that members of the public that did not play the games could still get involved, starting with *Assassin's Creed Renaissance* (2009), the 'book version' of the Ancestor Assassin story of *Assassin's Creed II* (2009). The real first steps in transmedia storytelling[16] were taken with the release of the short film *Assassin's Creed: Lineage* (2009), which introduced the viewer to the main protagonist of the second *Assassin's Creed* game, Ezio Auditore da Firenze, and, more importantly, to the storyworld of *Assassin's Creed*

---

[16] The special edition of the first *Assassin's Creed* game came with a short comic that takes place in the storyworld of the first game (both the modern as well as the historic part) and adds to the story. However, as it is not separately available it is usually seen as a paratext rather than a part of the transmedial story. There is also a non-canonical Penny Arcade *Assassin's Creed* comic about Altaïr.

II.[17] Also, for the French-speaking market, the graphic novel *Assassin's Creed 1 Desmond* (2009) was published that expanded both Desmond's story as well as the Mythos of the Pieces of Eden.[18]

To date, there are 10 main games[19], 20 other games, 8 graphic novels, 6 comic books and 3 comic book series, 4 series of novels, 4 short animated movies, 1 short fiction film, 1 feature film, and rumours of an animated TV series in cooperation with Netflix.[20] Most of these media texts expand the Mythos of *Assassin's Creed* by introducing new artefacts, such as the Shrouds of Eden, which have healing and regenerative properties, other Apples, which are used to manipulate people, and the Swords of Eden that not only give the bearer great charisma, but also negate the effectiveness of illusions. A notable exception are the mobile adaptations of the main games, which are also different in that they only use the storyworld and gameworld of the Ancestor Assassins and not Desmond's present-day world. Other exceptions are the mobile (multiplayer) spin-off games, which are clearly designed to give the player new opportunities to explore the game world—again only that of the Ancestor Assassins—but do not add anything to the storyworld. The new Pieces of Eden that were and are still being introduced often have religious associations, such as the pontifical staff of Pope Alexander VI (Rodrigo de Borja), the sword of Jeanne d'Arc, the Shroud of Turin, or the Apple from the Garden of Eden. Others are associated with mythical objects, such as the Chrystal Skulls, Arthur's sword Excalibur, or the Golden Fleece. The transmedial texts also give more information on the ancient and very advanced humanoid species, the Isu, who made the Pieces of Eden and other cutting-edge technological devices. We learn that the Isu created the human race to serve them as slave labour. Additionally, even though the enmity between the Isu and the humans grew, over time, some Isu and humans formed attachments, resulting in human progeny with special DNA, the so-called Precursor DNA (the Assassins), which accounts for their special abilities, such as Eagle Vision.[21] In 75,000 BC, a global catastrophe destroyed most of the Isu and the humans as well as their civilization and the greater part of their technology. However, in the course of the Mythos, as was already shown in the first game, it becomes clear that the Isu and their Pieces of Eden continue to interfere with humankind.

Of the games that introduce new information, *Assassin's Creed II* (2009) is notable because for the first time the player is confronted with the Isu themselves who reveal the major elements of the Mythos. The Facebook game *Assassin's Creed Project Legacy* (2010–2012) introduced several new Ancestor Assassins and Pieces of Eden, so that players would have a better idea of the multi-game storyworld before playing *Assassin's Creed Brotherhood* (2010). The online game *Assassins' Creed Initiates* (2012–2013) brought the information introduced in the main games together, while adding new information as well, so that player fans were well-prepared for *Assassin's Creed III* (2012), as this game would mean the demise of Desmond and the solution to the 21 December 2012 enigma. This also brought a major change in the storyworld in that the main protagonist in the modern-day part, the character through which the player 'entered' both the game world and the storyworld of the Ancestor Assassin, was no longer there. For the gameworld, this meant that it was now the player herself who 'enters' the world as an employee of Abstergo[22], making the gameplay experience in theory more immersive. In the storyworld, the player cooperates with the Assassins.[23] Notable new elements that were added to the Mythos, especially in *Assassin's Creed Black Flag* (2013) and *Assassin's Creed Rogue* (2014), are Precursor

---

[17] See Veugen 2016.
[18] *Assassin's Creed 1: Desmond* as well as *Assassin's Creed 2: Aquilus* (2010) and *Assassin's Creed 3: Accipiter* (2011) are part of the so-called *The Ankh of Isis Trilogy* (bundled in 2013). As the modern-day part tells an alternative version of Desmond's story, this set of graphic novels is considered non-canonical by many fans.
[19] *Assassin's Creed III: Liberation* was first released as a PS Vita game and only later ported to the PS3, Xbox, and PC. As it only takes place in the Animus, it cannot be considered a main game. The next main game, *Assassin's Creed Odyssey*, is already announced.
[20] See Appendix A for the complete list.
[21] Eagle Vision allows the Assassins, for instance, to distinguish between enemies and targets.
[22] In *Assassin's Creed Project Legacy*, the player already was an employee of Abstergo, but now to gather information on Pieces of Eden and other Ancestor Assassins.
[23] The player is now addressed with the 'title' Initiate and her handler is an Assassin called Bishop.

Sites, i.e., First Civilization Temples: "We haven't found an apple, but... a tree. These Temples hold the earth together like roots. Disturb them, and Haiti falls or... Lisbon. Or any other place the Manuscript shows" as Shay Cormac, the protagonist of *Assassin's Creed Rogue*, explains; blood vials which can be used to spy on the donor as long as the person is still alive,[24] but which, of course, also contain the DNA of that person; and Sages, human incarnations of the Isu Atjah. Sages have triple DNA consisting of a significantly higher percentage of the First Civilization genome, which means that Sages have an extraordinary affinity with Pieces of Eden.

With *Assassin's Creed III*, Ubisoft stepped Transmedia Storytelling up a notch. Along with the game, Ubisoft published two comic books, *Assassin's Creed the Chain* (2010–2011) and *Assassin's Creed the Fall* (2012), where the reader is introduced to Assassin-turned-Templar Daniel Cross and his Ancestor Assassin Nikolai Orelov. Cross is Desmond's main antagonist in *Assassin's Creed III* and Orelov is the protagonist of the game *Assassin's Creed Chronicles: Russia* (2016). The Oliver Bowden books, which so far had been adaptations of the Ancestor Assassin part of the games, from then on were no longer adaptations[25] but became counterparts to the games, either telling the story from the point-of-view of a Templar (Haytham Kenway, the father of Ratonhnhaké:ton/Connor the protagonist of *Assassin's Creed III* in *Assassin's Creed Forsaken* (2012) and Élise de la Serre, the childhood friend and later love interest of Arno Dorian the protagonist of *Assassin's Creed Unity* in the book with the same title (2014)) or what happened before, i.e., the story leading up to the moment the game starts (in *Assassin's Creed Underworld* (2015) for the game *Assassin's Creed Syndicate* (2015)).[26] More recent comic books and fictional novels not only introduce *Assassin's Creed* to a younger generation, they also use the new elements of the Mythos while adding Precursor Artefacts, Templars, and Assassins of their own.

7. The Ethos of *Assassin's Creed's* Transmedial World

As for the Ethos, the three tenets of the Creed, the player/reader/viewer expects them to hold true for all Assassins, but obviously outside of the games they can only be part of the storyworld and not the game world. Still, as will be shown, some of the non-interactive media texts use the tenets while several of the main games do not.

7.1. The Main Games

Already in the second *Assassin's Creed* game the three tenets are not mentioned.[27] In the storyworld of the game this is logical because the game's protagonist Ezio Auditore da Firenze is not raised as an Assassin. Still, in the course of the game, Ezio learns the skills he needs but not through formal training. As Desmond's friend Lucy tells Desmond that he learns the skills of his Ancestor Assassins through the so-called bleeding effect of the Animus, so does the player learn the skills needed in the game world by following instructions given to Ezio. The first is new, and morally questionable. In the new game world of *Assassin's Creed II*, money has become a necessity as Ezio has to buy armor and weapons, pay for travel and healthcare, etc. However, when he starts off as a 17-year-old youth who gets in a brawl with the Pazzi family, he is wounded and needs medical care. As he does not have any money, his older brother encourages him to loot the men they have just beat up. This ability to loot will become one of the ways to obtain money, valuables, and (special) objects in the game world of *Assassin's Creed*, as will the looting of chests, which are strewn all over the game world. Interestingly, Ezio can loot chests in plain sight without any consequences, but this does not hold true

---

[24] Originally only by a Sage in the so-called Observatory through a specially prepared Chrystal Skull. However, as the game shows, the Skull also works outside the Observatory and does not require the presence of a Sage.

[25] Apart from the book *Assassin's Creed Black Flag*, I will come back to this when discussing the books.

[26] Before *Assassin's Creed III*, the Assassins, both in the games as well as in the graphic novels, had names related to birds of prey, e.g., Ezio which is translated 'Eagle'. Interestingly, in the recent film, this tradition is reinstated: Callum (=dove, not a bird of prey of course but a bird) and Aguilar (=Eagle).

[27] For the years of publication/release of the separate media texts see Appendix A.

for (dead) bodies. Looting bodies will be commented on by nearby stage characters. Looting bodies in front of guards is inadvisable as the player will immediately get in a fight; so, in essence, tenet 3 'Never compromise the Brotherhood' is still in place even though it is not literally mentioned in the game. This also holds true for the other two tenets, 1 'Stay your Blade' and 2 'Hide in plain sight'. The first tenet becomes evident as soon as Ezio has a blade and the player inadvertently kills a stage character. The game will comment "Ezio did not kill civilians". The next time it happens, the player is desynchronized. Ezio learns the second tenet when he is wanted for murder early on in the game and is brought to a house of courtesans. Here, he is taught how to blend in with a group of people to remain undetected. Additionally, instead of Altaïr's scholars, Ezio now befriends courtesans, thieves, and mercenaries whom he can hire to distract guards. So, even though the tenets are not explicitly mentioned, through the story Ezio learns them step-by-step once the storyworld (and/or the game world) calls for the particular skill. Ezio also has no Assassination contracts. As mentioned before, he wants revenge for the murder of his father and brothers. However, when he has killed the person he holds responsible, he finds out that more people were involved, and when he kills those, other names are revealed, driving the story and Ezio's quest forward. Every step of the way, Ezio and the player learn new skills or information while growing from a 17-year-old boy to a seasoned Assassin of age 39 years. This is when he finally confronts the head of the Templar Order Rodrigo Borgia, i.e., Pope Alexander VI. However, instead of killing him, the now wiser Ezio 'stays his blade'. Not that Borgia is innocent; he was the brain behind the murders, but the wiser Ezio recognizes that Borgia (as a Pope) is no longer a threat and that his son Cesare is much more dangerous to the Assassins' cause. This raises the question of whether Ezio has somehow learned the tenets 'off-screen' so to say. This could also explain an apparent discrepancy in the game. About mid-way through the game, Ezio is in pursuit of Jacomo de Pazzi. When he has found him, he does not go in for the kill but says: "If I can stay my blade long enough to follow him he'll lead me to his Templar brothers, I'll have more names for my list".[28] "Stay my blade" is not a random phrase: to use this exact phrase one has to know the tenets. Ezio is the protagonist in two other main games, *Brotherhood* and *Revelations*, in which he grows from a master Assassin to a mentor of fame. In these games, the tenets themselves hold true (with the same consequences as in *Assassin's Creed II*), but, as in *Assassin's Creed II*, they are not mentioned explicitly.[29] Particular to *Assassin's Creed Revelations* is that the game also 'retells' Altaïr's story as recorded by Altaïr himself on another First Civilization object, the Memory Seal.[30] Additionally, although the first disk recalls the storming of the Assassin stronghold after Altaïr failed to retrieve the Apple of Eden, his being reminded of the three tenets is not on the Seal.

The tenets are also not mentioned explicitly in a number of the main games with an Assassin protagonist that followed. In fact, starting with *Assassin's Creed III*, the protagonist/player can no longer kill civilians (at least not in hand-to-hand combat, however hard many players have tried).[31] There is an exception: the player can still (inadvertently) shoot civilians, which leads to the usual "X did not kill civilians" and desynchronization when another civilian is shot, but this seems to be an element of the game engine rather than a conscious design decision. The second tenet, 'Hide in plain sight', still works for all the Assassins even though they are not 'taught' to do so.[32] However, tenet 3,

---

[28] Of those who are responsible for the murder of his father and brothers.

[29] As a mentor Ezio does, however, uphold the tenets. There is a more covert reference to the tenets in *Revelations*. On the door to Altaïr's library, underneath the original Assassin stronghold in Masyaf, it states in Arabic "Revere the blood of the innocent" and "Hide in the midst of the crowd".

[30] As already mentioned, in the first game Altaïr is an avatar and not a character with a background story etc. The Seals, in a sense, repair this by telling Altaïr's life story, how he grew up, his travels, his research into the Apple of Eden, etc., thus turning the erstwhile avatar into a fully fledged character. This story can also be found in the book *Assassin's Creed The Last Crusade*. Ubisoft also included the first *Assassin's Creed* game for fans who had not played the game before.

[31] In the storyworld of *Assassin's Creed III*, Ratonhnhaké:ton is half Native American. His tribe, the Kanien'kehá:ka, show respect to all living creatures and that is why he does not kill (initially also not Templars).

[32] In most games, there are on-screen instructions. Apart from not being detected and becoming anonymous, hiding places are most often used for stealth assassinations.

'Never compromise the Brotherhood', only applies to specific games.[33] This has to do with the fact that starting with *Assassins Creed III*, the up-to-then black and white portrayal of the Assassins and the Templars is greatly nuanced and the Brotherhood of Assassins has been severely diminished so that Assassins, such as Ratonhnhaké:ton (*Assassin's Creed III*), Arno (*Assassin's Creed Unity*), and Jacob Fry (*Assassin's Creed Syndicate*), do not feel as obligated to the Creed as Altaïr or Ezio. Edward Kenway, protagonist of *Assassin's Creed Black Flag*, is a civilian first before he becomes a pirate and for a very short time a Templar. He takes on the role of an Assassin he has killed for personal gain. Becoming rich and a man of status is his motivation for most of the game. However, several Assassins and the Sage he meets remark that he has some Assassin powers. Only at the end of the game does Edward decide to work with the Assassins and finally become one of them.[34] Arno (*Assassin's Creed Unity*) is 'taught' the tenets of the Creed, but only after ca. one quarter of the game has already passed. From the ensuing gameplay it becomes clear that this time the tenets are only there for the story. At first, Arno obeys the mentor, but when his love Élise is threatened, he no longer waits for orders but takes matters into his own hands, even bringing Élise, who is a Templar, to the Assassin council.[35] Because he has not consulted with the Brotherhood on several occasions, Arno is expelled from the order for exposing the Brotherhood (tenet 3). Still, not attracting attention and becoming anonymous remain important elements in the game world and are at times still linked to the storyworld as well. When Jacob Fry helps Charles Darwin in *Syndicate* and Darwin suggests that he might help with the mission, Jacob replies: "Oh with all respect, mister Darwin, I believe I will proceed alone. After all, we wouldn't want to attract any unwanted attention".

As far as pickpocketing is concerned, all Assassins can still pickpocket but Jacob and Evie Fry only pickpocket to steal special objects; they do not steal from civilians. There is no explicit explanation why they cannot; it is merely suggested that they feel more a part of the people than a part of the Brotherhood.[36] All Assassins can also still loot, but when Arno loots commoners, the spoils are meagre (spoons, forks, etc.) in keeping with the poverty of the French people at the time of the revolution. That Jacob and Evie were tutored by an Assassin father becomes also clear in the combination of storyworld and game world. The game is situated in Victorian London. Like Ezio, they have helpers, this time in the form of the Rooks, a gang of street thugs that Jacob founded. They also get help from street urchins who, as in the original Sherlock Holmes stories, source information and from the historic policeman Frederick Abberline. When Evie or Jacob or both have assassinated someone, they dip a white handkerchief in the blood of their victim in a similar motion to the one Altaïr used to stain the feather he was given as a token of his contract.

However, that the tenets have become increasingly less important can also be seen from the missions, which often call for X number of kills of soldiers, guards, ship's crew, etc. to gain 100% completion. This translates into awards and credits, which not only determine the player's ranking on the overall leader board but also enable the player to buy extra skills or armour in the game. A glitch in *Assassin's Creed III* means that Ratonhnhaké:ton often faces groups of more than fifty soldiers in circumstances where the fighting itself then attracts even more soldiers, clearly violating the third

---

[33] In fact, *Assassin's Creed Black Flag* is the only game that at the very end mentions the Assassin's Creed bureau.

[34] The gameworld and gameplay of *Assassin's Creed Black Flag* is more like that of *Assassin's Creed II* than *Assassin's Creed III*, as Edward can again use 'courtesans' to lure guards away and has more opportunities to blend in with crowds and sit on benches to remain undetected while waiting for his assassination victim.

[35] When his father is murdered, Arno is adopted by the Templar Grand Master of the Parisian Rite, Élise's father. From the book *Unity* it becomes clear that Élise from an early age knows that he is an Assassin, even though Arno does not know yet. The game and the book are very much written to show that both in the ranks of the Assassins as well as the Templars there are traitors and there are those, like Élise's mother, who want to end the feud between the two groups.

[36] In the book it becomes clear that the Creed has been ingrained in them by their father Ethan. Evie is the true believer of the two. She often reminds Jacob of what their father would have said or wanted. Jacob is more a brawler and fights more openly, thus violating tenets 2 and 3, although the British Brotherhood has been greatly diminished and there is no Assassin's bureau in London. Evie and Jacob report to Henry Green, who, as can be found out in the book *Assassin's Creed Underground*, in fact is Jayadeep Mir, the son of Arbaz Mir (*Assassin's Creed Brahman* and *Forsaken*).

tenet. However, even without the glitch, it is very hard to stealth assassinate in *Assassin's Creed III*.[37] Obviously, these elements, which also can be found in other games, are solely added to make the game harder to play. It is part of the game world and not of the storyworld, thus gradually moving the games away from Désilets' original idea that everything the player does drives the story forward (2007).

This is less the case in *Assassins' Creed Rogue*, which is truer to the original design of the first *Assassin's Creed* games. As if to remind us, the game starts with the words:

> Stay my blade from the flesh of the innocent.
> Hide in plain sight.
> Never compromise the Assassin Brotherhood.
> These are the tenets of the Creed.
> The principles I used to live by.
> was a young man then.
> The Seven Years' War was about to begin.
> could not have imagined what the future had in store for me...
> Nor the cost I would choose to bear...
> My name is Shay Patrick Cormac.
> This is my story . . .

Shay starts off as an Assassin, but the American Assassins and their leader Achilles increasingly act against the tenets in Shay's eyes. When Shay is tasked to get a piece of Eden from a Precursor Temple in Lisbon he causes a massive earthquake, killing hundreds of innocent civilizations. When he confronts Achilles with the disaster, Achilles still perseveres with finding the other Temples. This makes Shay turn away from the Brotherhood. In the course of the game, it becomes clear that even though Shay eventually takes the side of the Templars he does this because he still truly believes in the first tenet: Assassins are there to protect normal people, not to let them suffer. Shay also shows compassion towards the people he kills. He kills because there is no other way; he does not kill out of spite, hatred, or any other negative emotion. However, because some of the people he has to kill are Assassins, the gameplay can be quite challenging as Shay and the Assassins share the same skillset, including tenet 2 'Hide in plain sight'. Interestingly, when Shay has left the Brotherhood and happens to kill a civilian, instead of the obligatory "Shay did not kill civilians" the game now warns that killing civilians will put bounty hunters on his track.

Apart from the interesting reversal from Assassin to Templar, which contributes to the already mentioned nuancing of the black and white opposition, *Assassin's Creed Rogue* is also a very important game not only because of the new insights gained in the Mythos of *Assassin's Creed*, but also because the game adds to Achilles' backstory,[38] filling in gaps left by *Assassin's Creed III*. It also shows Haytham Kenway as Templar Master of the Templar's Order of the Colonial Rite and his near destruction of the Colonial Brotherhood of Assassins. Finally, it reveals that Shay is responsible for the death of Arno's Assassin father, which is Arno's 'call to adventure' in *Assassin's Creed Unity*. Similar to the opening, *Assassin's Creed Rogue* ends with Shay's words, but now they are spoken as a Templar:

> Uphold the principles of our Order, and all that for which we stand.
> Never share our secrets nor divulge the true nature of our work.
> Do so until death—whatever the cost.
> This is my new creed. I am Shay Patrick Cormac.

---

[37] In *Black Flag* I have killed 3016 opponents to date. Of course, Edward is not an Assassin. Still, in the book his mother asks him "How many men have died at your hand, eh?" Edward does not reply directly "I looked at her. The answer, of course, was countless" (p. 428). This basically acknowledges that only killing a select number of opponents is no longer part of being an Assassin in the games, even though in the scene in the book his mother disowns Edward publicly for his deeds.

[38] Amongst others reconfirming why Achilles calls Ratonhnhaké:ton Connor.

Templar of the Colonial... of the American Rite.

am an older man now, and perhaps wiser.

war and a revolution have ended, and another is about to begin.

May the Father of Understanding guide us all."[39]

7.2. The Mobile and Online Games

Of the mobile games, only those with new content are interesting. These are *Assassin's Creed Altaïr's Chronicles*, *Assassin's Creed Bloodlines*, *Assassin's Creed III Discovery*, *Assassin's Creed Liberations*, and the three *Assassin's Creed Chronicles* games: China, India, and Russia. The first two games have Altaïr as protagonist. *Chronicles* is a side-scrolling game and uses text boxes instead of speech. Although the game's story is credible as a prequel dated one year before the main game, the gameplay is not, especially the fact that you have to kill civilians to get their clothes. Apparently, the makers, Gameloft, were not aware of the tenets. More importantly, the restricted game world of the side-scroller did not call for a storyworld element to direct the player. The gameworld of the PSP game *Assassin's Creed Bloodlines* is very similar to that of the main game. The game includes a 'New game tutorial' that not only shows the button combinations for the various actions, it also teaches the player the three tenets, although they are somewhat rephrased:

Please note that following the assassin's creed,

your ancestor's way of life, will assist you with staying in sync.

The Creed consists of three tenets.

First: Never hurt an innocent person.

Second: Always be discreet.

Third: Do not compromise the clan.

Should you lose sync, you can restore synchronization

by reviewing key moments of your ancestor's life

or by respecting the creed.

So, similar to the main game, the player is instructed on how to 'behave' in the open-world setting of the game.

Assassin's Creed III Discovery is again a side scrolling game, with a similarly restricted game world as *Altaïr's Chronicles*. The gameplay is based mostly on combat. Hiding places are available but they serve as elements for stealth combat. In the tutorial, the player is taught the important moves the player character can make, but the tenets are not mentioned. In the game, which takes place in the storyworld of the main game 15 years after the murder of Ezio's father and brothers, Ezio mentions that his thirst for vengeance is still strong, but that his responsibility to the Assassin Brotherhood is stronger. In the game, you are constantly killing or dodging opponents and navigating and exploring the game world, which presents itself as a puzzle with switches and hidden passages. This reinforces the idea that the tenets are not necessary due to the game world restrictions of side-scrolling games.

The game world of the PS Vita game *Assassin's Creed Liberation* is very similar to that of the main games, and like the other mobile games, only uses the Ancestor part. The Ancestor in question (the Assassin player character) is Aveline de Grand Pré. She is not taught the tenets explicitly, but they still apply. Like the Assassins in the earlier main games, she can kill innocents, but will get the obligatory warning "Aveline did not kill civilians" and desync should it happen again. She can loot (dead) bodies—in fact, it is part of a mission—but as it is forbidden in the storyworld she cannot do so when guards are around. Pickpocketing is not only still possible, it is also a game skill, e.g., to collect

---

[39] "May the Father of Understanding guide us all" is part of the 'Creed' of the Templars. Note Shay's correction in line five: first he says Colonial (=Assassins) then he corrects it in American (=Templar). This basically reveals that even at the end of his life Shay still thinks of himself as an Assassin.

voodoo dolls.[40] The touchscreen of the PS Vita gives pickpocketing an extra dimension. As for the most recent *Chronicles* Games, they are interesting but mostly from a transmedia storytelling point of view as they link several of the already existing media texts.[41] The games are again fast-paced side-scrolling games, so even though the game world includes looting, at least in *Assassin's Creed Chronicles Russia*, you hardly bother. All three games have soldiers, guards, Templars, etc. but no real civilians, so accidentally killing those does not happen. However, in *Assassin's Creed Chronicles India*, for the first mission, the player is warned that: "This mission is different though. There are no Templars to deal with, only innocent [palace] guards who, under the Assassin's mantra, cannot be harmed".

The Facebook game *Assassin's Creed Project Legacy* was more of a turn-based strategy game where the player was an employee of Abstergo tasked with sifting through memories collected from different Assassins. In this way, the game did really expand the Mythos and Topos of the transmedial world. As such, the game world could not be set up as a flower box; it had to adhere to just texts and pictures. Most players thought of themselves as friends or even recruits of the Assassin Brotherhood, which was enhanced by the fact that Abstergo at times questioned the players to test their loyalty. Added to that, a mysterious character named Erudito used social media and actual 'Abstergo' merchandise to help the fan community to access deeper levels of the Abstergo mainframe. Unfortunately, the promised *Project Legacy 2.0* was never launched, but thanks to Erudito the players did get access to the last set of videos. Even though *Project Legacy* did not have a regular player character, one of the memories recounts the life of the Assassin Perotto Calderon, who was sent by Ezio to spy on the Borgias. He compromised the Brotherhood by falling in love with Lucrezia Borgia and had a son with her, Giovanni. As the child was sickly and deformed, Perotte stole a Shroud of Eden in the hope of curing the child, killing several of his fellow Assassins in the process, in all this violating tenet 3. The online game *Assassin's Creed Initiates* was an alternate reality game where the players both competed but also worked together to solve puzzles set in the storyworld of *Assassin's Creed* in the lead up to *Assassin's Creed III*. To solve some of the clues, the hive mind of the collective was needed as each player brought his or her own set of knowledge to the task. The game also had a world map and a time line, both of which were needed to solve the second part of the game. This even involved players going to actual locations to report to the community what could be found there.

7.3. The Books

Here, I will limit myself to the Oliver Bowden books as these are the ones that are the most closely linked to the games. The books are not participatory as they only involve the storyworld as discussed by Ryan. In discussing the books, I will again only focus on the tenets, as these form the basis of the Ethos of the Assassin storyworld.

In Ezio's storyworld, *Assassins Creed Renaissance* (the adaptation of the ancestor part of *Assassin's Creed II*), *Assassin's Creed Brotherhood*, and Ezio's part of *Revelations*, the tenets are not mentioned in concurrence with the games.[42] As already explained, *Revelations* is different as it also includes Altaïr's memory seals. There are two references to the Creed here; both are directly linked to the Assassins. Firstly, when Altaïr wants to burn the body of their mentor, his former friend Abbas protests: "But this is not our way! To burn a man's body is forbidden!" and blames Altaïr saying: "All your life you have made a mockery of the Creed! You bend the rules to suit your whims, while belittling and humiliating those around you!" This causes a fight among the Assassins when Altaïr shouts:

---

[40] Voodoo Dolls are only part of the game world. The reward for collecting all of them is a special outfit.

[41] Most notably the short animated film *Assassin's Creed Embers*, where Shao Jun, the protagonist of the *China Chronicles*, seeks out Ezio and receives a Precursor Box which features in all three *Chronicles* games.

[42] Even though the Ezio books are adaptations, they do all contain new parts as well. In *Renaissance*, they are relatively small, but in *Brotherhood* Ezio also goes to Spain to look for Cesare Borgia. In the mobile game *Discovery*, Ezio also travels to Spain but for a different reason. In *Revelations*, we learn what happened after *Brotherhood* and why Ezio travels to Constantinople. Then, his story from the game is told. However, the book ends with Ezio's last days as told in the short animated film *Embers*.

"Brothers ... Stop! Stay your blades!" (p. 222). When after many years, Altaïr returns to the Assassins' stronghold, he finds that many of the Assassins have turned from the Creed:

> You say these men are cruel,' said Altaïr. 'Has any man raised his blade
> against an innocent?' 'Alas, yes,' Cemal replied. 'Brutality seems to be
> their sole source of pleasure.' 'Then they must die, for they have
> compromised the Order,' said Altaïr. 'But those who still live by the
> Creed must be spared.' (p. 309).

Alongside *Revelations*, Oliver Boden also published *Assassin's Creed The Secret Crusade*. As this book tells Altaïr's life story, turning the erstwhile avatar in a true character, it also contains the passage about the three tenets. However, as it is a book, we also get Altaïr's thoughts, which puts a different light on the character of Altaïr: "There are rules. We are nothing if we do not abide by the Assassin's Creed. Three simple tenets, which you seem to forget. I will remind you. First and foremost: stay your blade ... ' It was to be a lecture. Altaïr relaxed, unable to keep the note of resignation from his voice as he finished Al Mualim's sentence. ' ... from the flesh of an innocent. I know.'"[43]

Assassin's Creed Black Flag begins with Edward's 'call to adventure', the reason he goes to sea and initially joins the crew of a privateer. The next two parts and most of part four tell the story of the game, adding his voyage back to England and explaining the premises of *Assassin's Creed Forsaken*. The book is interesting form a transmedial storytelling point of view because it links the storyworld of the games *Black Flag*, *Assassin's Creed III*, and *Syndicate* and the book *Assassin's Creed Forsaken*. It should be noted that the book much earlier than the game shows Edward's sympathy for the Assassins. In the first part of the book, which is not in the game, Edward is thwarted by a man wearing a ring with the symbol of a cross. The imprint of the ring is left on his face when the man hits him. When Edward is recruited into the Templar order he is given a similar ring and it dawns on him that it is the same ring the mysterious man was wearing, the man who not only struck him but also burned down his father's farmstead: "And suddenly I was thinking that whatever squabbles these people had with the Assassins, then, well, I was on the side of the Assassins." (p. 194).

Assassin's Creed Forsaken tells Haytham Kenway's life story from his own point of view. Like the *Black Flag* book, it includes part of the game as well. As Haytham is the son of Edward Kenway, the protagonist of *Assassin's Creed Black Flag*, he knows about the tenets. In fact, he knows a lot about the Assassins and even has a hidden blade, which Shay comments on in *Assassin's Creed Rogue* and which also explains why the player in *Assassin's Creed III*, where Haytham is the protagonist of the first part, believes him to be an Assassin. Interesting in *Forsaken* is that the book confirms Edward Kenway's scepticism towards the Brotherhood. When Haytham talks with Reginald Birch, his former Templar mentor, Birch remarks: "Of course, I knew your father felt differently to me concerning many—perhaps even most—of the tenets of the Order, but that is because he didn't subscribe to them".

The book *Assassin's Creed Unity*, like *Forsaken*, does not tell the Ancestor story of Arno the protagonist of the *Unity* game. The book is Élise de la Serre's diary with a few additions by Arno. As already mentioned, Élise is the daughter of François de la Serre, the Grand Master of the French Templars as well as the man who adopted Arno after Shay killed his father. As Élise is destined to become Grand Master herself, the tenets discussed in this book are those of the Templars and not those of the Assassins. Both *Forsaken* and *Unity* are clearly intended to show that Templars and Assassins are not that different. *Assassin's Creed Underworld*, finally, tells the story of Evie and Jacob Fry's father Ethan, who contrary to the preceding Assassins was born to the Creed. This also meant that he taught his children Evie and Jacob the tenets of the Creed, although this is not literally in the book and is only hinted at when the twins are concerned: "They had no servants. Ethan would not have allowed it, believing the very idea of retaining servants went against the tenets of the creed" (Kindle Location

---

[43] See Appendix B for the full dialogue.

2986). However, apart from Evie and Jacob, Ethan did also train the son of his friend Arbaaz Mir: Jayadeep. When Jayadeep fails his first mission, two of the three tenets are mentioned: "Jayadeep's actions had broken the tenets of the creed: he had been forced to surrender hiding in plain sight; worse, he had been forced to compromise the Brotherhood" (Kindle Locations 1032–1033).

7.4. The Comic Books and Graphic Novels

Of the many comic books and graphic novels, only three are closely linked to the games. As already explained, even though the graphic novels use the same storyworld and transmedial world, their legitimacy as part of the transmedia story is questioned. The Titan comics are part of transmedia storytelling but have no direct reference to a particular game. They were crated for a new, younger audience and expand on the transmedial world, both that of the present-day as well as the Ancestor part (with new Ancestors, Locations, Artefacts, and Sages). The three comics that have direct links to the games are *The Fall*, *The Chain*, and *Brahman*. *The Fall* and *The Chain*, which as already mentioned are directly linked to *Assassin's Creed III*, tell the story of Assassin-born Daniel Cross. Like Desmond, he was kidnapped by Abstergo but at a much younger age. Through prolonged exposure to the animus he suffers from constant 'hallucinations' caused by the bleeding effect. He escapes and is found by the Assassins who try to improve his condition. However, when he finally meets the Mentor the hallucinations take over and he kills the Mentor. After fleeing, he returns to Abstergo and the Animus. In *The Chain*, through his Assassin Ancestor Nikolai Orolov, he finds Ezio's Codex in which Desmond is mentioned. Despite the fact that he spends a long time with the Assassins, the tenets are never mentioned. *Brahman* is linked to the book *Assassin's Creed Underworld* and the games *Assassin's Creed Syndicate* and *Assassin's Creed Chronicles India*. As it is fairly recent, the storyworld uses an Abstergo headset, allegedly an entertainment device to replay the best parts gathered from the DNA of an Ancestor Assassin.[44] In the game *Assassin's Creed Black Flag*, the object of Abstergo, apart from getting information about Sages, Blood Vials, and the Observatory, is to create such an experience which in the game is called *Devils of the Caribbean* (alleged release date Summer 2014). In *Brahman*, when Jot Soora, an employee of Mysore Tech, is testing the Abstergo device for release on the Indian Market, he stumbles upon hidden code that can upload the actual memories of an Ancestor of the current wearer. So, as it turns out he was not randomly chosen to wear the headset as his Ancestor was linked to the Assassin Arbaaz Mir and should know the last location of the famous Koh-I-Noor diamond (another Precursor Artefact). As the Ancestor Assassin's memories are accessed in media res, there are no references to the tenets in the comic.

7.5. The (Animated) Films

The short films, whether animated or not, serve as introductions to and bridges between main games. Consequently, they do not give information about the tenets, not even *Assassin's Creed Lineage*, which introduces Ezio and his family and also shows what happened before *Assassin's Creed II*, which helps to understand why Ezio's father had to die. *Embers*, the short film that tells about Ezio's final days and death, introduces the Chinese Assassin Shao Jun, the protagonist of *Assassin's Creed Chronicles China*. The story of *Embers* can also be found in the book *Assassin's Creed Revelations*.

The tenets are also not in the feature film, but they are in the film's promotional material. The film was first announced to the fans on 21 December 2015 in a tweet by Ubisoft that showed the business card of Alan Rikkin, the CEO of Abstergo in the film. When the fans called the number on the card they heard a voicemail by Rikkin (Jeremy Irons) giving the website of Twentieth Century Fox (the film's distributer). On 25 March 2016, the Voicemail changed. It again began with a message by Rikkin but then hacking sounds were heard and the voce of Callum Lynch (Michael Fassbender), the modern

---

[44] This was also the premise of *Assassin's Creed Liberation*, where the data came from the very first participant, Subject 1 (Desmond is Subject 17). This was still in the experimental phase of the Animus Project.

day Assassin in the film, speaks the words: "These are the sacred tenets of our brotherhood: to stay your blade from the flesh of the innocent, to hide in the plain sight, and above all else, never to compromise the brotherhood". As Callum only in the last part of the film understands that he is part of the Brotherhood and is not taught the tenets in the film, it must be assumed that the events in the film took place before 25 March 2015.[45] Interesting about the film is that, unlike the games, 65% takes place in the present day. The film is an independent production in the transmedia storytelling world of *Assassin's Creed*: "'We essentially did them all on our own because we wanted to have an original script,' he said. 'It's a movie that's based on the game, but it's not a movie that is the game.'" (Makkuch 2016).

Still, the film adheres to the Mythos, Topos, and Ethos of the transmedial world even though there are discrepancies with the games. The Apple of Eden Abstergo is seeking in the film is the Apple of Adam and Eve. In the games, this Apple is Altaïr's Apple (Apple #2), which Ezio left hidden behind a wall in Altaïr's vault in the original Assassin's stronghold in Masyaf (in *Revelations*). However, as there are several Apples of Eden and the one in the film is simply referred to as Aguilar's[46] Apple, which apparently was not discovered until 1492, the year the historic part of the film takes place, we must assume that this is one of the other Apples. Another seeming discrepancy is that in the game *Assassin's Creed II Discovery*, Ezio is in Spain in 1491 to save Christopher Columbus from Torquemada and the Spanish Inquisition. The film is set one year later in 1492. Aguilar himself is pursued by the Inquisition and Torquemada and nearly escapes being burned at the stake. At the end of the historic part, Aguilar hands over the Apple to Columbus for safe keeping. In 2017, Aymar Azaizia, head of content since *Assassin's Creed II*, during a Reddit AMA discussion stated that the game was no longer canon in light of the story of the film (Azaizia 2017). However, later, after a discussion with the fan community, he changed his mind: "I declare that thanks to the light you put on the matter, Assassin's Creed (AC) Discovery should be considered as canon in the AC lore". (Azaizia 2017)[47]

Even though the tenets are not in the film, they are in the official novelization of the film. First, when the Assassins try to rescue Prince Ahmad[48] when his hiding place is discovered by the Templars, they implement tenet 2: "Now, the Assassins blended in effortlessly with the throng that stood, frightened and uneasy, awaiting the approach of the Templars. It was one of the tenets of the Creed: *Hide in plain sight*" [Italics in the original] (p. 50). Secondly, after Aguilar and Maria escape from the Inquisition, in their flight they land in the room of a family. Aguilar thinks: "Stay *your blade from the flesh of the innocent*. The first tenet of the Creed. These people would come to no harm through him or Maria" (p. 147). Finally, when the sultan betrays the Brotherhood by giving up the Apple for the life of his son, the prince, Aguilar has every right to kill him, especially as this action cost Maria's life. In the film, we only see the reaction of the sultan: "Forgive me". In the book, however, we also get Aguilar's thoughts: "*I could kill him right now*, Aguilar thought. He knew that Muhammad would not resist ... But Aguilar knew he would not kill the sultan. The first tenet of the Creed was '*Stay your blade from the flesh of the innocent*." (p. 199). The differences between the film and the book are obvious. The film is about showing, so there would have to be a scene in the film that could have lent credibility to Callum stating the tenets. The book, however, is about telling, which gives more room to explain actions and thoughts.

8. Conclusions

The transmedial world, as described by Klastrup and Tosca, is an abstract content system that is medium-independent. However, the Mythos, Topos, and Ethos of this transmedial world

---

[45] The film was released on 21 December 2016, a month and day with some significance in the *Assassin's Creed* transmedia storytelling world, as is of course the date of the Tweet.

[46] Aguilar is the Ancestor Assassin in the film.

[47] Showing the commitment of the fan community to keep the Mythos of the transmedial world intact. As already mentioned, in the book *Assassin's Creed Brotherhood*, Ezio returns again to Spain, but this takes place in March 1507, so after the events of the film.

[48] He is the son of the sultan and has been kidnapped to force his father, the keeper of the Apple, to hand it over to the Templars.

originally stem from the storyworld of the 'ur'-text. As the 'ur'-text of *Assassin's Creed* is the first game, also called *Assassin's Creed* (2007), apart from the storyworld there is also the game world, the represented version of the storyworld. As I argued, in the earlier games the storyworld and the game world are interwoven. However, the storyworld in games, by necessity, differs from the one described by Ryan in her book *Storyworlds Across Media*. The participatory mode of computer games means that special rules, values, and (mental) events in games are not 'independent' as in books or films but that they may influence the player's decisions and consequently her actions. By examining several media texts from the transmedial world of *Assassin's Creed*, focussing specifically on the Mythos and Ethos of this world, it became clear that on the one hand the transmedial world uses different media to expand the Mythos of the series, while, on the other hand, the Ethos of the storyworld influences player decisions in the game world. It also became clear that, throughout the series, the innovative idea of the original designer Patrice Désilets, where "everything that you can do with your freedom is basically driving the story forward" (2007), thus interweaving the storyworld and the game world, has been abandoned in favour of gameplay-driven challenges. In the game world, this manifested itself in less emphasis on the tenets of the Creed, arguably the most important element of the Ethos of *Assassin's Creed*. However, the tenets are not completely forgotten as the promotional material for the *Assassin's Creed* film and its novelization showed. However, these media texts 'show' and 'tell'; they do not direct.

Funding: This research received no external funding.

Conflicts of Interest: The author declares no conflict of interest.

Appendix A

Legend: * media introducing new Precursor Artefacts and/or information about the Isu.[A] adaptations.

Main games

PS3, Xbox360, PC (the dates given are for the console releases)
*ASSASSIN'S CREED (2007).
*ASSASSIN'S CREED II (2009).
*ASSASSIN'S CREED BROTHERHOOD (2010).
*ASSASSIN'S CREED REVELATIONS (2011).
*ASSASSIN'S CREED III (2012).
*ASSASSIN'S CREED IV BLACK FLAG (2013)
*ASSASSIN'S CREED ROGUE (2014)

PS 4, Xbox One, PC (the dates given are for the console releases)
*ASSASSIN'S CREED UNITY (2014)
*ASSASSIN'S CREED SYNDICATE (2015)
*ASSASSIN'S CREED ORIGINS (2017)

Games for handheld or mobile platforms

[A] ASSASSIN'S CREED (2007).
*ASSASSIN'S CREED: ALTAÏR'S CHRONICLES (2008, Nintendo DS)
*ASSASSIN'S CREED BLOODLINES (2009, PSP).
[A] ASSASSIN'S CREED II (2009).
[A] ASSASSIN'S CREED TWITTER ASSASSINATION EXPERIENCE (2009).
[A] ASSASSIN'S CREED II: MULTIPLAYER (2010)).
*ASSASSIN'S CREED II DISCOVERY (2009, Nintendo DS).
[A] ASSASSIN'S CREED BROTHERHOOD (2010).
[?] ASSASSIN'S CREED RECOLLECTION (2011)

^AASSASSIN'S CREED REVELATIONS (2011).
^AASSASSIN'S CREED III (2012).
*ASSASSIN'S CREED LIBERATIONS (2012, PS Vita)
*ASSASSIN'S CREED PIRATES (2013)
[?]ASSASSIN'S CREED MEMORIES (2014)
*ASSASSIN'S CREED CHRONICLES CHINA (2015, PS Vita)
*ASSASSIN'S CREED CHRONICLES INDIA (2016, PS Vita)
*ASSASSIN'S CREED CHRONICLES RUSSIA (2016, PS Vita)
[?]ASSASSIN'S CREED IDENTITY (2016)

Online games/databases
*ASSASSIN'S CREED PROJECT LEGACY (2010-2012, Facebook).
*ASSASSIN'S CREED INITIATES (2012-2013).

(Animated) short films
*ASSASSIN'S CREED: LINEAGE (2009). Simoneau, Y. (director). Ubisoft Montreal & Hybride.
http://assassinscreedlineage.us.ubi.com/.
*ASSASSIN'S CREED: ASCENDANCE (2010). Ubisoft Workshop (production). Ubisoft Entertainment.
http://www.megavideo.com/v/ZQV0Y3H2c2801992086a1c1ca1865c66522a82f41.
^(*)ASSASSIN'S CREED: EMBERS (2011). Ubisoft Workshop (production). Ubisoft Montreal. www.
youtube.com/watch?v=QL30864YID4.
^(*)ASSASSIN'S CREED: THE SYNDICATE (2015) Felix Gary Gray (writer), New Science (producer).
Ubisoft. www.youtube.com/watch?v=geNmfrPMhgg.
^(*)ASSASSIN'S CREED: FRENCH REVOLUTION (2017) Rob Zombie (writer), New Science (producer).
Ubisoft. www.youtube.com/watch?v=kEe219MWyOM.

Feature films
*ASSASSIN'S CREED (2016). Justin Kurzel (director). 20th Century Fox. Blu ray.

Oliver Bowden Books
Official *Assassin's Creed* series by Oliver Bowden published by Penguin books London.
^A *Assassin's Creed Renaissance.* (2009)
^{A (*)} *Assassin's Creed Brotherhood.* (2010)
* *Assassin's Creed The Secret Crusade.* (2011)
* *Assassin's Creed Revelations.* (2011)
* *Assassin's Creed Forsaken.* (2012)
* *Assassin's Creed Black Flag.* (2012)
* *Assassin's Creed Unity.* (2014)
* *Assassin's Creed Underworld.* (2015)
* *Assassin's Creed Origins Desert Oath.* (2017)

Other Books
*Kirbey Matthew J. (2016). *Last Descendants.* Scholastic Inc.
* Golden, Christy. (2016). *Assassin's Creed Heresy.* San Francisco Ubisoft.
^A Golden, Christy. (2016). *Assassin's Creed official movie novelization.* San Francisco Ubisoft.
*Golden, Christy (2016) *Assassin's Creed Regression in Assassin's Creed official movie novelization.*
San Francisco Ubisoft.
*Kirbey Matthew J. (2016). *Last Descendants: Tomb of the Kahn.* Scholastic Inc.
*Kirbey Matthew J. (2017). *Last Descendants: Fate of the Gods.* Scholastic Inc.

Graphic Novels (French editions)
published by Les Deux Royaumes Paris.

Ankh of Isis Trilogy. Artists Eric Corbeyron & Djillali Defali
* *Assassin's Creed: 1 Desmond.* (2009)
* *Assassin's Creed: 2 Aquilus.* (2010)
* *Assassin's Creed: 3 Accipiter.* (2011)

The Hawk Trilogy. Artists Eric Corbeyron & Djillali Defali
* *Assassin's Creed: 4 Hawk.* (2012)
* *Assassin's Creed: 5 El Cakr.* (2013
* *Assassin's Creed: 6 Leila.* (2014)

Assassin's Creed: Conspirations
**Tome 1: Die Glocke* (2016). Artistes Guillaume Dorison & Jean-Baptiste Hostache
**Tome 2: Le Projet Rainbow* (2017). Artistes Guillaume Dorison & Patrick Pion

Comic Books
*Kerschl, K. & C. Stewart (2011). *Assassin's Creed: The Chain.* Ubisoft.
*Kerschl, K. & C. Stewart (2012). *Assassin's Creed: The Fall.* Ubisoft.
(*)Kerschl, K. & C. Stewart (2012). *Assassin's Creed: Subject Four.* Ubisoft.(compilation of *Assassin's Creed: The Fall* and *Assassin's Creed: The Chain*).
*Kerschl, K. & C. Stewart (2014). *Assassin's Creed: Brahman.* Ubisoft.
*Col del, A & C. McCreery (2015) *Trial by Fire. Assassin's Creed series.* Titan Comics.
*Col del, A & C. McCreery (2016) *Setting Sun. Assassin's Creed series.* Titan Comics.
*Lente van F. & D. Calero (2016) *Black Cross. Templar series.* Titan Comics
*Col del, A & C. McCreery (2017) *Homecoming. Assassin's Creed series.* Titan Comics.
*Lente van F. & D. Calero (2017) *Cross of Water. Templar series.* Titan Comics
*Watters D & A. Plaknadel (2017) *Common Ground. Uprising series.* Titan Comics
*Edgington I. (2017) *Assassin's Creed Reflections. Assassin's Creed series.* Titan Comics.
*Watters D & A. Plaknadel (2018) *Inflection Point. Uprising series.* Titan Comics
*Watters D & A. Plaknadel (2018) *Finale, Uprising series.* Titan Comics
*Toole. A. (2018) *Assassin's Creed Origins.* Titan Comics.

Other publications
Assassin's Creed Encyclopaedia 1st edition (2011). Ubisoft
Assassin's Creed Encyclopaedia 2nd edition (2012). Ubisoft
Assassin's Creed Encyclopaedia 3rd edition (2013). Ubisoft
**Assassin's Creed Unity: Abstergo Entertainment—Employee Handbook* (2014). Ubisoft

Appendix B

The two guards on either side of Altaïr stepped forward and took his arms. His muscles tensed. He braced himself against them but did not struggle. 'What are you doing?' he said warily. The colour rose in Al Mualim's[49] cheeks. 'There are rules. We are nothing if we do not abide by the Assassin's Creed. Three simple tenets, which you seem to forget. I will remind you. First and foremost: stay your blade . . . ' It was to be a lecture. Altaïr relaxed, unable to keep the note of resignation from his voice as he finished Al Mualim's sentence. ' . . . from the flesh of an innocent. I know'. The crack of Al Mualim's palm across Altaïr's face echoed from the stone of the courtyard. Altaïr felt his cheek

---

[49] Al Mualin is Ezio's mentor and head of the Brotherhood.

burn. 'And stay your tongue unless I give you leave to use it', roared Al Mualim. 'If you are so familiar with this tenet, why did you kill the old man inside the Temple? He was innocent. He did not need to die'. Altaïr said nothing. What could he say? I acted rashly? Killing the old man was an act of arrogance? 'Your insolence knows no bounds', bellowed Al Mualim. 'Make humble your heart, child, or I swear I'll tear it from you with my own hands'. He paused, his shoulders rising and falling as he took hold of his anger. 'The second tenet is that which gives us strength', he continued. 'Hide in plain sight. Let the people mask you so that you become one with the crowd. Do you remember? Because, as I hear it, you chose to expose yourself, drawing attention before you'd struck'. Still Altaïr said nothing. He felt the shame squat in his gut. 'The third and final tenet', added Al Mualim, 'the worst of all your betrayals: never compromise the Brotherhood. Its meaning should be obvious. Your actions must never bring harm upon us: direct or indirect. Yet your selfish act beneath Jerusalem placed us all in danger. Worse still, you brought the enemy to our home. Every man we've lost today was lost because of you'. Altaïr had been unable to look at the Master. His head had remained on one side, still smarting from the slap. But as he heard Al Mualim draw his dagger he looked at last. 'I am sorry. Truly, I am,' said Al Mualim. 'But I cannot abide a traitor'. No. Not that. Not a traitor's death. His eyes widened as they went to the blade in the Master's hand: the hand that had guided him since him childhood. 'I am not a traitor,' he managed. 'Your actions indicate otherwise. And so you leave me no choice'. Al Mualim drew back his dagger. 'Peace be upon you, Altaïr', he said, and plunged it into Altaïr's stomach. (pp. 55–57).

References

Adams, Ernest. 2003. The Construction of Ludic Space. Paper presented at Level Up Digital Games Research Conference, Utrecht, The Netherlands, November 4–6.

Aristotle. 1996. *Poetics. Penguin Classics*. Translated and Introduced by Malcolm Heath. London: Penguin Books.

Azaizia, Aymar. 2017. Reddit AMA. Available online: https://redd.it/60pj33 (accessed on 31 May 2018).

Bordwell, David, and Kirsten Thompson. 2001. *Film Art An Introduction*, 6th ed. New York: McGraw–Hill.

Désilets, Patrice. 2007. Assassin's Creed Developer Diaries #3: Freedom. YouTube Video. Available online: http://www.youtube.com/watch?v=boQo9iL8ado (accessed on 2 April 2016).

DidYouKnowGaming. 2014. "Assassin's Creed". NormalBoots.com. YouTube Video. Available online: http://www.youtube.com/watch?v=d2UQk8EXPtM (accessed on 26 May 2018).

Egenfeldt-Nielsen, Simon, Jonas Heide Smith, and Susana Pajares Tosca. 2013. *Understanding Video Games. The Essential Introduction*, 2nd ed. New York: Routledge.

Herman, David, Mafred Jahn, and Marie-Laure Ryan, eds. 2005. *Routledge Encyclopaedia of Narrative Theory*. London and New York: Routledge.

Hutcheon, Linda. 2013. *A Theory of Adaptation*, 2nd ed. London/New York: Routledge.

Iser, Wolfgang. 1980. *The Act of Reading. A Theory of Aesthetic Response*. Baltimore: The John Hopkins University Press.

Jenkins, Henry. 2003a. "Transmedia Storytelling" in the "Digital Renaissance". In *MIT Technology Review*. Boston: The MIT Press.

Jenkins, Henry. 2003b. Game Design as a Narrative Architecture. In *First Person: New Media as Story, Performance, and Game*. Edited by Noah Wardrip-Fruin and Pat Harrigan. Cambridge: The MIT Press.

Jenkins, Henry. 2006. *Convergence Culture: Where Old and New Media Collide*. New York: New York University Press.

Jenkins, Henry. 2007. Transmedia Storytelling 101. Confessions of an Aca-Fan. Available online: http://henryjenkins.org/2007/03/transmedia_storytelling_101.html (accessed on 3 September 2015).

Juul, Jesper. 2005. *Half-Real: Video Games between Real Rules and Fictional Worlds*. Cambridge: The MIT Press.

Klastrup, Lisbeth, and Susana Tosca. 2004. Transmedial Worlds—Rethinking Cyberworld Design. Paper Presented at the 2004 International Conference on Cyberworlds, Tokyo, Japan, November 18–20; pp. 409–16.

Klastrup, Lisbeth, and Susana Tosca. 2009. MMOGs and the Ecology of Fiction: Understanding LOTRO as Transmedial World. Paper present at the 2009 DiGRA International Conference: Breaking New Ground: Innovation in Games, Play, Practice and Theory Brunel University, London, UK, September 1–4.

Machinima. 2010. Assassin's Creed Part 1: Sneaking in. All Your History are Belong to Us. YouTube Video. Available online: http://www.youtube.com/watch?v=fEdiVREmjko (accessed on 23 April 2014).

Makkuch, Eddy. 2016. Assassin's Creed Movie Producers Have Plans for Two Sequels. Gamespot. Available online: https://www.gamespot.com/articles/assassins-creed-movie-producers-have-plans-for-two/1100-6439840/ (accessed on 31 May 2018).

Mulligan, Jessica, and Bridgette Patrovsky. 2003. *Developing Online Games: An Insider's Guide*. Boston: New Riders.

Murray, Janet. 1999. *Hamlet on the Holodeck: The Future of Narrative in Cyberspace*, 2nd ed. Cambridge: The MIT Press.

Ndalianis, Angela. 2005. Television and the Neo-Baroque. In *The Contemporary Television Serial*. Edited by Lucy Mazdon and Michael Hammond. Edinburgh: University of Edinburgh, pp. 83–101.

North, Nolan. 2015. *Metrocon Friday Panel*. Tampa: YouTube video.

Rajewski, Irina. 2005. Intermediality, Intertextuality, and Remediation: A Literary Perspective on Intermediality. *Intermédialités*, 43–64. [CrossRef]

Ryan, Marie-Laure. 1991. *Possible Worlds, Artificial Intelligence, and Narrative Theory*. Bloomington: Indiana University Press.

Ryan, Marie-Laure, and Jan-Noël Thon, eds. 2014. *Storyworlds across Media: Towards a Media-Conscious Narratology*. Lincoln/London: University of Nebraska Press.

Samsel, Jon, and Darryl Wimberley. 1998. *Writing for Interactive Media: The Complete Guide*. New York: Allworth Press.

Shippey, Tom. 1982. *The Road to Middle-Earth: How J.R.R. Tolkien Created a New Mythology*, 3rd ed. New York: Houghton Mifflin.

Veugen, Connie. 2005. 'A Man, lean, dark, tall': Aragorn Seen Through Different Media. In *Reconsidering Tolkien*. Edited by Thomas Honegger. Zollikofen: Walking Tree Publishers, pp. 171–209.

Veugen, Connie. 2011. Computer Games as a Narrative Medium. Ph.D. dissertation, Vrije Universiteit Amsterdam, Amsterdam, The Netherlands.

Veugen, Connie. 2014. Altaïr Ibn-La'Ahad, Arab Assassin or All-American Game Hero? In *Magazine Stichting Instituut voor Maatschappelijke Verbeelding*. Edited by Heidi de Mare.

Veugen, Connie. 2016. Assassin's Creed and Transmedia Storytelling. Special Issue on Transmedia and Games, *International Journal of Gaming and Computer Mediated Simulations* 8: 1–19.

Wolf, Mark J. P., ed. 2012. *Encyclopaedia of Video Games. The Culture, Technology, and Art of Gaming*. Oxford: Greenwood.

Article

'Things Greater than Thou': Post-Apocalyptic Religion in Games

Lars de Wildt * , Stef Aupers, Cindy Krassen and Iulia Coanda

Institute for Media Studies, KU Leuven, Leuven 3000, Belgium; stef.aupers@kuleuven.be (S.A.);
cindy.krassen@kuleuven.be (C.K.); iulia.coanda@kuleuven.be (I.C.)
* Correspondence: lars.dewildt@kuleuven.be (L.d.W.); Tel: +32-16-37-92-98.

Received: 3 May 2018; Accepted: 18 May 2018; Published: 23 May 2018

Abstract: In the literature on religion in games, two broad types of religion have been depicted: on the one hand, historical religions—Christian, Muslim and Buddhist narratives, tropes and symbols—and, on the other hand, fiction-based religion, referring to fantasy, myth and popular culture. In this article we aim to describe, analyze and explain the emergence of a new, unacknowledged repertoire. Building on two case studies—*Fallout 3* and *Horizon: Zero Dawn*—we argue that modern technology (computers, AI, VR, androids) itself is becoming a sacred object of veneration in fiction, specifically in post-apocalyptic games that imagine man-made annihilation. Although the themes and topics differ, this emergent form of techno-religion in game narratives is generally located in a post-apocalyptic setting. Although they are fictitious, we conclude that such narratives reflect developments in real life, in which technology such as artificial intelligence is feared as an increasingly powerful, opaque force.

Keywords: post-apocalypse; video games; religion in games; *Horizon: Zero Dawn*; *Fallout 3*

Aloy: *"Why are the lands beyond Nora territory called 'tainted'?"*

Teersa: *"Is it not obvious? Our land is sacred. We live in sight of the one Goddess, All-Mother—source of all that lives. Beyond her sight lies a vast fallen land, spiritually tainted. That is why it is against tribal law to leave. But this blessing will protect you."*

1. Revelations of a New World

Video games allow us to imagine worlds beyond our own. Much like religions have offered us the ability to think beyond our mundane daily lives, turning on our computers or consoles can offer us a different world. The elective affinity between religion and games has not gone unnoticed in academia. On the one hand, it has been widely argued that games *function* as religion since, as Huizinga argued, "into the confusion of life it brings a temporary, limited perfection" (Huizinga 1970, p. 12). On the other hand, game texts are brimming with religious narratives, symbols, tropes and plots and are as such encoded with 'ultimate meanings' that are negotiated, reconstructed and reversed while playing (Schaap and Aupers 2017).

The traditional function of religion—ultimate meaning-making in the face of this-worldly illness, suffering and death (Weber 1948; Berger 1967)—thus becomes an important asset in game design (cf. Wagner 2012; Leibovitz 2014). Not always are game worlds and the narratives they display hopeful, however. This paper considers the case of the 'post-apocalyptic' game genre. How is such a deeply religious concept—the end of the world most closely associated with the eponymous New Testament book—made into a genre for entertainment, and what place does religion have within the post-apocalyptic worlds portrayed? Prompted by previous theorizations of religion in fictional media, we propose that in order to understand the way the post-apocalypse is treated in video games, we must turn to 'science fiction-based' religion, a category of religious representation that falls beyond the scopes of history- and fiction-based religion. That is, while ample academic scholarship reflects on games' representation of Biblical, Islamic and other historical religions, as well as on the fictional religions of *Skyrim* or Tolkien that are based on the fantasy genre, there is little attention given to a new kind of religiosity around technology, specifically in its dystopian, sometimes fearful guise (cf. Geraci 2012). Given the explorative nature of this study, we focus on game texts as source material, before looking at their players or developers: a game-immanent approach rather than an actor-centered one (Heidbrink et al. 2014; Zeiler 2018; Aupers et al. 2018; cf. De Wildt and Aupers 2018). By highlighting *Fallout 3* and *Horizon: Zero Dawn* as two popular, theoretically relevant case studies from the past 10 years, this paper will explore whether and how religion is represented in a world where society and humanity have been nearly, if not completely erased. In short, we will ask: How do video games present religion in the post-apocalypse and, particularly, how is religion positioned vis-à-vis future technologies in the game world?

2. Religion in Games: History, Fantasy and Future

Overall, the research on religion in games is concerned with recognizing religious beliefs in games: how religious beliefs occur; how 'superempirical' gods (and other entities) and their followers are represented; and how religious elements and narratives are incorporated in interactive worlds. In other words, 'religion in games' research studies the occurrence of religion in the narrative or representative content of games—or the "narratological" layer of games, for lack of a better term (cf. Aarseth 2001; Frasca 2003; Murray 2005; cf. De Wildt 2014; e.g., Bosman 2016). Examples abound. Scholars such as Vit Šisler employ cultural approaches to religion in order to identify how the Islamic faith and its followers have been represented differently in Western and Middle Eastern games (Šisler 2006, 2008, 2009); whereas Masso and Abrams have done the same for Judaism (Masso and Abrams 2014). Other research has focused more directly on how narratives from world religions are incorporated and changed by game designers, such as Robert W. Guyker's analysis of *Journey*'s use of shamanistic tropes recurring throughout pre-modern and non-Western religions (Guyker 2014); and Bosman and Poorthuis' tracing of the occurrence and adaptations of Lilith and the Nephilim (Judeo-Christian mythological characters) throughout Judaic, Christian, Islamic and occult literature as well as various games, each considered equally (Bosman and Poorthuis 2015).

While these research examples and their case studies draw on what Davidsen calls "history-based" religion, or conventional world religions that "claim to refer to events that have taken place in the actual world" such as the Christian Gospels (Davidsen 2013, p. 386), most games rely instead on fictional religions. We use the term "fiction-based" here as opposed to "history-based," where the latter refers to long-standing religious practices such as Christianity, Islam, Hinduism and the other big world religions. The conceptualization of "fiction-based" and the contrast with history-based religions springs from the sociological literature on contemporary religious practices around modern fiction, such as Tolkien-based religions, Jediism, Matrixism and so on (Davidsen 2013; cf. Possamai 2005). Although this distinction is empirically and theoretically problematic from some societal perspectives, such as those that regard the Bible as potentially fiction just as much as other fiction is potentially sacred (cf. De Wildt and Aupers 2017), the distinction is helpful as an analytical construct. That is, it allows us to differentiate between established traditions vis-à-vis those religions that were made up for a modern fictional work, without diminishing how meaningful either can be.

2.1. Fantasy Fiction-Based Religion: A Strong Bias

Fiction-based religion is a staple in video games and provides frequent narrative background and ludic contexts to make games meaningful for players. Research by Tanya Krzywinska, for example, shows through a combination of ethnography and content analysis that the different fictional religious traditions in *World of Warcraft*—invented belief systems ranging from the monotheistic "Church of the Holy Light" to the kinds of totemic and animistic nature worship organized around fictional deities—provide invaluable drama and cosmological conflict through the beliefs of non-playable characters and the narrative backgrounds of players' characters (Krzywinska 2006). More radically, Markus Wiemker and Jan Wysocki argue that 'god' games—where players take the position of the omniscient, powerful God of a society—draw from a wide array of cultural influences to shape their own alternative belief systems based on game-specific own morals, miracles and divine manifestations (Wiemker and Wysocki 2014).

However, as these and other case studies show, much work about in-game religion that is not grounded in established, history-based religions, is about fiction-based religion in games, particularly of the fantasy genre (e.g., Aupers 2007; Bainbridge 2013; Copier 2005; Fine 1983; Gregory 2014; etc.). In his essay "On Fairy Stories," the 'Father of Fantasy' J.R.R. Tolkien argues that there is a fundamental human need to imagine alternative fantasy worlds. In this essay, as much as through his own fictional work, Tolkien expresses a need for fiction to "enchant" us, to grant us recovery, escape and consolation from our daily lives (Tolkien 1939; cf. Curry 1999). Fantasy fiction-based religion in media texts—films, series and games—may be considered a product of the romantic imagination. Born from the work of Tolkien, fantasy can be categorized as "deeply nostalgic [. . .] an emotionally empowering nostalgia" (Curry 2005, p. 126) or an "archaic nostalgia" (Jameson 1975, p. 161) for a world that is infused with spiritual values, meaning, magic and enchantment. Indeed: the imaginary past in which fantasy fiction-based religion is set, presupposes the omnipresence of religion, magic, and beliefs in spiritual forces in nature. Alongside historical religions, fantasy thus also presents religious worlds as something romantic, and deeply nostalgically associated with rural, pseudo-medieval and magical pasts.

Tolkien practiced what he preached. Middle Earth, the location of his trilogy *Lord of the Rings*, which was first published in 1954, is both fantastic and realistic, both mythical and rational, and is by far the most influential work in the fantasy genre. Its main narrative—featuring creatures like hobbits, elves, and wizards as main protagonists—is mainly based on Norse mythology and embraces a "polytheistic-cum-animist cosmology of 'natural magic'" (Curry 1998, p. 28). These 'pre-modern' religious worldviews are, Tolkien felt, important since "the 'war' against mystery and magic by modernity urgently requires a re-enchantment of the world, which a sense of Earth-mysteries is much better placed to offer than a single transcendent deity" (Curry 1998, pp. 28–29). Middle Earth, in short, was in part invented to counter modern processes of disenchantment but, ironically, became fully embraced by the modern world since the 1960s. The literary work and mythopoeic approach of Tolkien also spilled over to the game industry and became, as such, a typical example of a "transmedial" phenomenon (Jenkins 2006). Myth-making, in the context of computer games, became a matter of technical design. Turkle argues: "The personal computer movement of the 1970s and early 1980s was deeply immersed in Tolkien and translated his fantasy worlds into hugely popular (and enduring) role-playing games" (Turkle 2002, p. 18). Indeed, Tolkien died in 1973, but around that same time his enchanting world was reproduced in cyberspace. In 1976 a Stanford hacker, Donald Woods, and a programmer, Will Crowther, developed *Adventure*, the first text-based role-playing game on the computer. *Adventure* "turned out to be one of the most influential computer games in the medium's early history" (King and Borland 2003, p. 31). An important shift came in the 1980s when Trubshaw and Bartle developed the '*Multi-User Dungeon*' (MUDs) that made it possible to collectively explore this textual world. Between the end of the 1970s and the beginning of the 1990s, text-based role-playing games and MUDs were booming. Some examples that are directly derived from the work of Tolkien are *The Shire* (1979), *Ringen* (1979), *Lord of the Rings* (1981), *LORD* (1981), *Ring of Doom* (1983), *Ringmaster* (1984), *The Mines of Moria* (1985), *Bilbo* (1989), *The Balrogian trilogy* (1989) and *Elendor* (1991). In 1996 and 1997, respectively, *Diablo* and *Ultima Online* were launched on the Internet—the latter generally understood as the first three-dimensional Massively Multiplayer Online Role Playing Games. In the last decade such fantasy games became immensely popular, whether multi- or single-player. Well-known examples are *Everquest* (1999), *Asherons Call* (1999), *Dark Age of Camelot* (2001), *World of Warcraft* (2004), *Lord of the Rings Online* (2007), *The Elder Scrolls* series including the hit *Skyrim* (2011) and the MMO *TES:O* (2014), the *Dragon Age* series, most recently titled *Inquisition* (2014), and so on—all of which, without exception, harken back to a faux-medieval Tolkienesque fantasy world of religion and enchantment.

2.2. Science Fiction-Based Religion: A Blind Spot

The focus on fantasy in academia, we argue, blinkers other, unacknowledged genres that constitute fiction-based religion in games. As opposed to fantasy fiction, science fiction narratives present futuristic universes devoid of religious meaning. Indeed: tapping into current trends and extrapolating these to the future, sci-fi worlds *seem* to be dominated by scientific reasoning instead of faith and technological practices, methods and artefacts instead of magic. More than anything else, science fiction would seem to exemplify the "disenchantment of the world" (Weber 1948). To paraphrase Max Weber, like in the real world, in futuristic sci-fi universes such as *Star Trek*:

> "One need no longer have recourse to magical means to master or implore the spirits, as did the savage, for whom such mysterious powers existed. Technical means and calculation perform the service" (Weber 1948, p. 139)

Such (evolutionary) arguments about rationalism, science, and technology as an "irreligious power" (Ibid., p. 142), are deeply institutionalized in the social sciences, and may account for the fact that debates on fiction-based religion generally show a bias towards the fantasy genre and a blind spot for the sci-fi genre.

Notwithstanding countless recent studies showing that the dichotomy science/technology versus religion is theoretically and empirically problematic (e.g., Latour 2012; Noble 1999; Davis 1998), particularly since the cultural logic of modernization spawns its own religions, spiritualities and magical re-enchantments (Aupers and Houtman 2010), there are ample indications that the science fiction genre is infused with religion, myth and magic. Much of the golden age of sci-fi between the 1930s and the 1970s was utopian, informed by a typical modern belief in scientific progress, space exploration and technological control over nature; if religion was mentioned, it was generally depicted as an outdated, irrational uncivilized worldview (Bleiler 1990; Fitting 2010). The genre of cyberpunk—allegedly pioneered by Philip K. Dick in the 1970s (Davis 1998), and developed by Vernor Vinge, William Gibson and Neal Stephenson in the 1980s and 1990s (Cavallaro 2000), we argue, exemplifies an important shift in which science fiction opens up to religion, magic and enchantment. More fundamentally, we theorize, science fiction-based religions indicate a radical and unacknowledged ontological shift in the perspective on religion: religious, spiritual or occult phenomena are no longer located in nature (as in history- or fantasy-based religion), but in the man-made technological world.

What, then, was the role of the cyberpunk genre in the formation of science fiction-based religion? It is already a mainstay in literature that cyberpunk both reflected emergent technologies in the 1980s—information and communication technology, virtual reality, Artificial Intelligence—and influenced it (Dery 1996). The key element is virtual reality. Inspired by observations in an arcade hall and predating the World Wide Web, William Gibson dubbed the term 'cyberspace' in his novel *Neuromancer* (1981) to signify a digital space opened up by connected computers or, rather: "a tailored hallucination" promising the "bodiless exultation of cyberspace" to its consumers. Alternatively called "the Other plane" (by Vernor Vinge in 1981) and "the metaVerse" (by Neal Stephenson in 1993), the man-made ontology of cyberspace became the pinnacle of the religious imagination in cyberpunk and beyond. As an immaterial space beyond time and place, it was considered in the 1990s as "metaphysical space" (Heim 1993), "new Jerusalem" (Benedikt 1992, p. 14) and a "paradise where we will be angels" (Stenger 1992, p. 52). As one of the protagonists in Gibson's later novel *Mona Lisa Overdrive* speculated about the omnipresence and opacity of cyberspace: "Is the Matrix God?"

This religious imaginary is not restricted to the ontology of cyberspace. At the heart of the cyberpunk narratives, we find the assumption that our human life-world, including our virtual environment, is totally permeated with autonomous technologies to the extent that people can no longer make valid distinctions between reality and fantasy; humans and AI; technology and magic. "Cyberpunk," Cavallaro argues in this respect, "charts an ambivalent mythopoeia in which new forms of life are seen to emerge from technology and, at the same time, the digital universe is permeated by mysticism and occultism" (Cavallaro 2000, pp. 53–54). Characters in cyberpunk novels constantly encounter creatures and entities that may be either artificially intelligent or spiritual. Case, the protagonist of Gibson's *Neuromancer*, for instance meets 'Flatliner'—a deceased hacker haunting cyberspace—and his digitally reincarnated girlfriend Linda. Gibson's second novel, *Count Zero*, introduces the Loa—voodoo-gods that appear, send messages and disappear again. Are they Gods or malicious programmes? Indeed: in Neal Stephenson's *Snowcrash*, artificial intelligences are 'speaking in tongues'—instigating religious viruses amongst the passive population.

This hovering between technology and spirituality—or more specifically the framing of powerful and opaque technologies as themselves religious or enchanting—is a key feature of cyberpunk novels in the 1980s and 1990s. This science fiction-based religion has gone mainstream ever since. Hollywood blockbusters—from *The Lawnmower Man* (1993), *ExistenZ* (1999), *The Matrix* (2000) to *Transcendence* (2014), increasingly feature the message that, while nature may be under the control of humans, "technology is God" (Dinello 2005).

3. Post-Apocalyptic Religion

Science fiction-based religion, then, from cyberpunk novels to Hollywood blockbusters, seems to indicate an ontological turn from the sacred situated in nature to the sacred situated in technology. Notwithstanding the 'disenchantment of the world,' omnipotent and opaque technology invokes religious imaginary that is by and large unacknowledged in the literature. This brings us to our case-studies. If the cyberpunk of the 20th century dealt with 20th-century concerns of 'virtual reality' and computer viruses in a religious-spiritual way, how does the science fiction of the 21st century deal with 21st-century concerns about technology? This paper selects two case studies featuring a post-apocalyptic world: the 1950s 'atompunk' setting of *Fallout 3* and the faux-prehistorical 'stonepunk' of *Horizon Zero Dawn*. The analysis is guided by the question: How do video games present religion in the post-apocalypse and, particularly, how is religion positioned vis-à-vis future technologies in the game world?

The question is motivated by two concerns, based on the theoretical framework above. First of all, science fiction-based religion places the sacred in an often dystopian future, rather than in a fantastical or historical past. Secondly, science fiction-based religion places the sacred into the technological, rather than the (super)natural. As a consequence, these dystopian futures are often motivated by a fear of the potential of technology. In line with this, post-apocalyptic games such as *Fallout* and *Horizon* invariably show a world destroyed by man-made technological disaster. Fallout 3, released by Bethesda in 2007 to great acclaim, shows a world destroyed by the atomic bomb, filled with robots still running (over 200 years after being manufactured) on atomic energy, but with only small pockets of humans left to inhabit the earth alongside them. *Horizon: Zero Dawn* takes place 1000 years after the invention of 'Biomatter Conversion'—the ability for machines to infinitely reproduce and fuel themselves by consuming grass, humans and other animals—causes the apocalypse, in which small tribes populate an earth dominated by self-reproducing robots and rare wildlife. Both games revolve around humans, including the player, coping with the dominance of these technological inventions in a world where humans face near-extinction.

3.1. Fallout 3: "Why Do You Worship the Bomb?"

> Confessor Cromwell: *"The Church of the Children of Atom is based on the idea that each single atomic mass in all of creation contains within it an entire universe. When that atomic mass is split, a single universe divides and becomes two—thus signifying the single greatest act of Atom's creation.*

Occasionally, a divine event occurs and trillions upon trillions of new universes are created. The last such event took place here, 200 years ago. Where most of the lost children of Atom see that event as simple war and devastation, we see creation and unification in Atom's Glow."

Lone Wanderer [Player-character]: *Why do you worship the bomb?*

Confessor Cromwell: *"Those who were called to Atom during the Great Division were very fortunate. They were permitted to aid in the process of Atom's creation. We seek the same, both in symbol and in fact and the 'bomb,' as you call it, represents Atom's capacity for creation. We kneel before it and ask that Atom call us to aid him. We pray that out of our meager bodies, he will create new life."*

The year is 2277 AD. Exactly 200 years ago, the United Nations was dissolved, China occupied Alaska and the USA have annexed Canada. The year 2077 brings about a worldwide nuclear war that destroys most of the important human settlements around the world. The *Fallout* series is staged in an alternative historical timeline after the fallout of a nuclear war between China and the USA. The sociocultural context surrounding this war is that of a society that has kept the culturally conservative aesthetic of the 1950s but developed different technology with the help of its newly found nuclear energy supply. The envisioned world places uranium at the center of societal change, as the most important human resource and the main reason for a full-scale global conflict.

In this context, the game assigns two key figures as symbols of the world's technological advancement: artificial intelligence (especially robots) and the atomic bomb. The *Fallout* games develop these technological artifacts and weave them into their main storylines, where they come to take completely different positions in society. While both robotic developments and missiles are created with the help of nuclear power, the rocket symbol attains a more sacralized position in this society's post-apocalyptic development. Most typically, we see this in the emergence of the "Church of the Children of Atom." Their worship of atomic energy is not ostensibly a religion rooted in a long tradition, but is fundamentally part of a traumatizing contemporary reality: an undetonated warhead in a world destroyed by atomic bombs.

Nuclear power, deified as Atom, is worshipped to have destructive and metamorphic, cleansing properties: "We must suffer to truly feel Atom's embrace, to lay broken before Him, and feel the gentle wash of the Glow." While the pre-existing, pre-apocalyptic religions are practically extinct, the Church of the Children of Atom is a post-war religious cult that worships 'Atom' as their singular divine agent, which is omnipresent, omniscient and omnipotent. Atom is everywhere, knows everything, and has the power to affect the properties of different bodies in the world. As the game's loading screen—which acts as a type of narrator, normally dispensing game-play tips and lore from an extra-diegetic, objective perspective—occasionally explains: "The Church of the Children of Atom believe the war of 2077 was actually a great holy event perpetuated by their god, Atom."

Starting with *Fallout* 3, the player is introduced to Church of the Children of Atom in Megaton—not coincidentally also the name for an explosive measurement unit. The town, which is likely one of the first that players encounter (cf. Bainbridge 2016), is host to an undetonated atom bomb, discovered by survivors in the wasteland of what was formerly Washington, D.C. Megaton was built around the bomb, which the inhabitants came to fear, respect and eventually worship (Figure 1). The centrality of this religion to Megaton can most literally be seen through its map location, at the center of the settlement (Figure 2). Town and Church are effectively led by Confessor Cromwell, who can be seen in Figure 1 preaching Atom's power to all who can hear:

"Give your bodies to Atom, my friends. Release yourself to his power, feel his Glow and be Divided.

Yea, your suffering shall exist no longer; it shall be washed away in Atom's Glow, burned from you in the fire of his brilliance.

Come forth and drink the water of the glow. For this ancient weapon of war is our salvation, it is the very symbol of Atom's glory. Let it serve as a reminder of the division that has occurred in the past."

Here, Atom is said to come and divide our cells, ending our earthly suffering. Atom is present anywhere, from the "infinite worlds" inside our every cell, to the huge radiation storms, powerful ecological consequences of the nuclear fallout that plagues the wasteland. Thus, the Church was created and fortified in Megaton where its first settlers took shelter in the crater in the 23rd century—and it has spread across the United States since then, as the appearance of the Church attests to in various places in *Fallout 4*, which takes place barely 10 years later.

Figure 1. Confessor Cromwell preaching and praying next to the atom bomb.

Figure 2. Megaton's map (*Fallout* Wikia n.d.).

Fallout 3 presents a world in which the near-complete destruction of human civilization means that most scientific and traditional institutions have disappeared. After the apocalypse, the raw power of nuclear energy can only be understood as phenomenal. Additionally, the disappearance of any necessary knowledge of nuclear power—most appliances from before the apocalypse still work—makes it into a magical, incomprehensible power. Its destructive potential can only be imagined, while its altering effect on mutated humans and animals can still be seen. While the Church of the

Children of Atom deifies this potential, *Fallout 3* contrasts it with another religious institution, that of a more romantic spiritual cult, the Treeminders. The Treeminders are a community in Oasis—an immediate visual opposite to Megaton: verdant, sprawling and multi-levelled. It can only be accessed through an arduous and hidden mountain path. There, rather than a loudly preaching Confessor Cromwell at the center of Megaton, stands a soft-spoken Tree Father Birch, who guards the entrance and invites the player inside. The two religions even act as symmetrical gameplay options, in that the player has the option to fully destroy either town (cf. Bosman 2017), Oasis and Megaton, to violently erase the worship of these antithetic gods (destruction vs. creation).

As opposed to Atom, the Treeminders deify nature, embodied in the shape of 'The Great One,' a talking tree. The Great One—or as he's also called The Lord, Him, The One Who Grows, Gives, and Guides, and The Talking Tree, or simply Harold – is the product of a retrovirus exposure that was supposed to create resistance to radiation but instead created mutated humans. The retrovirus' effect on Harold is that a tree started growing out of him until he became one with it (Figure 3).

Figure 3. Harold, The One Who Grows, Gives and Guides, talking to the player.

Harold, however, has no pretensions of being a god and is not happy with the cult's veneration of him. His mutations gave birth to the entire forest of Oasis, an achievement considered a miracle in the destitute Wasteland. On a ludic level, the player can decide to let the tree die (a wish expressed by Harold as well) and completely destroy the last kernels of this spiritual and romantic cult; or instead to let him selflessly live to create new forests. Whereas nature was killed by the atom bomb (the god of the Children of Atom), the initial retrovirus that was supposed to make humans resistant to Atom's radiation fights back through Harold.

In the more recent *Fallout 4*, the Church of the Children of Atom is now present in a totally irradiated environment, The Glowing Sea (Figure 4). Upon meeting the leader of the cult's base in the Glowing Sea, players may ask "Holy Ground? Atom? What's going on here?" The explanation is that "Atom reached out and touched this world, bringing his Glow to us. It remains to this day, a reminder of his promise. Infinite worlds through division." The survival of the cult in the normally instantly fatal environment is rationalized as being a supernatural gift:

"That is Atom's unique gift to us, the true believers.

He has brought us here to this place, a place that cannot harm us, so that we may worship him. So that we may spread his word to others.

That is our calling. To deliver Atom's message to a world that does not wish to hear it. To show Atom's power to all."

Figure 4. Atom's place of worship, next to a radiated water crater, in the Glowing Sea.

In the *Far Harbor DLC*, players can join the church after completing a quest that resembles an initiation ritual, to seek the "Sacred ELEMENTS, guide to Atom's HOLY word" (Figure 5), which turns out to be the Periodic Table (Figure 6). Upon doing so, players meet The Mother of the Fog, the Children's spirit leader sent from Atom to guide them. The MoThEr (Figure 7) spirit is the figure shrouded in mist (atomic glow) who passes down Atom's will and guides the player to the periodic table, their Bible.

Figure 5. The scroll that guides believers to Atom's "HOLY word."

In all, the *Fallout* games imagine a world destroyed by nuclear war in which previous institutions, religious and otherwise, have been destroyed. In this context, one of the first settlements the player of *Fallout 3* encounters is Megaton, where one religious group is central. This group, the Church of the Children of Atom, worships Atom: a masculine, incomprehensibly opaque deification of atomic power. Atom is presented as omnipresent, omniscient and omnipotent and is worshipped by building a religion around an undetonated nuclear bomb (in *Fallout 3*) and later by expanding church sites to irradiated lands (*Fallout 4*). In its reverence of atomic power, exemplified through the glorification of the periodic table, ideas of division and theories of atoms found "within" everything, the Church presents a parody of a contemporary 'science—religion' divide in popular culture. Even its direct contrast, the religion of the Treeminders, which opposes the Children of Atom thematically (revering nature instead of science), should be seen as a way of dealing with the consequences of man-made nuclear fall-out through religious metaphors. Both, importantly, appear possible only against the background of the total erasure of previous historical religious institutions.

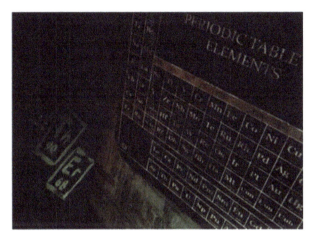

Figure 6. The Periodic Table that serves as the holy text of the Church of the Children of Atom.

Figure 7. The MoThEr aids the player in their quest to become a member of the Church of the Children of Atom.

3.2. Horizon: Zero Dawn, "Mother Nature as an AI and the Ultimate Killer App"

Elisabeth Sobeck: *"What if we could give life—a future? What if we could build a kind of seed, from which, on a dead planet, life could blossom anew? This is the aim—the hope—of Project: Zero Dawn: to create a super-intelligent, fully-automated terraforming system—and bring life back from lifelessness. What would such a system require? At its core, it would need a true AI. Fully capable*

of making the trillions of decisions necessary to reconstitute the biosphere. An immortal guardian,
devoted to the re-flourishing of life. We call it GAIA. Mother Nature as an AI."

Another recent game that explores technology through several religious metaphors is *Horizon:*
Zero Dawn. The storyline of *Horizon* revolves around a post-apocalyptic world set in the 31st century,
wherein human life as we know it has gone extinct. The old civilization created (military) machines,
technology, and AI that became uncontrollable, got corrupted, and went completely haywire thereby
consuming biomass and destroying all life on earth in the process.

In a last attempt to save the earth, a small group of programmers, scientists and scholars developed
an independent AI system called GAIA that is tasked with recreating a sustainable earth and biosphere.
GAIA consists of several subsystems with names such as HADES, ARTEMIS, DEMETER, and so on,
each with their own function to rebuild (human) life on earth in the future. The diegetic setting for the
31st century, however, is a world dominated and ruled by overdeveloped machines that are on top of
the food chain and that become increasingly dangerous and destructive. Humans, on the other hand,
find themselves somewhere at the bottom of the food chain. Once more they live in what appear to
be 'pre-historic' tribes where they try to survive as hunters and gatherers. In this setting, the player
controls and leads a young woman named Aloy through the game world to protect her tribe against
hostile tribes and to unravel the truth about a long lost civilization, called the Old Ones – to be equated
with current, contemporary American civilization (the game takes place more specifically around
Colorado Springs.

Not only the living conditions of humans are reduced to pre-historic manners and lifestyles, some
of the tribes also rely on rather primitive forms of religion. The religion of Aloy's tribe, which frames
much of the game from beginning to end, is one of matriarchal monotheism centered around technology
and AI. Unbeknownst to the fictional characters due to a total loss of knowledge regarding technology,
what they are glorifying as a Goddess was once human-made. The tribe in question, the Nora,
are controlled by matriarchs; whereas the primary antagonists make up a predominantly male,
militaristic cult called the Eclipse, who fittingly worship a subsystem called HADES.

The Nora worship what they consider to be a goddess, namely "All-Mother." In the mission
'Mother's Heart,' however, it immediately becomes clear for the player and Aloy that All-Mother
is nothing more than a huge mechanical door controlled by an AI that 'speaks' with a female-like
computer-generated voice (Figures 8 and 9). To many modern players, the All-Mother immediately
reminds them of our contemporary voice interfaces: not much more than a door-guarding version of
Apple's *Siri* or Amazon's *Alexa*. The door is hidden deep within a mountain that is considered to be
sacred ground and is therefore forbidden territory for all Nora except the matriarchs. Although Aloy
understands at first glance that the goddess is a door, the matriarch accompanying her is convinced that
the door is divine and cannot comprehend, nor is willing to believe, that her goddess is human-made.

The same counts for the Eclipse who worship the main antagonist of the game, a metal devil
called "HADES" that communicates with a male-like computer-generated voice. In the mission 'Deep
Secrets of the Earth' it is called "the ultimate killer app" by its maker as HADES' original function
was to reset the earth in case GAIA's attempts of creating a new sustainable world resulted in failure:
"HADES takes the biosphere back to 0, square one, a clean slate. [. . .] It is extinction on demand,
death on speed dial." In the mission 'To Curse the Darkness' it is revealed that the Eclipse believe
HADES is a god and, therefore, they execute his commands. These encompass the (re)assembly and
the repair of killer machines; as well as the assassination of Aloy, making HADES the prime antagonist.
In doing so, his cult-followers believe that HADES will eventually help the Eclipse in controlling
and commanding the dangerous machines roaming the wildlands so they can use these machines to
conquer the world. They do not realize that HADES controls and uses them with the goal of causing
another apocalypse that will destroy humanity once and for all—including them.

Figure 8. Aloy tries to explain to a matriarch that All-Mother is actually a door.

Figure 9. Aloy in front of an activated "All-Mother"—a glorified, but artificially intelligent door lock.

Both the All-Mother and HADES, then, are confused for wise, utopian agents, even though their goals are clear and their algorithms do not encompass more than that. HADES is the "extinction failsafe protocol" for GAIA, the head AI charged with repopulation; the All-Mother is the Nora's name for GAIA's digital door-guard. Machines and extremely intelligent AI have thus become so incomprehensible for 31st-century humans that they are considered to be gods and goddesses and are worshipped with utter devotion.

The metaphor of gods and goddesses for AI and machines is taken one step further as the player discovers more of *Horizon's* plot. As mentioned in the first paragraph, the previous civilization (Old Ones) realized that humanity would go extinct and, in one last attempt to save the earth and some form of life in the future, they created GAIA:

"A super intelligent, fully-automated terraforming system. [. . .] [a] true AI. Fully capable of making the trillions of decisions necessary to reconstitute the biosphere. An immortal guardian, devoted to the re-flourishing of life. We call it GAIA. Mother Nature as an AI."

The religious metaphor already comes to the fore in the names given to GAIA's subsystems, all based on the names of ancient Greek gods and goddesses (Figure 10; Table 1): APOLLO, DEMETER, POSEIDON, and so on. Additionally, it is evident in their functions. For instance, in the mission 'The Heart of the Nora' the player and Aloy discover that after the apocalypse, humanity was recreated by one of GAIA's subsystems and machines in cradle facilities called ELEUTHIA, after the Greek goddess of childbirth and midwifery. In these facilities the genetic codes of the Old Ones are preserved and used to breed new human beings. The machines are programmed in such a way that they can nurture these new humans into fully-grown adults that are able to procreate themselves and the facilities are equipped with anything needed to sustain these new human beings ranging from food, toys, and even an internal educational system called APOLLO that was supposed to teach humans everything about the extinct civilization (Figures 11 and 12).

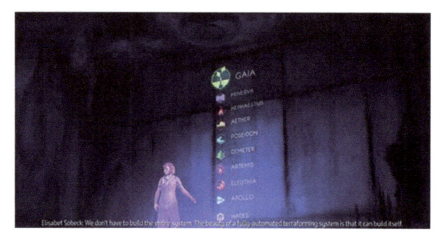

Figure 10. GAIA and her subsystems named after Greek gods and goddesses, and one Roman goddess.

Figure 11. A hologram explains to Aloy and the player how cradle facilities (ELEUTHIA) work.

Yet, AI and machines are not only capable of assembling human beings and recreating the biosphere. Even before the apocalypse, the AI of machines was developed enough to learn how to make themselves more powerful and how to "procreate." As these systems were developed without a backdoor in their programming, the Old Ones called destruction upon themselves as they could not stop the machines from reproducing, and feeding on bio-matter from plants to animals to humans. This process continues after the apocalypse. As a result, so-called "machine cradles" are scattered throughout *Horizon's* game environment. These machine cradles function as factories wherein new machines are assembled and programmed. In this way, the survival of the murderous machine population is guaranteed.

Table 1. An overview of the most important AIs and their primary mythological origins (*Horizon Zero Dawn* Wikia n.d.; Smith 1872; Grimal 1996).

AI	Description	*Mythology*
AETHER	AETHER is the subfunction of GAIA dedicated to detoxifying the Earth's ravaged atmosphere.	Personification of the upper sky.
APOLLO	APOLLO is the subfunction dedicated to the archival of human history and culture, and the education of new generations of humans born in Cradle facilities.	Greek god of the sun and light, music, truth and prophecy, healing, poetry.
ARTEMIS	ARTEMIS is the subfunction dedicated to the creation and reintroduction of animal life onto a newly-terraformed Earth.	Greek goddess of the hunt, wild animals, wilderness, childbirth, virginity and protector of young girls.
DEMETER	DEMETER is the subfunction dedicated to the replanting of the Earth from cryopreserved seed stocks.	Greek goddess of the harvest and agriculture
ELEUTHIA	ELEUTHIA is the subfunction dedicated to the cloning and raising of humans from genetic stock at specially designed and prepared Cradle facilities scattered across the Earth.	Greek goddess of childbirth and midwifery.
GAIA	GAIA is the main A.I. overseeing repopulation of the earth. GAIA and her subordinate functions are tasked with re-terraforming the Earth back to its pre-apocalyptic state.	Personification of the Earth.
HADES	HADES is the "extinction failsafe protocol"—the last resort for GAIA, which would allow it to destroy and reset the terraforming process when an undesirable outcome is detected.	Greek god of the dead, of the Underworld, darkness, the Earth, fertility, riches, mortality, afterlife and metal.
HEPHAESTUS	HEPHAESTUS is the subfunction dedicated to the construction of underground Cauldron facilities that would build the machines needed to complete the terraforming project.	Greek god of blacksmiths, metalworking, carpenters, craftsmen, artisans, sculptors, metallurgy, fire, and volcanoes.
MINERVA	MINERVA is the subfunction dedicated to the construction of massive communications arrays to broadcast the deactivation codes to the berserk apocalyptic robots.	Roman goddess of wisdom and strategic warfare.
POSEIDON	POSEIDON is the subfunction dedicated to detoxifying the Earth's poisoned seas and oceans.	Greek god of the Sea and other waters; of earthquakes; and of horses.

Thus, machines and AI are not only incomprehensible and destructive, but also more powerful, productive, and creative than humans. The old civilization could not save itself from the machine-apocalypse and had to rely on AI, subsystems, and machines to safeguard the existence of a possible future humanity and to recreate life on earth. In the same way, humans in the 31st century are only able to exist because they were created by machines in special cradles facilities controlled by a powerful, overarching AI system and subsystems. In that sense, humans no longer dominate and control life, AI and the machines they once created and developed, but it is AI and machines that are in the position to sustain or destroy the biosphere and life in general.

Finally, although some humans like Aloy by accident come to use technological objects, it is a world that has fundamentally come to fear technology. At the same time, the name Aloy itself echoes an alloy, any combination of two metal materials—just as the player controls the cyborg combination of Aloy's body and the technological projections of the 'focus'. A Focus is a small augmented reality device that Aloy finds at the beginning of the game, which can provide wearers with a multi-purpose 3D neural interface and communication possibilities (Figure 13). These small devices were developed by the Old Ones to simplify interactions between humans, and with machines, technology. They react to the voice and gestures of the person using the device—much like a fictionalized Google Glass. In one of the first playable parts of the game, Aloy finds a Focus in the ruins of what once used to be a workplace or bunker of the Old Ones. This little device is then used by Aloy and the player to discover relevant and interesting objects in the game environment, to scan documents and holograms left by the Old Ones, and to distinguish between friends and foes. However, as these ruins are considered to be cursed by the Nora, the little device is also seen as something dangerous. On the other hand, among the Eclipse, the Focuses have a divine connotation as these are given to them by HADES and the devices allow them to communicate with each other, as well as directly with HADES.

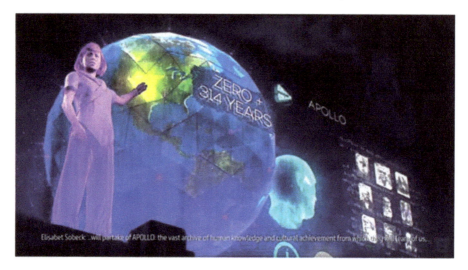

Figure 12. A hologram explains the educational APOLLO archive.

Figure 13. Aloy as a child with her "Focus" (the little triangular device above her ear).

Horizon: Zero Dawn thus portrays a post-apocalyptic world in which technology, machines, and AI are worshipped and feared by human tribes for two main reasons. On the one hand, AI, machines and technology are more intelligent, developed, creative, and powerful than humans. On the other hand, AI, machines, and technology are opaque and incomprehensible: humans lack the historical and technological knowledge to understand these inventions—resorting to worship their power in ignorance.

4. Conclusions

The fictional worlds of both *Fallout* and *Horizon* show similar imaginations of how to deal with technology: through metaphors of divinity. In the *Fallout* series, the Church of the Children of Atom substantially deifies the Atomic bomb, personifying it as a masculine god that is incomprehensible, everywhere, all-knowing and all-powerful. This "ancient weapon of war is our salvation," and shall usher in a time through the "fire of his brilliance"—playing on both meanings of brilliance as intelligent and glowing—in which you may "release yourself to his power, feel his Glow and be Divided." Rather than just being one possible imagination of religion in the post-apocalypse, the Children of Atom show a deeply familiar way for human societies to deal with the incomprehensible, omnipresent, omniscient and omnipotent nature of 'Atom.' This conception of Atom by the Church as such echoes many divine descriptions in the Bible such as Psalm 145:17, describing the god of Abrahamic traditions as "righteous in all his ways, and faithful in all he does." It additionally mirrors the Biblical God's supposed *omnipresence* (Psalm 139:7–10; Jeremiah 23:24; 1)—"Behold, heaven and the highest heaven cannot contain You, how much less this house which I have built" (Kings 8:27)—his *omniscience*—"His understanding is infinite" (Psalm 147:5) and he "knows all things" (1 Jn.3:18–20)—and his *omnipotence* (Rev.19:6; Eph.3:20):

> "He is wise in heart and mighty in strength, who has defied Him without harm? It is God who removes the mountains, they know not how, when He overturns them in His anger; who shakes the earth out of its place, And its pillars tremble; who commands the sun not to shine, and sets a seal upon the stars; who alone stretches out the heavens and tramples down the waves of the sea; who makes the Bear, Orion and the Pleiades, and the chambers of the south; who does great things, unfathomable, and wondrous works without number." (Job 9:4–10)

How similar in strength and scope is the discourse on Atom?

> "Behold! He's coming with the clouds! And every eye shall be blind with his glory! Every ear shall be stricken deaf to hear the thunder of his voice!
>
> Each of us shall give birth to a billion stars formed from the mass of our wretched and filthy bodies."

Even when we contrast the Church of the Children of Atom to their obvious counterpart, the role of religion in making sense of the post-apocalypse becomes clear. That is, whereas the Treeminders form a Church based on nature instead of science—worshipping a forest, rather than the periodic table—and on creation instead of destruction. Both are ways of coping with man-made disaster, and the atomic power that led to the barren post-apocalyptic wasteland of *Fallout*. More importantly, both are specifically new, uniquely technology-driven ways of coping with the apocalypse that are enabled only after the erasure of pre-existing institutions and traditions of worship after the fallout.

In *Horizon: Zero Dawn*, too, we see a similar situation. The Nora and Eclipse both worship and follow leftover, pre-apocalyptic inventions of Artificial Intelligence because they are incomprehensible to their primitive societies. They *seem* wise, but the game provides little reason for why the Nora and Eclipse started following them. Similarly to *Fallout*, these technological innovations are presented to post-apocalyptic humans as incomprehensible, destructive *and* creative, powerful *and* productive;

all of which seem to lead to no other choice within these fictional worlds than to worship them. The machines of *Horizon: Zero Dawn*, much like Atom and the Treeminders' deified Harold, were both misunderstood but nonetheless seen as creators and controllers of life: incomprehensible, omnipresent, omniscient and omnipotent.

We argue that these games show religious faith and worship applied not to historical, mythological gods or the natural world, but to the very technological innovations that brought on the apocalypse. *Fallout* and *Horizon* are far from the only games to employ metaphors of divinity in order to make sense of the destructive and awe-some power of technologies. Indeed, similar patterns can be found in a variety of post-apocalyptic games, from *NEO Scavenger*'s Church of the Blue Frog, *Fallen Earth*'s tech-obsessed religion, *Metro 2033*'s cults and churches, *Final Fantasy X*'s Yevon religion, the *Destiny* series' Traveller and its prophet the Speaker, *NieR: Automata*'s devoutly religious "Machines," lead by Adam and Eve. Such post-apocalyptic games, we argue, exemplify the under-acknowledged alternative of "science fiction-based religion" next to the well-documented and commercially well-represented traditions of history-based and fantasy (fiction-)based religion. As opposed to those traditions' nostalgic framing of religion, science fiction-based religion has been represented since the 1980s as a way of making sense of technologies and their implications for humans. That is, technology is consequently framed as an opaque force with god-like powers—whether it is cyberspace, the matrix, the atomic bomb or self-reproducing artificial intelligence—these are 'things greater than thou.'

The religious imagery about such powerful technologies, we demonstrated, is perceived as highly ambivalent. They are potentially destructive and constructive; frightening and fascinating; divine and demonic. In the analysis of, what he calls, 'posthuman technologies' in contemporary science fiction, Daniel Dinello (2005) argues that this ambivalence is key. On the one hand, AI, biotech, VR or nanotechnology promise humans "techno-heaven"—engineered salvation from the biological body and even an "immortal mind" (Noble 1999). On the other hand, it may bring us 'techno-hell'—computers taking over and, ultimately, bringing about an apocalypse: the 'Singularity' (Kurzweil 2005), the "rapture of the nerds" (Popper 2012) or "apocalyptic AI' (Geraci 2012). From the academic perspective of religious studies and the sociology of religion, this ambivalence may be the core of the religious sentiment underpinning science fiction-based religion (Aupers 2009; Aupers et al. 2008). In *The Threshold of Religion* (Marett 1914), Robert Marett explained the birth of 'nature religion' by the fact that 'primitives' found themselves confronted with a natural environment they could neither understand nor control their natural environment; they therefore experienced it as an overpowering, mysterious force ('mana') that invoked the basic the basic religious emotion of 'awe,' a combination of fascination and fear: "of all English words awe is, I think, the one that expresses the basic religious feeling most nearly" (Ibid., p. 13). The theologian Rudolf Otto (Otto 1987), in turn, depicted the 'holy' as the Other—motivating a sense of 'fascinans' and 'tremendum.' Nowhere does this trembling awe and fascinated devotion—for Atom, for Artificial Intelligence—come together as obvious as in the genre of *Fallout* and *Horizon*. Not nature, but technology now seems to be the pinnacle of religious sentiments of 'awe'.

In conclusion, then, these two games typify a science fiction-based religiosity that reveres technology of the future—omnipresent, omniscient, and omnipotent technologies that invoke religious feelings of fear and fascination. Science fiction, however, feeds on science faction: these texts about an apocalyptic world governed by technologies comment on, speculate about and make sense of emergent technologies in contemporary society—atomic bombs, AI and VR. More than that, they reproduce some of the dreams and nightmares formulated by technological pioneers in Silicon Valley—such as those of 'posthumanists' like robotics specialist Moravec (1988) or futurist Ray Kurzweil (2005), theorizing about AIs as 'mind children,' 'uploading consciousness' or the 'singularity.' By playing apocalyptic games *about* machines *on* machines, players inhabit digital worlds that imagine ways to deal with the super-humanly powerful and intelligent technologies that will surround us, or already do. The God metaphor, so it seems, plays an essential role in this imagination.

Author Contributions: L.d.W. and S.A. conceived of the paper. C.K. and I.C. did the primary work on gathering and analyzing the material case studies. Theoretical framing and final analysis were performed by all four co-authors in collaboration, with the final editing being done primarily by L.d.W. All authors contributed substantially throughout the process.

Funding: This research received no external funding.

Acknowledgments: The authors would like to thank Yeheng Pan, Marie Figoureux and Thom Frissen for their support and significant aid throughout the process of writing. Special thanks go out to XL Noodles for hosting many a disillusioned author's necessary break.

Conflicts of Interest: The authors declare no conflict of interest.

References

Aarseth, Espen. 2001. Computer game studies, year one. *Game Studies* 1: 1–15.

Aupers, Stef. 2007. "Better than the real world". On the Reality and Meaning of Online Computer Games. *Fabula* 48: 250–69. [CrossRef]

Aupers, Stef. 2009. The force is great: enchantment and magic in silicon valley. *Masaryk UJL & Tech* 3: 153.

Aupers, Stef, and Dick Houtman. 2010. Religions of Modernity: Relocating the Sacred to the Self and the Digital. In *Religions of Modernity*. Leiden: Brill, pp. 1–30.

Aupers, Stef, Houtman Dick, and Peter Pels. 2008. Cybergnosis: Technology, Religion and the Secular. In *Religion: Beyond a Concept*. New York: Fordham University Press.

Aupers, Stef, Schaap Julian, and Lars de Wildt. 2018. Qualitative In-Depth Interviews: Studying Religious Meaning-Making in MMOs. In *Methods for Studying Video Games and Religion*. Edited by Vit Sisler, Kerstin Radde-Antweiler and Xenia Zeiler. London: Routledge.

Bainbridge, William Sims. 2013. *EGods: Faith versus Fantasy in Computer Gaming*. Oxford: Oxford University Press.

Bainbridge, William Sims. 2016. *Virtual Sociocultural Convergence*. Basel: Springer International Publishing.

Benedikt, Michael. 1992. *Cyberspace: First Steps*. Cambridge: MIT Press.

Berger, Peter. 1967. *The Sacred Canopy: Elements of a Sociological Theory of Religion*. New York: Doubleday.

Bleiler, Everett Franklin. 1990. *Science-Fiction, the Early Years: A Full Description of More Than 3,000 Science-Fiction Stories from Earliest Times to the Appearance of the Genre Magazines in 1930: With Author, Title, and Motif Indexes*. Kent: Kent State University Press.

Bosman, Frank. 2016. The Word Has Become Game: Researching Religion in Digital Games. *Online Heidelberg Journal of Religions on the Internet* 11: 28–45.

Bosman, Frank. 2017. There Is No Solution! "Wicked Problems" in Digital Games. *Games and Culture* 1–7. [CrossRef]

Bosman, Frank, and Marcel Poorthuis. 2015. Nephilim: The Children of Lilith. The Place of Man in the Ontological and Cosmological Dualism of the Diablo, Darksiders and Devil May Cry Game Series. *Online-Heidelberg Journal of Religions on the Internet* 7: 190–207. [CrossRef]

Cavallaro, Dani. 2000. *Cyberpunk and Cyberculture*. London and New Brunswick: Athlone Press.

Copier, Marinka. 2005. Connecting worlds. Fantasy role-playing games, ritual acts and the magic circle. Paper presented at DiGRA 2005 Conference: Changing Views—Worlds in Play, Vancouver, BC, Canada, June 16–20.

Curry, Patrick. 1998. *Defending Middle-Earth: Tolkien, Myth & Modernity*. London: Harper Collins Publishers.

Curry, Patrick. 1999. Magic vs. enchantment. *Journal of Contemporary Religion* 14: 104–12. [CrossRef]

Curry, Patrick. 2005. Tolkien and his critics: A critique. *Root and Branch—Approaches Towards Understanding Tolkien* 119: 81–148.

Davidsen, Markus Altena. 2013. Fiction-based religion: Conceptualising a new category against history-based religion and fandom. *Culture and Religion* 14: 378–95. [CrossRef]

Davis, Erik. 1998. *TechGnosis. Myth, Magic and Mysticism in the Age of Information*. New York: Three Rivers.

De Wildt, Lars. 2014. Precarious play: To be or not to be Stanley. *Press Start* 1: 1–20.

De Wildt, Lars, and Stef Aupers. 2017. Bibles and BioShock: Affording Religious Discussion on Video Game Forums. In *Proceedings of the Annual Symposium on Computer-Human Interaction in Play*. New York: ACM, pp. 463–75.

De Wildt, Lars, and Stef Aupers. 2018. Playing the Other: Role-Playing Religion in Videogames. *European Journal of Cultural Studies* 21. forthcoming.

Dery, Mark. 1996. *Escape Velocity: Cyberculture at the End of the Century*. New York: Grove Press.

Dinello, Daniel. 2005. *Technophobia!: Science Fiction Visions of Posthuman Technology*. Austin: University of Texas Press.

Fallout Wikia. n.d. Available online: http://fallout.wikia.com/wiki/Fallout_Wiki (accessed on 1 May 2018).

Fine, Gary Alan. 1983. *Shared Fantasy: Role Playing Games as Social Worlds*. Chicago: University of Chicago Press.

Fitting, Peter. 2010. Utopia, dystopia and science fiction. In *The Cambridge Companion to Utopian Literature*. Cambridge: Cambridge University Press, p. 135.

Frasca, Gonzalo. 2003. Ludologists love stories, too: Notes from a debate that never took place. Paper presented at Digital Games Research Conference, Utrecht, The Netherlands, November 4–6.

Geraci, Robert. 2012. *Apocalyptic AI: Visions of Heaven in Robotics, Artificial Intelligence, and Virtual Reality*. Oxford: Oxford University Press.

Gregory, Rabia. 2014. Citing the Medieval: Using Religion as World Building Infrastructure in Fantasy MMORPGs. In *Playing with Religion in Digital Games*. Edited by Heidi Campbell and Gregory Price Grieve. Bloomington: Indiana University Press.

Grimal, Pierre. 1996. The Dictionary of Classical Mythology. Hoboken: Wiley-Blackwell.

Guyker, Robert William. 2014. The Mythic Scope of Journey. A Comparative Assessment Concerning the Spirit at Play and Cybernetic Shamanism. *Online-Heidelberg Journal of Religions on the Internet* 5: 317–52. [CrossRef]

Heidbrink, Simone, Tobias Knoll, and Jan Wysocki. 2014. Theorizing religion in digital games. Perspectives and approaches. *Online-Heidelberg Journal of Religions on the Internet* 5: 5–51. [CrossRef]

Heim, Michael. 1993. *The Metaphysics of Virtual Reality*. Oxford and New York: Oxford University Press.

Horizon Zero Dawn Wikia. n.d. Available online: horizonzerodawn.wikia.com/wiki/Horizon_Zero_Dawn_Wikia (accessed on 1 May 2018).

Huizinga, Jopie. 1970. *Homo Ludens*. London: Paladin.

Jameson, Fredric. 1975. Magical narratives: romance as genre. *New Literary History* 7: 135–63. [CrossRef]

Jenkins, Henry. 2006. *Convergence Culture: Where Old and New Media Collide*. New York: NYU Press.

King, Brad, and John Borland. 2003. *Dungeons and Dreamers: The Rise of Computer Game Culture. From Geek to Chic*. New York and Chicago: McGraw-Hill.

Krzywinska, Tanya. 2006. Blood Scythes, Festivals, Quests, and Backstories: World Creation and Rhetorics of Myth in World of Warcraft. *Games and Culture* 1: 383–96. [CrossRef]

Kurzweil, Ray. 2005. *The Singularity Is Near: When Humans Transcend Biology*. London: Penguin.

Latour, Bruno. 2012. *We Have Never Been Modern*. Boston: Harvard University Press.

Leibovitz, Liel. 2014. *God in the Machine: Video Games as Spiritual Pursuit*. West Conshohocken: Templeton Foundation Press.

Marett, Robert Ranulph. 1914. *The Threshold of Religion*. London: Methuen and Co. Ltd. First published 1909.

Masso, Isamar Carrillo, and Nathan Abrams. 2014. Locating the Pixelated Jew. In *Playing with Religion in Digital Games*. Edited by Heidi Campbell and Gregory Price Grieve. Bloomington: Indiana University Press.

Moravec, Hans. 1988. *Mind Children: The Future of Robot and Human Intelligence*. Boston: Harvard University Press.

Murray, Janet Horowitz. 2005. The last word on ludology v narratology in game studies. Paper presented at International DiGRA 2005 Conference: Changing Views—Worlds in Play, Vancouver, BC, Canada, June 16–20.

Noble, David. 1999. *The Religion of Technology: The Divinity of Man and the Spirit of Invention*. New York and London: Penguin Books. First published 1997.

Otto, Rudoolf. 1987. *Das Heilige. Über das irrationale in der idee des göttlichen und sein verhältnis zum rationalen*. München: Verlag CH Beck. First published 1917.

Popper, Ben. 2012. Rapture of the Nerds. The Verge, October 22. Available online: https://www.theverge.com/2012/10/22/3535518/singularity-rapture-of-the-nerds-gods-end-human-race (accessed on 1 May 2018).

Possamai, Adam. 2005. *Religion and Popular Culture: A Hyper-Real Testament*. No. 7. Brussels: Peter Lang.

Schaap, Julian, and Stef Aupers. 2017. 'Gods in World of Warcraft exist': Religious reflexivity and the quest for meaning in online computer games. *New Media & Society* 19: 1744–60.

Šisler, Vit. 2006. Representation and self-representation: Arabs and Muslims in digital games. In *Gaming Realities: A Challenge for Digital Culture*. Athens: Fournos.

Šisler, Vit. 2008. Digital Arabs: Representation in Video Games. *European Journal of Cultural Studies* 11: 203–20.

Šisler, Vit. 2009. Palestine in pixels: The holy land, Arab-Israeli conflict, and reality construction in video games. *Middle East journal of Culture and Communication* 2: 275–93.

Smith, William. 1872. *Dictionary of Greek and Roman Biography and Mythology*. London: John Murray.

Stenger, Nicole. 1992. Mind Is a leaking Rainbow. In *Cyberspace: First Steps*. Edited by Michael Benedikt. Cambridge: MIT Press, pp. 49–58.

Tolkien, John Ronald Reuel. 1939. *On Fairy-Stories*. Oxford: Oxford University Press, pp. 3–84.

Turkle, Sherry. 2002. Our Split Screens. *Etnofoor* 15: 5–19.

Wagner, Rachel. 2012. Godwired: Religion, Ritual and Virtual Reality. London: Routledge.

Weber, Max. 1948. Science as a Vocation. In *From Max Weber: Essays in Sociology*. Edited by Hans Heinrich Gerth and Charles Wright Mills. London: Routledge, pp. 129–56.

Wiemker, Markus, and Jan Wysocki. 2014. 'When people pray, a god is born ... This god is you!' An Introduction to Religion and God in Digital Games. *Online-Heidelberg Journal of Religions on the Internet* 5: 197–224. [CrossRef]

Zeiler, Xenia. 2018. Level Up: Methods for Studying Video Games and Religion. In *Methods for Studying Video Games and Religion*. London: Routledge, pp. 3–13.

Article

Play, Game, and Videogame: The Metamorphosis of Play

Javier Gil-Gimeno *, Celso Sánchez-Capdequí and Josetxo Beriain

Department of Sociology, Public University of Navarra, Campus Arrosadia s/n, 31006 Pamplona, Spain;
celso.sanchez@unavarra.es (C.S.-C.); josetxo@unavarra.es (J.B.)
* Correspondence: fcojavier.gil@unavarra.es

Received: 2 April 2018; Accepted: 12 May 2018; Published: 17 May 2018

Abstract: The question, the Fragestellung, which drives this paper is, can football video-games be analyzed from a religious perspective? We can answer positively, at least, provisionally. First, in order to demonstrate our approach, we will take into account the different conceptions on play drawn along sociological theories. Second, we will analyze Francis M. Cornford's contribution to the already forgotten but essential work by Jane Ellen Harrison, Themis: The Social Origins of the Greek Religion, in which he established an elective affinity between the origin of the Olympic Games and the annual ritual dedicated to the Daimon-God Dionysus, in which he was elected the best Kouros (Young hero-King) of the year. At the very beginning, play, ritual, and competitive games (helped by self-reflexivity as well as collective reflexivity) were united, and that constellation is still there in modern times with the creation of modern sport. Third, in modern advanced societies the football game-sport creates meaning, and succeeded throughout two main processes such as the sportification and progressive rationalization of violence. Fourth, we built an ideal type of two competing strategies, in which created a new type of hero, the sports hero, the modern celebrity. Finally, fifth, we analyze how in our digitalized societies the football videogames are a sort of play on the play of which comes out a religious transcendence associated with it, "Throughout the videogame I become myself in my idol". We explain this comparing two ideal types, the Dionysian-Messi versus the Apollonian-Ronaldo.

Keywords: play; game; football videogames; religion; ritual practices

---

1. Introduction

Play is one of the many realities that shape the world. One might even say it constitutes a world within the world, since it predates human culture. Animals played long before humans did. What is striking is that, amongst animals whose social structure with a varying degree of strong hierarchy, such as canines and primates, play is characterised by a sense of parity. Indeed, its purpose is to reduce inequalities associated with size, strength and social status. Play is egalitarian. Here, one can see a certain notion of justice, there is a series of rules and expectations that help neutralise the differences between individual animals, intended to maintain the harmony of the group (Bekoff and Jessica 2009, p. 121). Neither *homo erectus* nor their successor, *homo sapiens*, can equal the strength or speed of animals; nor can they match their skill at climbing trees or manipulating objects with their feet. Nonetheless, they have surpassed them by developing novel, speedy body postures and complex gestures, which can be used in dance, swimming, gymnastics, tool-building, mime, and gesture. What is truly surprising about the emergence of this new set of evolutionary skills, however, is that, although the product of imagination and learning, they are paradoxically manifested as the outcome of a useful uselessness of the immature. That is to say, these actions, which are functionally and pragmatically useless (either to children or to adults) are distinctively human and profoundly valuable (useful).

There are times and places in which "Human beings don't live in the real world" (Gopnik 2009, p. 19), such that they create a separate space-time, a world outside that other serious and pragmatic world of the everyday. This is the world of play.

2. An Analytical Vision of Play

In a work that had great sociological influence, George Herbert Mead [1934] (1962, pp. 152–64) introduced a crucial distinction between unregulated *play* and the regulated *game*. The aim of play, developed spontaneously by children, is to maximize pleasure. In the game, in contrast, the child—and by extension the adult—adopts the same attitude as everyone else involved in the same game. That is to say, he *follows the rules of the game*, in the terms established by Ludwig Wittgenstein (1988, p. 74). This attitude finds its expression "in taking the role of the other, playing at the expression of their gods and their heroes, going through certain rites which are the representation of what these individuals are supposed to be doing. The process is one which develops, to be sure, into a more or less definite technique and is controlled" (Mead [1934] 1962, p. 153). In accepting the roles of the others, players assume what is expected of them in their role and in their relation to the shared collective goal. They fully adopt and accept the organized guidelines of the team or the ensemble, which are born out of the 'generalized other' as a single entity to which the players belong, thus creating an 'us', an *esprit de corps*. In order to play in a team, the child must move from specific thought to abstract thought, allowing him or her to accept the rules not as 'mine', or 'yours', but as 'ours'. Whereas the search for pleasure is egocentric, *directed at oneself*, the search for group recognition and the collective excitation generated by the game among the spectators is *directed at others* (Elias and Dunning 1992, p. 251).

We have seen how play transgresses the limits of pure biology and physics, creating a sense, a meaning. By exceeding the bounds of the biological 'instinct', it creates a novel instance, the 'spirit'. As Johan Huizinga says in his *Homo Ludens*: "In the making of speech and language the spirit is continually 'sparking' between matter and mind, as it were, playing with the wondrous nominative faculty. [. . .] Thus, in giving expression to life man creates a second, poetic world alongside the world of nature" (Huizinga [1949] 1980, p. 4). However, before trying to define what play is, we should first establish what it is not. Play is not opposed to the serious; a child who plays does so seriously. Although one part of unregulated play provokes laughter that does not mean that they are the same. Nor should play be identified with the comic, which is related to the foolish, basically because play is not foolish. According to J. Huizinga [1949] (1980), it is a free activity, it is freedom. Play is not coercively activated. It represents a certain suspension of 'ordinary' life, a supra-logical counter-world, which transcends the logic of the normal-serious world, an interlude in everyday life. It creates its own space and its own time and generates an order that is parallel to (and, sometimes, in conflict with) the common order, as is the case with the carnival/Mardi-Gras celebration. In the game there is a clear tension, a sense of chance, uncertainty, contingency, or puzzle, all of which have to be confronted with bodily strength, stamina, inventiveness, daring, and cunning. When two contending groups (i.e., two teams) come together, this is manifested as a struggle, a fight between two polarities to which violence is progressively sublimated to become contest in pursuit of triumph and/or the breaking of a record.

Child's play is the most elementary form of play, but, as G. H. Mead has shown, it is transformed into more complex forms of game. As J. Huizinga puts it: "Archaic society, we would say, plays as the child or animal plays. Such playing contains at the outset all the elements proper to play: order, tension, movement, change, solemnity, rhythm, rapture. Only in a later phase of society is play associated with the idea of something to be expressed in and by it, namely, what we would call 'life' or 'nature'. Then, what was wordless play assumes poetic form. In the form and function of play, itself an independent entity which is senseless and irrational, man's consciousness that he is embedded in a sacred order of things finds its first, highest, and holiest expression. Gradually the significance of a sacred act permeates the playing. Ritual grafts itself upon it; but the primary thing is and remains play" (Huizinga [1949] 1980, pp. 17–18). As we shall explain in greater detail, using the evolutionary methodology developed by Merlin Donald (1991), the mimetic-imitative aspects of play are gradually complemented by higher and more advanced mythical-symbolic and theoretical forms. In other words, "in myth and ritual the great instinctive forces of civilized life have their origin: law and order, commerce and profit, craft and art, poetry, wisdom and science. All are rooted in the primeval soil of play" (Huizinga [1949] 1980, p. 5). 'The sacred' does not exist as a prior idea or belief in mysterious or supernatural beings; instead it is *only through ritual that it comes into existence*. The existence of 'the sacred' precedes the essence-belief in the sacred: "Only through the appropriating event of the ritual does the sacred (and its figures: demons, gods and men) emerge as something different to the secular." (Beriain 2015, pp. 4–7).

The act of ritual communion clearly unifies the group, but *around what*? Action, emotional energy, and shared feelings cannot be sustained for long when they are activated merely by constituting an intensification of the collective existence. It is here that society itself intervenes through a process of symbolic sublimation in which the symbol is objectivized. As G. H. Mead [1934] (1962) notes, the symbol is the mark of the transition from pure biological stimulus to *symbolic* re-presentation. It is an immensely consequential evolutionary feat, since it transforms the mimetic action into *symbolic action*, "thus extending the lifetime of ritually intensified sentiments" (Collins 2004, p. 34). Indeed, "Social sentiments could have only a precarious existence. Though very strong as long as men are together and influence each other reciprocally, they exist only in the form of recollections after the assembly has ended, and when left to themselves, these become feebler and feebler; for since the group is now no longer and active, individual temperaments easily regain the upper hand [. . .] Thus these systems of emblems, which necessary if society is to become conscious of itself, are no less indispensable for assuring the continuation of this consciousness" (Durkheim [1912] 1965, p. 263). The intention is to celebrate the solidarity of the group, attending to the sentiments of all its members and, probably, marking the identity of the group in opposition to others. *In-group* solidarity and *out-group* solidarity are human options that recur at all levels, e.g., in hunters and gatherers, groups of schoolchildren, football teams, and even nation-states. There are innumerable references to play in sacred texts, but both J. Huizinga [1949] (1980) and Robert N. Bellah in his latest work (Bellah 2011, pp. 109–10) view the Second and Seventh books of Plato (1980) *Laws* as the most relevant observations on play and its capacity to mediate domains of meaning, the sacred and the secular, and on the figures involved, gods and men. In the Second book, Plato explains the value of festivals and links their origin to children's play:

> "This education [based on the proper ordering of passions in childhood] which consists in correctly trained pleasures and pains tends to slacken in human beings, and in the course of a lifetime becomes corrupted to a great extent. So, taking pity on this suffering that is natural to the human race, the gods have ordained the cycle of festivals as times of rest from labour. They have given as fellow celebrants the Muses, with their leader Apollo, and Dionysus -in order that these divinities might set humans right again. Thus, men are sustained by their festivals in the company of gods" (Plato 1980, p. 36).

Finally, this passage from Book VII highlights the importance of play for Plato in the origin of ritual and myth:

> "I say that man must be serious with the serious. God alone is worthy of supreme seriousness, but man is made God's plaything, and that is the best part of him. Therefore, every man and woman should live life accordingly and play the noblest games and be of another mind from what they are at present [. . .] For they deem war a serious thing, though in war there is neither play nor culture worthy the name which are the things we deem most serious. Hence all must live in peace as well as they possibly can. What, then, is the right way of living? Life must be lived as play. Playing certain games, making sacrifices, singing and dancing, and then a man will be able to propitiate the gods, and defending himself against his enemies and win in the contest" (Plato 1980, p. 193).

3. From Play and Ritual Practice in the Social Genesis of the Olympic Games to Modern Sport

Without losing sight of the fact that ritual is itself no more than an evolved form of serious play—that is to say, a game—let us now examine the Hymn of the Kouretes in Ancient Greece. This will enable us to analyse *ritual as that complex form of game*, whose rationalized version was originally represented by the Olympic Games. The Hymn was the founding landmark or appropriating event, which we can use to identify the social genesis of the game. The Hymn of the *Kouretes* (Harrison 1912, pp. 1–29) provides an example of that *primitive rite of tribal initiation (Eniautos-Daimon)* (Harrison 1912, p. 16), which *performatively expresses* the Greek worldview. Based on archaeological findings, Jane E. Harrison recovers the syntax of ritual and explores its profound interpretative meaning. The Hymn comprises three phases (Harrison 1912, p. 9 and following). In the first phase, the *invocation*, the god—originally Dionysus and later Zeus—is challenged as an immortal child or *Kouros*. In the second phase, *ritual performativity*, the participants (*Kouretes*), armed with shields and in an emotional frenzy, tear the child from his mother, conceal him, 'kill' him, cut him to pieces and scatter his remains to the wild[1]. Finally, in the third phase, the child reappears, he is brought back to life, revived and becomes the *bearer of the collective wellbeing*.

Let us now examine how the religious character underlying the origins of the ancient Olympic Games (those staged between 776 and 393 BC) first arose. British philologist Francis M. Cornford contributed a chapter to Harrison's (1912) study on the origins of the Olympic Games in Classical Greece, which we will use to help focus our study. Cornford sets out two ideas that are fundamental to understanding the religious origin of the games: firstly, the link with a festival held to honour Dionysus and later Zeus, and second, the subsidiary role played by the sporting competition in this celebration. We shall examine these two ideas together.

As F. M. Cornford notes, in their origins, the Olympic Games were not associated with the festival as a whole, nor with its overall significance, but merely with a specific part, i.e., the annual selection of the "*Kouros*" or best of the young men. As part of the ritual festival, a race was held to choose this 'best among the young men', who would subsequently be honored with the singing of the Hymn of the *Kouretes*, accompanied by a ritual dance. These, then, are the origins of the Olympic Games. Essentially, there were two privileges associated with victory in the race to choose the *Greatest Kouros*. Firstly, the right to hold the title for a year (or a given period),[2] showing a clear continuity between this event and the festival related to the rebirth of the *Eniautos-Daimon* or annual spirit. The winning *kouros* was reborn as an adult being who could participate in society and, thanks to his victory, play a key role in it. The second privilege was associated with that role. The year's *kouros* was charged with heading the procession in which the community led a sacrificial bull to the altar of the god, where the central part of the rite was performed.

So, as F. M. Cornford says, "Had we begun this chapter with the statement that the triumphal procession, or *komos*, was the original kernel of the Olympic Games, it would have seemed, in the strict sense of the word, preposterous. But in view of the facts we have analysed and of the previous discussion of the Dithyramb (p. 205), it will not perhaps now seem paradoxical to suggest that this procession, with its sacrifice and eating of a bull, its hymn to the hero, and the concluding feast in the banqueting chamber, was the central rite, to which the foot-race of the Kouretes was a mere preliminary". (Cornford 1912, p. 256). As J. Huizinga rightly notes, "The rite is a *dromenon*, which means 'something acted', an act, action. That which is enacted, or the stuff of the action, is a *drama*, which again means act, action represented on a stage. Such action may occur as a performance or a contest" (Huizinga [1949] 1980, p. 14). The cult is a dramatic representation. Indeed, "At the great

---

[1] Note the parallels between the dismembering and the subsequent recreation in nature found in the Hymn of the Kouretes and the figure of Dionysos/Zagreo in Euripides' *Bacchae*, which follows the same mythological narrative.

[2] Although we do not know with certainty whether the rite was held every year, the victor held the title of *Kouros* for a specific period of time.

seasonal festivals the community celebrates the grand happenings in the life of nature by staging sacred performances, which represent the change of seasons, the rising and setting of the constellations, the growth and ripening of crops, birth, life and death in man and beast". (Huizinga [1949] 1980, p. 15).

Originally in the Olympic Games, which began with a foot race "for the kingdom" (Cornford 1912, p. 255), the *Kouros* of the Cretan Hymn analyzed here is depicted as the *leader of his daimons*. "The race, whose original purpose was simply to determine who should be the greatest Kouros or King of his year, developed by successive accretions into the elaborate athletic sports, which in later times came to be the central feature of the whole festival" (Cornford 1912, p. 256). Long Live King Heracles (Hercules)! He is the *Daimon* embodied in the *winner of the race* who, to a great extent, stands as the object of worship. The *Olympic victor* was the *daimon* of his year, the *local hero and king* (Cornford 1912, pp. 256–57) of the games, normally held in spring. In Cornford's explanation, we can clearly see the process whereby the part is substituted for the whole, where a single section of the original religious rite—the foot race to choose the *Kouros* of the year—mutates into a lay ritual ceremony converted into a global mass phenomenon, i.e., the modern Olympics. As Cornford himself says, "The race, whose original purpose was simply to determine who should be the greatest Kouros or King of his year, developed by successive accretions into the elaborate athletic sports, which in later times came to be the central feature of the whole festival" (Cornford 1912, p. 256), it becomes a competitive de-ritualized Olympic, act.

J. Huizinga identifies two levels of play in social life. One lies below the threshold of consciousness and is dominated by an "only pretending" (Huizinga [1949] 1980, p. 8) that forges reality. In another, conscious level, the skill and determination inherent to precarious social balances are regulated. In Huizinga's words, "In play we may move below the level of the serious, as the child does; but we can also move above it-in the realm of the beautiful and the sacred" (Huizinga [1949] 1980, p. 19).

Since time immemorial, its presence has formed part of the *unwritten history* of humankind in which the conditions of human representation and their mother element, *theory*, are forged. Play—and more specifically, its primordial version, the rite understood as a rhythmic, ensemble, and coordinated expression of dramatic movements constituting ordered coexistence—is established in the pre-narrative substratum as a pattern for ordering a human life which is born *prematurely and without instinctive specialisation* (Gehlen 1980, p. 150). Ritual play lays the foundations for a forced creativity to which the human condition is called due to its congenital plasticity and existential opening. The basis of the game as a tool for creating social order in the absence of the theoretical guidelines of superior knowledge is the emotional agitation caused by a nature that confers on man an instinctive, precarious, and barely mature skillset. This is translated into a life experience centring on "an unlimited field *of surprise*, in which the first thing that is needed is some orientation" (Gehlen 1980, p. 151). Such orientation cannot be achieved from the underlying agitation and can only be channelled by an external instance regulating social behavior. The connatural in-adaptation of man to the world expressed in an overabundance of weak instincts and a boundless hyper-stimulation leads to the formation of mechanisms for coordinating action and attention based on the emergence of institutions that regulate uncertain behaviour. In the presence of superior thinking, man urgently needs to determine existential indeterminacy.

The Canadian psychologist Donald (1991) provides an explanatory framework in which play contributes to the formation of human consciousness. He describes evolution and the acquisition of skills without resorting to the classic notion of evolutionism centring on selection of the species. Donald proposes a *non-evolutionist vision of evolution* in which the acquisition of new faculties and skills does not result in the disappearance of earlier ones. The emergence of new faculties signifies an internal reorganisation of the overall picture of human representations and the possibility that in specific historical episodes, one may predominate over the rest without this involving deterministic and finalistic explanations. "The modern mind is thus a hybrid structure containing vestiges of earlier stages of human emergence, as well as new symbolic devices that radically altered its organization"

(Donald 1991, p. 4). In any case, the course of events does not follow a deterministic pattern based on the notion of need.

Donald offers an evolutionary approach based on four cultural phases: episodic, mimetic, mythic, and theoretic culture. Each one is integrated into, and enriches, the next. As R. N. Bellah, one of the sociologists most closely associated with Donald's thinking, puts it, "nothing is ever lost" (Bellah 2011, p. 72). Thus, we can see the metamorphosis of play, born as an imitative process tending to self-satisfaction, and transformed, thanks to the invention of human symbolic and narrative capacity, into a ritually regulated game, which is in turn transformed through sporting rationalization in modern societies into a scientific and technically perfected game, which still retains both its ritual and its imitative dimension. It may change, and, indeed, the rules and styles of play, and even the associated rituals, do change. However, what does not disappear is the game as such.

At the same time, the sports modulate their own self-image with the help of design, fashion, and advertizing. For in its narrative, the myth extols certain actors and feats from social life. It remains present in the narratives, chronicles, and legends which shape that world and which satisfy the contemporary actor's need for a dialogue with figures and archetypes that go beyond the routine bounds of everyday life. Players of football or any other sport are the new expressions of a secular sanctity, which depicts symbolic features of the human adventure, such as challenge, ambition, frustration, etc. The accounts of universal religions have not disappeared, but they are no longer the only ones. They are accompanied by secular myths, which emphasise the limits of existence. Now, however, they have a new and previously unknown element—*self-reflexivity*—which translates not only into a ritual secular game organized from human reasoning for an audience in need of new shared hopes, but also into the possibility (now clearly consummated) that the spectators themselves can form part of the game. In this new space of global interaction of individual virtual games, they no longer merely observe, they also act out *being like* the player who best matches their view of the world, which is the case of the real player on the videogames. In contrast to the collective mythifications, individual self-mythifications arise which are again capable of balancing forces and reducing the differences between competitors. This dissolving of differences is the result of virtual technology, which transforms *the playing field* in that its limits are not established by divine imposition, but by individual will. It is that will that decides what match is to be played, who the teams will be, what kit they will wear and how long the match will last. In short, the myth has been opened up to multiple uses. No longer is it managed by a centralized authority, but by the imagination of the actors. In a way, the individual *participates* in the new myths of football. He or she recreates them. Individuals see themselves as being a central part of the myth. They no longer act out founding scenes of the community, they represent themselves by re-enacting them.

4. Football, Industrialisation and the 'Sportification' of Play: The Social Genesis of Football as a Modern Sport

Both the Industrial Revolution of the mid-eighteenth century and the notion of introducing games as a regular extra-curricular activity in private schools (as promoted by Thomas Arnold in 1830), gave a clear incentive to the large-scale development of sport throughout the Victorian era in England. This was followed, in the late nineteenth and early twentieth centuries, by the restoration of the Olympic Games in Athens (1896) and a reawakened interest in nearly all competitive sports, including football (Elias and Dunning 1992, p. 162). In their magnificent studies of the evolution of sport and, more specifically, of football at the end of the Middle Ages and the beginning of the Modern Age in England, N. Elias and Eric Dunning point to the dual process whereby on the one hand, a rural population of peasants in different degrees of servitude were transformed into more or less free peasants and, on the other, a new class of untitled landowners arose, forming what became known as the gentry (Elias and Dunning 1992, p. 227).

It was in this context that the game (specifically football) emerged, as a local entertainment for a population of more or less free peasants, sponsored by local landlords, who were not always members of the nobility. There was no national framework of competition because the state was relatively unformed in the development of late-seventeenth and early eighteenth century British society, and the aristocracy and gentry 'were the State', using its apparatus to serve their own interests. Industrialization, combined with a new strengthening of the state, broke down this dynamic. The result was greater *pressure to create forms of sports participation targeted* not at a *local, but a national audience, and oriented towards victory or the overcoming of records.* There was a major shift from amateur to professionalized sport, which progressively broke through national barriers and took on a global perspective (Elias and Dunning, pp. 247, 262–63). However, there was no single reason for this transformation and rationalization in sport, but a set of different factors.

Another was clearly the '*sportification*' of the pastime (Elias and Dunning 1992, p. 34), in other words, the transformation of the pastime into sport, practised in the spare hours not devoted to waged labour. Such activities, which included horse racing, tennis, boxing, athletics races, football, and rugby, required players to perform methodical exercise to keep fit. A whole series of new *rules and means of arbitrations* had to be introduced to ensure *fair play* and increase the competitiveness of the competing teams.

The emergence of sport as a physical struggle—as against the traditional agonal struggle—is associated with the pacification of cycles of violence (Elias and Dunning 1992, p. 39). It brought an end to factional and sectarian fighting. Contributing to this development was the triumph of a unique social formation, the English gentry, together with new forms of parliamentary government based on democratic debate, in other words, on the game of political persuasion. Another contributing factor was undoubtedly the *monopolization and relatively solid, stable and impersonal control of the means of violence by emerging nation-states* (Fukuyama 2018, pp. 15–25) contrasting with traditional agonal forms of struggle, one of whose most characteristic examples is the Spartan *pancration*, where adversaries fought with their whole bodies—hands, feet, elbows, knees, neck, head, and even teeth. 'Pancratiasts' were even allowed to gouge out their opponents' eyes. They could trip them up, take hold of their noses, feet, or ears, dislocate their fingers and arms, and even use strangleholds. The wrestlers suffered terrible injuries, and some died as a result. The most brutal of games was that played by the *epheboi* of Sparta (Dress 1968, p. 83).

As for the meaning and structure of football, there are Marxist writers, such as Bero Rigauer (1969) who argue that in industrialized societies, sport is increasingly characterized by a quest for successes, reflected in a tendency to beat records, incited by the 'bourgeois spirit' of the dominant class, which seeks to commercialize the area of leisure and recreation. Other authors, such as Gregory P. Stone (1971) argue that all sports are affected by two opposite principles, play and exhibition. The problem arises, according to Stone, when the exhibition—oriented towards spectators or viewers—ends up destroying the recreational nature of sport. This is what has happened in the case of the Harlem Globetrotters, a basketball team known not for their titles, but for their exhibition matches. Although the two approaches illuminate important dimensions of the game, they do not get to the heart, the core, of a modern sport such as football. We believe that the concept of "balance of dichotomous tensions" coined by Elias and Dunning (1992, p. 250) and by Dunning (2009, pp. 15–27) accurately stresses the basic meaning of the game, by placing it within *the dynamic tension (in-group versus out-group)* (Elias and Dunning 1992, p. 268), i.e., *between two players or groups of players at once antagonistic and interdependent* within *a double mutual contingency.* There are a number of polarities, which take place in and through the game. Chief among them are the polarities between opposing teams, between attack and defence, between cooperation and tension between the two teams, between cooperation and competition within each team, between an emotional identification with one's own team and rivalries with the opposition, between individual aggression and the restraining of such aggression by the rules, between performance and results, between game and mass spectacle, or between players (the game) and managers (money-business).

The key of sports in general and of football in particular would be in the unloading of our energy and in the concomitant projection of energy towards the world. Thus, our own personal unloading of energy brings about the energy reloading of the other as observer, emerging as a result of that a dynamic loop between the player and the co-player, between the football players and the public, between the team and its symbolic equipment. All teams symbolize with their 'colours' to the people to whom are referred, to the clan or tribe with their attributes, to the daimon-spirit of the place. Thus, the Athletic of Bilbao has a Basque symbology, the Barça has a Catalan symbology, and the Real Madrid has a central or Castillian, Spanish or universal symbology, as has the Spanish language. Today, the Real Madrid would be a symbol of Spain, which floats in its own turbulences, a symbolism which personifies at best the "madridista" supporter and tennis player, Rafael Nadal.

One undoubtedly relevant factor in the development of football as a mass phenomenon has been its *'functional democratization'*. In a process that began in the North and Midlands, lower status (middle and working class) organizers, players, and spectators emerged, breaking the monopoly of the "public school élite" (Elias and Dunning 1992, p. 260) of the country's ruling class. A new inter-class ethic of amateur sport began to take hold, increasingly existing alongside professionalising sport.

The increase in the size of the social conglomerates-cities, noted by Herbert Spencer, favored the creation of *"chains of interdependence"*, greater connectivity between individuals and between social circles, as Émile Durkheim noted. This created a modern structure of social interdependence, which at the same time generated a demand for interregional, national, and transnational sport. But, unlike Elias and Dunning (1992) who believe that in today's culture, sport is ultimately developing towards record-beating and pure performance, we do not believe that there is any such ultimate and one-way trend towards seriousness (Huizinga [1949] 1980), nor do we feel that sport should be seen as something bourgeois, or class-based (Rigauer 1969). Rather, there subsists a *dynamic tension between opposing forces*, between game and *performance*, between amateur and professional, between art in motion and pure technique.

In the first part of this paper, we analyzed the emergence of the hero in the competitive game, identified in ritual practice with the *daimon*, with the magic potential, embodied by the group, to later become an Olympic God. We shall now take a last methodological step by analyzing the *play on play* of football video games. We shall compare two currently opposing ideal types, the Dionysian model of the *trickster* Lionel Messi and the new Apollonian Herakles, embodied by Cristiano Ronaldo.

5. Football and the Sacred. Cristiano Ronaldo and Lionel Messi as Weberian Ideal Types

Michel Maffesoli remarks that footballers are "emblematic figures" (Maffesoli 2009, p. 204) of postmodern societies. An emblem is "a symbol or representation typifying or identifying an institution or quality, etc." (Concise Oxford Dictionary of Current English (Oxford Dictionaries 1992, p. 381)). In *Elementary Forms of Religious Life* (Durkheim [1912] 1965), É. Durkheim presents the emblem as being closely related to the religious in totemic societies. Based on our deliberations above, we shall now analyze whether behind the footballer, viewed as an emblematic figure, it is possible to see some type of religious component.

In order to continue conceptually furnishing this issue we shall examine another of the classical studies on the origins of religion, Wilhelm Wundt's *Elements of Folk Psychology*, first published in 1912. W Wundt establishes three figures or forms directly linked to the religious in what he calls the 'primitive man' stage: demons, heroes, and gods, and he describes the relationships of cause and effect between them. What differentiates a god or hero from a demon is that the latter is an impersonal force, it "lacks the attribute of personality" (Wundt [1912] 1916, p. 367). As for the other two categories, the difference between them lies in the fact that the hero, "as thoroughly human, shares the universal lot of man as regards dwelling-place, length of life, and liability to sickness and death" (Wundt [1912] 1916, p. 367) whereas gods have both a human and a super-human personality; they are immortal and live in a special dwelling place, normally located outside this world. We shall not concern ourselves here with the aptness of Wundt's definition or deciding whether it is subject to the evolution of scientific knowledge on the subject. However, we can say that his definition of the hero establishes elective affinities with the footballer, seen as an emblem, as M. Maffesoli noted.

For W. Wundt, the hero is "an idealized man" (Wundt [1912] 1916, p. 370). Football players have a series of attributes that are greatly valued socially: youth, vigour, skill, competitiveness, fame, recognition, and wealth. *This fact of possessing socially-recognized virtues is what turns them into emblems*, since it favors the possible expression of processes of objectivation which is ultimately what any form of idolization (hero, god, spirit, or other) points to. Footballers cannot be called spirits or gods, but here we wish to analyze whether they might be considered to be heroes of modern societies. For the moment, we consider that W. Wundt's definition to be fitting.

But what type of hero would a footballer be? And can all footballers be considered to be heroes? The answers to these two questions contain the two main paths of action we wish to explore in this section. We shall answer the first question using the genealogy and classification of the hero offered in W. Wundt [1912] (1916), updating it with the addition of a last category, and we shall discuss the second issue at greater length below. However, we believe some form of introduction is important here. First, we must introduce a small differentiation. Compared to the rest of society, the footballer is considered privileged. However, in spite of being privileged compared to a non-footballer, if we reduce the margin of action, focusing exclusively on footballers, we have seen that not all football players are heroes in the strict sense of the word. Only those who are outstanding in this socially valued art can be said to achieve this status.

Just as only one *kouros* could be the victor in a race in honor of Dionysus, as F. M. Cornford (1912) notes, the status of hero can only be attained by the greatest among the great. *Heroism is essentially linked to achievement*, to the performing of different actions, of feats. "The *hero*/player must be the other to be capable of inverting *the same*[3]" (Verdú 1980, pp. 19–20). Thus, the football hero is that one who stands out, who does things that the rest do not, who has something that others do not. In other words, they embody an ideal. In today's footballing universe, two figures bear the sublime, Cristiano Ronaldo and Lionel Messi. Both have attained the pinnacle of their profession, but they have done so by playing sometimes radically different models or patterns. Therefore, our second line of action in this section will be to turn these two players into two archetypical categories or Weberian ideal types. This exercise should reveal two different and exclusive modes, two 'paths to be consecrated', two forms of accomplishing the hero status through the actions performed in the footballing 'field'.

5.1. The Football Hero

Just as M. Donald (1991) speaks of different 'stages' in human evolution, we can also follow W. Wundt [1912] (1916) in seeing different phases in the historical development of the hero. He proposes three: *the hero of the sagas, the redeeming hero, and the saint hero*. We shall add a fourth category, which we shall use to link the German psychologist's thinking to the subject of our study, *the secular hero*, one of whose representatives is the football hero.

We shall start with the *saga hero*. This is a *kouros*, but not a "lad" (Wundt [1912] 1916, p. 335). "He is a man in the prime of his life" (Wundt [1912] 1916, p. 335). Although his youth is one of his characteristic features, this freshness is not the axis around which the virtue he represents revolves. Rather, it comes from a blend of a not overly-ripe maturity and youth without inexperience. He is "a being of transcendent power and strength" (Wundt [1912] 1916, p. 336). His strength comes from his youth, but he derives his power from a combination of experience and vigor. The second category, the *redeeming hero* "represents an offshoot of the hero saga, springing up at those times when the religious impulses are dominant" (Wundt [1912] 1916, p. 339). In other words, just as the saga hero had played a central role in the transition from myth to logos and from magic to religion, the redeeming hero, fundamentally, is a being of religious good tidings. Likewise, the redeeming hero is "a personality who is throughout exalted above human stature, but who, nevertheless, attains to divinity only through his striving, his suffering, and his final victory." (Wundt [1912] 1916, pp. 339–40). This in turn suggests an

---

[3]   Original italics.

other-worldly religious goal or purpose (attaining divinity), which is achieved through fundamentally human means. We believe that the strength of Wundt's classification lies in the historicity (humanity) of figures such as Jesus of Nazareth or Prince Siddhartha Gautama, rather than in their reborn or iconic versions as the 'anointed' (Christ), or the 'enlightened' one (Buddha). Thirdly, we have the figure of the *saint hero*. Such heroes attain sacred status without abandoning their human nature. Their achievements are related to that fact of "awakening [. . .] to a pure religious life" (Wundt [1912] 1916, p. 340). Their actions are always confined to the sphere of the human. One might ask what the difference is between Buddha and the saints. In terms of their heroic action, there is practically none at all, as they both seek religious perfection through intervention in the everyday. However, according to M. Weber the difference lies in the fact that Siddharta was reborn (Weber [1922] 1978) as Buddha; he ended up acquiring a divine status, he is invested by the charisma, whereas saints are not.

When W. Wundt talks about heroes, he is referring to the primitive stage, yet his definition need not be limited to this phase though, which, he writes, mankind has already passed. If the hero is 'man in idealised form', in all societies we will find subjects capable of bringing essentially human skills to the sphere of the ideal. We have therefore decided to introduce a fourth type, the *secular hero*. A person may be considered a *secular hero* if, as Charles Taylor (2007) argues, he lives his life—and thus his heroic actions— in the context of an *immanent frame*. Here it is important not to confuse immanence with an absence of idolization. Behind the hero—like the demon or the god—one can see the ineffable, the mysterious, the tremendous, the transcendental. These aspects, which are closely linked to the sacred—as authors such as Rudolf Otto [1917] (2012) and Ingolf Dalferth (2017) have noted—have not disappeared from the scene in modern and secular societies, rather they have been transformed (Lenoir 2005), taking on different guises. According to a number of writers on the subject, such modern-secular embodiments of the sacred include the following: the person (Durkheim [1898] 1973; Joas 2014), revolutionary cults (Mathiez [1904] 2012), and the civil 'sphere' (Bellah [1967] 2007). Likewise, the sacred keeps cropping up both in the public dimension (Casanova 1994) and in the private (Luckmann 1973; Beck 2009; James [1902] 1986).

Zygmunt Bauman sees processes of individuation as the characteristic feature of modernity. "To put it in a nutshell, 'individuation' consists of transforming human 'identity' from a 'given' into a 'task' and charging the actors with the responsibility for performing the task and for the consequences (also the side-effects) of their performance" (Bauman 2000, p. 32). In this backdrop, subjects who are capable of standing out, of approaching perfection in the execution of this task acquire a different status; they become ideal men, or heroes in Wundt's terms. The status they achieve is not divine because they are still human, but this does not prevent us from identifying dynamics of immanent idolization which appear as a consequence of their achievements, of the fact of having succeeded in "a search for personal maturity and social relevance" (Bellah 1969, p. 81). For all of these reasons, we consider *the modern backdrop to be a fertile terrain for heroism and for the emergence of individual religious forms*, as we shall see in the following sections.

5.2. Cristiano Ronaldo and Lionel Messi as Weberian Ideal Types

As we have seen, both the religious and the heroic have a place in modern, secular societies. However, as we know, not all social practices afford access to heroic status in equal terms. There are some who, due to their social importance—as in the case of monotheistic religions in the phase of the 'historical religions' (Bellah 1969) or sacrifice in agro-pastoral societies (as Marcel Hénaff (2010) notes) —facilitate the transition along and towards the 'paths of consecration'. To-day, sport in general and football in particular help to fulfil that function, essentially because of the importance they have attained as symbols of the civilizing process (Elias and Dunning 1992), as guarantors of controlled violence, shifted into a form of leisure—in short, into something very closely associated with regulated play, with the game.

As we have said, in today's footballing universe, two players stand above the rest, Cristiano Ronaldo and Lionel Messi. Although both can be said to have triumphed in the idolizing modern task of achieving social relevance through the exemplary exercise of their profession, each exemplifies a different way of acquiring hero status. Here it may be helpful to objectify their different defining attributes by referencing two Weberian ideal types (Weber [1922] 1978). For the moment, then, we shall turn away from specific footballers and seek to describe and investigate two (also specific) means of attaining heroic status in modern societies, in this case through the game of football. We shall divide this task into three phases. Firstly, we shall apply the Nietzschean dialectic between the Apollonian and the Dionysian to these two players, and secondly, we shall clothe Cristiano Ronaldo in the garb of the ascetic and Lionel Messi in that of the trickster. Finally, we shall explore how their numbers (7 and 10 respectively) also offer relevant information on their attributes and the 'paths of consecration' they have travelled.

In *The Birth of Tragedy* (Nietzsche [1872] 1980), Friedrich Nietzsche presents two "spirits" (Nietzsche [1872] 1980, p. 24), which commonly clash dynamically in social life and which are key for explaining how mythical-archetypical genus arises. These are the Apollonian (linked to the Greek god Apollo) and the Dionysian (associated with Dionysos). Our interest here is not in analyzing the tension between these two 'forces' or 'spirits', but in associating each of them with one of the two players we are studying. *Cristiano Ronaldo represents the Apollonian spirit* expressed through the element of wilfulness. Through this capacity, which combines decision, intention, and sacrifice, he builds order, harmony, and a "monument of achievements" (Nietzsche [1872] 1980, p. 39). Cristiano Ronaldo is an example of *wilfulness*, of 'professionalism' placed at the service of football. He is the first to arrive at the training sessions and the last to leave. He has sculpted each of his muscles to get the most from it, to place it at the service of his profession and to extend his sporting career to the maximum. His will for perfection, to continuously reinvent himself, has led to success and the heroic path. He is unquestionably a *self-made man*. *Lionel Messi*, on the other hand, *embodies the Dionysian spirit*. Despite the undeniable will, effort, and professionalism, which he brings to his task, his fundamental 'strength' lies not in these features, but in the *innate*. Messi seems driven—intoxicated, even—by a force, which, by definition, lies outside his capacity to control it, which goes beyond his will. That force chose him long before he himself learned to handle it. Indeed, it is his capacity to control it that makes him a magician (Weber [1922] 1978). This strength is very closely linked to the Weberian *charisma* (Weber [1922] 1978) or the *mana* that Mauss [1924] (1979) analyzes.

We can see elective affinities between these aspects and the second pair of concepts through which we shall construct the ideal types embodied by Cristiano Ronaldo and Lionel Messi, the worldly ascetic and the *trickster*. *Cristiano Ronaldo is the maximum representative of worldly asceticism oriented towards football*. For M. Weber, "The person who lives as a worldly ascetic is a rationalist, not only in the sense that he rationally systematizes his own conduct, but also in his rejection of everything that is ethically irrational, aesthetic, or dependent upon his own emotional reactions to the world and its institutions. The distinctive goal always remains the alert, methodical control of one's own pattern of life and behaviour" (Weber [1922] 1978, p. 544). As we saw in the last paragraph, Cristiano Ronaldo applies a rational method for steering his life towards the achievement of his goals. His 'alert control' and method-based approach are key to understanding his achievements. Lionel Messi, in contrast, is no worldly ascetic. His heroic status is associated with certain specific aspects of another archetype, analyzed in depth by authors such as Carl G. Jung [1954] (2005), Emmanuel Lizcano (2018), and Paul Radin (1972), the *trickster*. Although C. G. Jung [1954] (2005, p. 248) stresses the unconscious (a notion which, as we have seen, is very closely linked to the Dionysian element), the area of greatest coincidence between the figures of Lionel Messi and the *trickster* is in the aspect of the "*sower of chaos*[4]" (Lizcano 2018, p. 2). Lionel Messi specializes in creating chaos in his adversaries' defensive systems, in resorting to the unpredictable or to the never-before-seen to 'mock' his enemies. His capacity to disrupt and the ease with which he achieves it are two of his clear defining features. Even his name

---

[4]   Our italics.

might seem to presage his archetypical condition, he is *Lío (mess in Spanish)*-nel Mess-i, in other words, a double generator of chaos. "He is a disrupter" (Lizcano 2018, p. 10).

Cristiano Ronaldo's shirt number is 7, and Messi's is 10. In the imaginary of football, *7* is reserved for the forwards, for the *strikers* or goal-scorers, whereas *10* is for *mid-fielders*. Historically it has been associated with *footballers with exceptional technique*, men who have brought something different and novel to the game. They are normally more the creators of goals than the scorers. At the same time, it is interesting to examine briefly at the symbolic value these two numbers have in the specific imaginary of Real Madrid and Barcelona. Real Madrid has forged its character and much of its identity on its number 7s. They have been representatives of effort, of determination, and of never giving up on a ball or a match, in short, of attaining their achievements through absolute commitment. That is the recipe behind their winning nature and what 'sets their fans alight'. Apart from Cristiano Ronaldo, two other key players have worn this number, Juan Gómez 'Juanito' and Raúl González Blanco. No other shirt has such a symbolic charge as Real Madrid. As we see, there is a communion between the attributes with which we have defined Cristiano Ronaldo, the symbolism of the number, and the identity of the club. In the case of Barcelona, the dynamic is different. We would not go so far as to say that the number 10 has the same symbolic role as the 7 in Real Madrid, but if we look at some of the players who have worn the short—Diego Armando Maradona, Romario, Rivaldo, Ronaldinho, and of course Lionel Messi himself—we can see that it has certainly had a specific weight in the creation of Barça's history and, therefore, in the forging of its identity. Barcelona's followers particularly appreciate this type of refined, high-quality player. Indeed, this type of player fits very well into the passing game and a mastery of ball possession that characterizes the team. Real Madrid's style, on the other hand, is closer to a stampede, intensity and speed, catharsis.

Cristiano Ronaldo and Lionel Messi are both representatives of the secular hero, but we can see some analogies between them and Wundt's prototypes (Nietzsche [1887] 1990). Cristiano Ronaldo is more of a saintly hero, whose deeds in the world (like the 'good Protestant' of the story) has afforded him holy status, while Lionel Messi is a redeeming hero, touched by the magic wand of charisma. Both have affinities with the saga hero, they are men in the 'prime of their life', superior to their fellow footballers and to other mortals through their attainment of heroic status.

6. The Religious in Football Video Games

Having set out some of the keys that will enable us to examine football from a religious perspective or from the point of view of the creation of sacredness, in this section we shall go one step further, extrapolating this analysis to the universe of football video games. We shall start by briefly considering the world of the video game in general. We shall then go on to explore whether we can find any mechanism of idolization linked to the playing of football video games.

6.1. The Game of the Game

According to the Spanish Video Game Association (AEVI[5]), the video game market grew worldwide by 8.5% in 2016 and now has global sales of 99.6 billion dollars. Europe is an industry leader and Spain is among the ten countries with the highest consumption of video games on the continent. Video games are the leading audio-visual leisure activity in Spain. Spaniards spend 6.2 h a week playing video games. And another relevant statistic is that the top-selling video game in Spain in 2016 was FIFA 2017, rising from eleventh place in 2015 for the previous year's version. In January 2018, FIFA (2018) is still the country's top seller. The subject matter is football.

This is a suitable juncture to focus on the fundamental aspect of this section. What do we seek to draw from this reflection? *That video games, viewed as a game of the game, represent a new phase in the process of culture creation.* In his *Homo Ludens*, J. Huizinga argues that "culture arises in the form of

---

[5]   For more information, see: www.aevi.org.es.

play, that it is played from the very beginning" (Huizinga [1949] 1980, p. 46). If we add both his own analysis on the recreational genesis of culture and the schemas for understanding social evolution provided by N. Elias [1939] (1968) and M. Donald (1991), we can see that—like culture—play adopts increasingly complex forms as it evolves. That greater complexity inherent to the creation of culture and society is what led to the rise of second-order thinking in Ancient Greece—in the context of the Axial Age—as Yehuda Elkana (1986) has shown.

Both the historical development of play—the associated incorporation of complexity—and the importance it has acquired in today's societies, can be said to have led to the emergence of a dynamic that parallels the expression of second-order thinking. This dynamic does not so much stress reflexivity (that is to say, a logic centring on thinking the game), but another logic in which *a second-order game* emerges, based on a previous game. This second-order game, played on or over itself, is magnificently exemplified by the football video game.

6.2. The Football Video Game as a Bridge between the Sacred and the Secular

N. Elias and E. Dunning remark that "what humans seek in their mimetic recreational activities is not to release tension but rather to experience a specific type of tension, a form of excitement which, as St Augustine clearly understood, is often associated with fear, sorrow and other emotions we try to avoid in our everyday life" (Elias and Dunning 1992, p. 106). This statement echoes the fine distinction drawn by É. Durkheim [1912] (1965) between sacred and profane states. Through mimetic and later symbolic recreational activity, the person who leads their 'everyday life' in the profane state gains access to the sacred state. This quote highlights the mediating role of play as a nexus, serving as a vehicle permitting travel between the spheres identified by É. Durkheim. Play can therefore have the same function of communication that was played by sacrifice (Hénaff 2010). Sacrifice might therefore be described as a 'sacred game', a term used by J. Huizinga [1949] (1980). However, what we are trying to elucidate is not whether we can find 'sacred games' (we believe this has been sufficiently proven) but rather whether behind football video games we can find that horizon of sacredness that so clearly lay behind sacrifice.

The first thing we should note is that video games in general and football video games in particular are not video-*plays* but video-*games*. Playing a *game*, as G. H. Mead [1934] (1962) notes, implicitly involves the interiorization of a 'generalized other', of a set of rules and guidelines for collective action. *The game is always played with others* (regardless of in this game the main contest in being played by a real player and a virtual player). Both the sacred game and the video game are always games, not play. G. H. Mead argues that there are "certain rites that are a representation of what supposed gods and heroes to do" (Mead [1934] 1962, p. 153). Although a player who switches on their *Play Station* or *X-Box* and sits down in front of the screen to 'control the movements' of the players need not necessarily be recreating an action that has taken place in the past, nonetheless what is depicted might perfectly well have happened or happen. What they experience is a simulation of a match, showing the electronic fortunes and misfortunes of real footballers, designed to be as faithful as possible to their originals, in terms of their physical appearance and skill sets. They are created in this way so that the experience is as real as possible.

However, although every sacred game is a *dromenon* (i.e., it is enacted), as we argue in Section Two (sic J. Huizinga), not every representation bears the hallmarks of the sacred. We must therefore use another key if we wish to establish effectively a connection between the sacred/religious and football video games. The Dutch historian writes, "The rite, or 'ritual act' represents a cosmic happening, an event in the natural process. The word 'represents', however, does not cover the exact meaning of the act, at least not in its looser, modern connotation; for here 'representation' is really *identification*, the mystic repetition or *re-presentation* of the event" (Huizinga [1949] 1980, pp. 14–15). For Huizinga the key that turns a representation into a sacred game is that through it a process of *mediation between the sacred and the secular* is produced. We believe that this identification also occurs in the performance that occurs in the football video game, which we shall analyze using two formulas.

Firstly, the digital game allows the player to virtually control the threads of existence. The game allows them to become an agent capable of controlling all aspects involved in the action, a demiurge. By doing this, they can decisively influence the result. By controlling the game of the game, they become the symbolic dominator of the world of football. Through this action, which occurs as a result of the virtual play, the player accedes to a state that would be off-limits to him in his condition as a secular subject. In this way, he transcends his limited human nature. So the player of the videogame has an enhanced personality, a technically increased control of the game. Secondly, the game of the game is a mechanism of intermediation through which the player becomes the footballer he is controlling. These two formulas of symbolic and virtual identification refer back to an essentially quasi-religious horizon.

So, whether through the video game the player becomes a demiurge or whether, he wears the mask of the hero, just like a religious ritual, the identification lasts as long as the performance is played out. During this time, the player changes state. This state is conceived as "a *totius substantiae* transformation" (Durkheim [1912] 1965, p. 54), something which É. Durkheim links to the sacred state. For, through the video game, they experience a renaissance (Weber [1922] 1978). Even if it is limited to the time in which the action takes place, it is no less religious than those in which that temporary state becomes permanent, such as the pope's change of name on acceding to the throne of St. Peter. They appear "under a new form" (Durkheim [1912] 1965, p. 54)—in this case that of the icon they operate via the controls or the demiurge capable of changing the sequence of things—while he is 'filled' with the sacred.

7. Discussion

In short, although, as J. Huizinga [1949] (1980) notes, over time the game has been gradually stripped of its sacred nature, we have shown how some of the elements involved in football video games can be analyzed in terms of the sacred. This does not mean that football video games can be said to be a religion; that would exceed our arguments here. However, it does mean that we can see certain dynamics in them that point towards the religious. These dynamics, as we have explained, have a transcendental component understood as an 'individualized reconnection'. This idea was magnificently expressed by Ernst Troeltsch, who created a religious category to complement the classic classifications of Church and Sect, i.e., mysticism. According to this notion "The world of ideas which had hardened into formal worship and doctrine is transformed into a purely personal and inward experience" (Troeltsch [1911] 1931, p. 992). É. Durkheim pointed out the same idea in this paragraph, "Not only are these individual religions very frequent in history, but nowadays many are asking if they are not destined to be the pre-eminent form of the religious life, and if the day will not come when there will be no other cult than that which each man will freely perform within itself" (Durkheim [1912] 1965, p. 61). This category, which has been widely used in subsequent studies in the area of human and social sciences (Luckmann 1973; Warner 2005; Beck 2009), perfectly identifies the religious process that occurs in the *game of the game* of football. In this type of religiosity, we do not encounter gods to be emulated, but living heroes/icons with whom to identify, such as Cristiano Ronaldo and Lionel Messi, who, like Hercules and Achilles, are not gods.

J. Huizinga [1949] (1980) also tells us that culture originates and develops in and through play. This means that religion, seen from the perspective of a *sacred game*, is one of the first complex forms in which the *game* was embodied, following its primitive and infantile phase as *play*. Arising out of this consideration, perhaps, over and above the religious component associated with football video games, we should note that the fundamental aspect of these games of games is, evidently, that they are played. Having said this, we believe that it would be very wrong to consider that the forms that appear after the stage of the *sacred game* are necessarily stripped of elements of sacredness. This would be to misunderstand the importance of Merlin Donald's (1991) analyses in understanding both our own thesis and the evolution of societies.

In this order of things, the reflection on the religious character of the virtual videogame is closer to the model of *privatized religion*, in Troeltsch [1911] (1931) and Luckmann's (1973) terms. We talk about a religious experience, which does not need the hot, thick, atmosphere of the rituals performed above and explained mainly by Durkheim. The individual would be the producer and the product, the God and believer at once, of a religious experience in which there is no break-up with the daily world. The religious experience of the virtual videogame does not match with the definitions of religion made by Clifford Geertz (1993) and Robert N. Bellah (2011) in which the main features are the ritual enhancement of the collective life linked to a general order of life.

In the videogame, or *game on the game*, the enhanced collective emotions of the real football game vanished being substituted by an identification game of the real player with the virtual player in a sort of mimesis where the former tries to be like the later, where a process (a neo-magical or new age process, we might say) of privatization of emotions is mobilized. This process arises within the new digitalized societies where the ritual dimension is hidden and where the public, the spectator, is missed, and where the dimension of the actor-player and the actor-public are substituted by an isolated real actor-player who interacts with a virtual actor-player, with an avatar, in a sort of each other mirroring play in which they mirror themselves *ad infinitum*. The playing field shifts into a screen in which the player (oneself) is a double of his idol and there is not anymore the public, the outside spectator, but another player (virtual), which is the main star of a game on the game. The play is been played between two players mainly, one real and the other virtual, and the first tries to be like the second.

Author Contributions: Conceptualization, J.G.-G., J.B., C.S.-C.; Methodology, J.G.-G., J.B., C.S.-C.; Software, J.G.-G., J.B.; Validation, J.G.-G., J.B., C.S.-C.; Formal Analysis, J.G.-G., J.B., C.S.-C.; Investigation, J.G.-G., J.B., C.S.-C.; Resources, J.G.-G., J.B., C.S.-C.; Data Curation, J.G.-G.; Writing-Original Draft Preparation, J.G.-G., J.B., C.S.-C.; Writing-Review & Editing, J.G.-G., J.B., C.S.-C.; Visualization, Javier Gil-Gimeno, J.B.; Supervision, J.G.-G., J.B., C.S.-C.; Project Administration, J.G.-G., J.B., C.S.-C.

Conflicts of Interest: The authors declare no conflict of interest.

References

Bauman, Zygmunt. 2000. *Liquid Modernity*. Cambridge: Polity Press.

Beck, Ulrich. 2009. *El Dios Personal*. Barcelona: Paidos.

Bekoff, Marc, and Pierce Jessica. 2009. *Wild Justice. The Moral Lives of Animals*. Chicago: Chicago University Press.

Bellah, Robert N. 1969. Religious Evolution. In *Sociology and Religion*. Edited by Norman Birnbaum and Gertrud Lenzer. Upper Saddle River: Prentice-Hall, pp. 67–83.

Bellah, Robert N. 2007. Religión Civil en América. In *Las Contradicciones culturales de la modernidad*. Edited by Josetxo Beriain and Maya Aguiluz (coords.). Barcelona: Anthropos, pp. 114–38. First published 1967.

Bellah, Robert N. 2011. *Religion in Human Evolution. From the Paleolithic to the Axial Age*. Cambridge: The Belknap Press of the Harvard University.

Beriain, Josetxo. 2015. Genealogía afirmativa' del hecho religioso en perspectiva sociológica. *Revista Española de Investigaciones Sociológicas (REIS)* 151: 3–22.

Casanova, José. 1994. *Public Religions in the Modern World*. Chicago: Chicago University Press.

Collins, Randall. 2004. *Interaction Ritual Chains*. Princeton: Princeton University Press.

Cornford, Francis M. 1912. The Origin of the Olympic Games. In *Themis, a Study of the Social Origins of Greek Religion*. Edited by Jane E. Harrison. Cambridge: Cambridge University Press, pp. 212–59.

Dalferth, Ingolf. 2017. *Trascendencia y mundo secular*. Salamanca: Sígueme.

Donald, Merlin. 1991. *Origins of the Modern Mind. Three Stages in the Evolution of Culture and Cognition*. Harvard: Harvard University Press.

Dress, Ludwig. 1968. *Olympia. Gods, Artists and Athletes*. London: Pall Mall.

Dunning, Eric. 2009. Figurational Sociology and the Sociology of Sport. In *Sociology of Sport and Social Theory*. Edited by Earl Smith. London: Human Kinetics, pp. 143–53.

Durkheim, Émile. 1973. Individualism and the Intellectuals. In *Émile Durkheim on Morality and Society*. Edited by Robert N. Bellah. Chicago: Chicago University Press, pp. 43–58. First published 1898.

Durkheim, Émile. 1965. *The Elementary Forms of Religious Life*. New York: The Free Press. First published 1912.

Elias, Norbert. 1968. *The Civilizing Process. Sociogenetic and Psychogenetic Investigations*. London: Blackwell. First published 1939.

Elias, Norbert, and Eric Dunning. 1992. *Deporte y ocio en el proceso de la civilización*. México: Fondo de Cultura Económica.

Elkana, Yehuda. 1986. The Emergence of Second-order Thinking in Classical Greece. In *The Origins and Diversity of Axial Age Civilizations*. Edited by Shmuel N. Eisenstadt. New York: State University of New York Press, pp. 40–64.

Fukuyama, Francis. 2018. The Last English Civil War. *Daedalus* 147: 15–25. [CrossRef]

Geertz, Clifford. 1993. Religion as a cultural system. In *The Interpretation of Cultures: Selected Essays*. Geertz: Fontana Press, pp. 87–125.

Gehlen, Arnold. 1980. *El hombre*. Salamanca: Sígueme.

Gopnik, Alison. 2009. *The Philosophical Baby. What Children's Minds Tell Us about Truth, Love, and the Meaning of Life*. New York: Farrar, Strauss and Giroux.

Harrison, Jane E. 1912. *Themis. A Study of the Social Origins of Greek Religion*. Cambridge: Cambridge University Press.

Hénaff, Marcel. 2010. *The Price of Truth*. Standford: Standford University Press.

Huizinga, Johan. 1980. *Homo Ludens. A Study of the Play-Element in Culture*. Boston: Routledge and Kegan Paul. First published 1949.

James, William. 1986. *Las variedades de la experiencia religiosa*. Barcelona: Península. First published 1902.

Joas, Hans. 2014. *The Sacredness of the Person*. Georgetown: Georgetown University Press.

Jung, Carl G. 2005. Acerca de la psicología del trickster. In *Los arquetipos y lo inconsciente colectivo*. Madrid: Trotta. First published 1954.

Lenoir, Fréderic. 2005. *Las metamorfosis de dios. La nueva espiritualidad occidental*. Madri: Alianza.

Lizcano, Emmanuel. 2018. El *trickster* o la burla recreativa. In *Lo demónico, el duende y el daimon*. Edited by Luis Garagalza. Barcelona: Anthropos, Aceptado, en proceso de edición.

Luckmann, Thomas. 1973. *La religión invisible*. Salamanca: Sígueme.

Maffesoli, Michel. 2009. *Iconologías. Nuestras idolatrías postmodernas*. Barcelona: Península.

Mathiez, Albert. 2012. *Los Orígenes de los cultos revolucionarios*. Madrid: CIS. First published 1904.

Mauss, Marcel. 1979. *Sociología y antropología*. Madrid: Tecnos. First published 1924.

Mead, George H. 1962. *Mind, Self and Society from the Standpoint of a Social Behaviorist*. Chicago: University of Chicago Press. First published 1934.

Nietzsche, Friedrich. 1980. *El Origen de la tragedia*. Buenos Aires: Adiax. First published 1872.

Nietzsche, Friedrich. 1990. *Genealogía de la moral*. Madrid: Alianza. First published 1887.

Otto, Rudolf. 2012. *Lo santo. Lo racional y lo irracional en la idea de dios*. Madrid: Alianza. First published 1917.

Oxford Dictionaries. 1992. *Concise Oxford Dictionary of Current English*. Oxford: Oxford University Press.

Plato. 1980. *The Laws*. New York: Basic Books.

Radin, Paul. 1972. *The Trickster. A Study in American Indian Mithology*. New York: Schocken Books.

Rigauer, Bero. 1969. *Sport und Arbeit*. Frankfurt: Suhrkamp.

Stone, Gregory P. 1971. American Sports: Play and Dis-play. In *The Sociology of Sport: A Selection of Readings*. Edited by Eric Dunning. London: Cass.

Taylor, Charles. 2007. *A Secular Age*. Cambridge: The Belknap Press of Harvard University Press.

Troeltsch, Ernst. 1931. *The Social Teachings of the Christian Churches*. London: Allen and Unwin. First published 1911.

Verdú, Vicente. 1980. *El fútbol. Mitos, ritos y símbolos*. Madrid: Alianza.

Warner, R. Stephen. 2005. *A Church of Our Own: Disestablishment and Diversity in American Religion*. New Brunswick: Rutgers University Press.

Weber, Max. 1978. *Economy and Society*. Los Angeles: University of California Press. First published 1922.

Wittgenstein, Ludwig. 1988. *Investigaciones filosóficas*. Ciudad de México: UNAM-Crítica.

Wundt, Wilhelm. 1916. *Elements of Folk Psychology*. London: George Allen and Unwin. First published 1912.

Article

Critique with Limits—The Construction of American Religion in *BioShock: Infinite*

Jan Wysocki

Institute of Religious Studies, Heidelberg University, Akademiestr. 4-8, 69117 Heidelberg, Germany; jan.wysocki@zegk.uni-heidelberg.de

Received: 1 April 2018; Accepted: 3 May 2018; Published: 7 May 2018

Abstract: Released in 2013, *BioShock: Infinite* is a blockbuster first-person shooter which explores topics of American nationalism and religion. This article examines how religion is represented within the game and how motifs from American religious history are used to construct its game world. After an overview of the game's production process and a literature review, several specific religious and historical motifs are discussed. Through a dissection of the aesthetic and narrative dimensions of the game, the article analyzes elements of religious history from which the developers of *Infinite* drew their inspiration, such as the biblical motif of Exodus or the still-popular concept of millennialism. The analysis shows how the game uses familiar but simultaneously transformed American imagery, such as a religiously legitimated American Exceptionalism in which George Washington, Thomas Jefferson, and Benjamin Franklin are worshiped as saintly figures. *Infinite* plays with popular notions of evangelical religion, mixed with themes related to so-called dangerous cults and sects. In this construction, *Infinite* strangely vacillates between a biting liberal caricature of religiously fueled nationalism and a nod to widespread moderate mainstream values in which unusual religious movements are negatively portrayed. The article argues that a critique of a mainstream religious movement such as evangelical Christianity is not possible for a multi-billion-dollar industry which is wary of critical topics that may potentially estrange its broad consumer base. In such instances, critique can only be applied to forms of religion that are already viewed as strange by the popular discourse.

Keywords: American history; critique of religion; cults; digital games; Evangelicalism; new religious movements; stereotypes

---

1. Introduction

BioShock: Infinite (short: *Infinite*) is the third installment of an economically and critically successful video game series. It was highly anticipated by both consumers and game critics prior to its long-awaited release in 2013. The high expectations for the game stemmed largely from its lead designer, Ken Levine, whose reputation was that of an auteur of supposedly mature and artful games (Parker 2017, p. 745). His work included positions at Looking Glass Studios and, later, Irrational Games, where he was responsible for the *BioShock* series. Levine and Irrational Games' contributions to this series were known for their deep atmosphere as well as their attempt to tackle philosophical and political themes within the genre of first-person shooters. The first *BioShock* (2007), for example, featured a critique of an ultra-liberal political and economic order, in which a society was determined by bare-bones rules and largely by economic power. The game's environment was set in a submarine utopia where an absolute free society, the ultimate meritocracy, was hoped to take shape (Kuhn 2016). In the game, this utopia had collapsed because of intra-societal struggle as well as drug abuse and was the stage for the adventures of the player's quiet main character.

Both critics and scholars have commented upon *BioShock*, engaging in lengthy discussions about its artistic quality. The game has been often framed as a validation of the argument that games can be serious art, not merely hollow entertainment products. Players of *Bioshock* have expressed that the audio-visual style and story, as well as the political and moral themes that it presented, elevated it into a higher sphere of meaningful and thought-provoking cultural products (Clarkson 2009; Parker 2017). Ken Levine has even occasionally been portrayed as the game industry's equivalent of the famous film director Orson Wells (Bissell 2013). The second installment of the series, *BioShock 2*, presented similar themes as its predecessor; however, failed to merit the level of praise accorded to the first game. This can be partially attributed to the development of *BioShock 2* by 2K Marin, a different studio then that which produced the first game; the game's production also did not involve Ken Levine. In this regard, Levine's legacy set highest expectations for the third part of the series, *Infinite*.

Infinite takes the player away from the game's undersea roots and plants her in a sky-based setting, where another form of utopian (or rather dystopian) order has been established. This time, Levine and his team decided to use the game to comment on racism, nationalism, and religious extremism. The antagonist of *Infinite* is Zachary Hale Comstock, a self-declared prophet who rules over a fictional city in the sky; it is inhabited by an all-white middle and upper class, one which exploits its black, Asian, and Irish working population. This apartheid state rests on religious commandments, focusing on the will of a prophet as well as to the exceptional role of the United States.

Following the release of *Bioshock*, the game attracted the interest of numerous commentators and was discussed as a vanguard of the games-as-art argument; however, *Infinite* fared poorly in comparison. Its decidedly neutral stance on politics was regarded as hypocritical, as it depicted the fight against racism and exploitation as negatively as exploitation itself (Pérez-Latorre and Oliva 2017). Additionally, the game was proactively advertised as delivering a "serious, sophisticated political commentary" (Parker 2017, p. 754); however, according to numerous critics, the game failed to deliver on such a promise.

Such themes and their presentation within the game are natural subjects for treatment within the contemporary study of religion. Through an examination of religious motifs in different media, the study of religion can contribute to a fuller understanding of the role of religion within contemporary society. With the meteoric rise of a highly grossing global industry such as digital games, this medium can provide information about shared important themes within society, ranging in perspective from media producers, to audiences who receive and interact with such media, or other media outlets that comment on digital games (Heidbrink et al. 2014, pp. 15–17; Campbell and Grieve 2014).

This article explores *Infinite* from the perspective of religious studies, which investigates the ways in which religion is constructed in and through media. For example, in the fashion of Cultural Studies as proposed by Russel T. McCutcheon (2007), religion is understood as a system of signs and symbols defined by specific historical and social contexts that convey a special meaning to its actors. One possible route of the study of religion is to determine the perspective of contemporary society regarding religion and how this view developed historically. In this case, the analysis of *Infinite* is not only an attempt to find out how religion is constructed generally within media but also an examination of how certain events, characters, etc. from religious history are used, combined, and transformed to generate a specific image of religion for a mass media audience.

This article is not the first to consider *Infinite* as a means by which to explore the study of games or the study of religion. *Infinite* has been discussed in several game studies publications with topics ranging from its usage of alternate histories (Lizardi 2014), an analysis of its neoliberalist qualities (Pérez-Latorre and Oliva 2017), to its media construction as a "prestige game" (Parker 2017). Several works explores *Infinite*'s themes of utopia and dystopia (Bosman 2014) or its stance on death and redemption with specific regard to the game's recurring theme of baptism (Bosman 2017). Other studies have analyzed how the game offers the opportunity for its audience to discuss religion on internet forums (De Wildt and Aupers 2017). Concurrently, *Infinite* has been used as an example to convey methodologies for general games research from the point of view of the study of religion (Heidbrink et al. 2014). In contrast, this article tackles the question of how the game is positioned in the broader discussion about potential for religious critique. It explores how *Infinite* depicts themes from different religious backgrounds, critiquing certain religious movements, as well as how the designers of a multi-billion-dollar entertainment product use the critique of religion for the benefit of their product. On the other hand, it also explores how game developers avoided any critique that would have lead to a loss in revenue.

The article surveys the themes of *Infinite* and analyzes the sources from religious history out of which the designers adopted material to construct *Infinite*'s religiously infused game world. As such, the role that Christian evangelical traditions have had on American history will be illuminated. In particular, the figure of the prophet Comstock will be used as a common thread: how this character encompasses certain stereotypes of evangelical religion as well as narratives about so-called sects, cults, and allegedly dangerous forms of religious organizations. The discussion will explore how, on the one hand, *Infinite* is upfront in its critical depiction of religiously fueled nationalism; on the other hand, it will be made evident that the game does not so much provide a radical critique of evangelical religion but merely states a mainstream view as to how American values can be perverted through cultic religions. Accordingly, *Infinite*'s critique is part of a common perspective of the American self-conception. It does not so much challenge its audience in its alleged demonstration of the ills of the connection among religion, nationalism, and racism. It rather represents an opinion about religion on which the American discourse already largely agrees. The paper concludes with thoughts about why it is crucial for a multi-million-dollar project like *Infinite* to avoid any critique of mainstream religion, as the members of such are a possible and hoped-for target audience.

2. Mirrors of American Religion in *Infinite*

To understand the connection of the game to religious imageries as well as its overall connection to religious discourses, it is helpful to work with a methodology that differentiates several dimensions of a game. As proposed by Heidbrink et al. (2014), religion in digital games can be considered according to four different perspectives which comprise the following: aesthetics, gameplay, game world, and gaming culture. Each layer can be considered separately to clearly analyze specific parts of the connection between religious discourses and the studied game. At the same time, those layers should not be viewed in isolation; rather, they are like interlocked cogwheels that make up the comprehensive media product that is a digital game. In this study, those four layers will be utilized to answer the question where and how religious symbols and language is used to construct the game, as well as how the game provides a construct with which to define religion.

2.1. Aesthetic Representations of Religious Themes

As an audio-visual medium, digital games present their content through aesthetics: characters and their movement as well as landscapes, architecture, and lighting are visually depicted in the game world; audible components include spoken conversation between characters, the voice of a narrator, sounds of nature, and the overall environment, music, and other sound effects. *Infinite*'s game world is built upon aesthetics which can be associated with specific, identifiable symbols of American Christianity. To provide an overview of the game's aesthetic representation of religion, the following section will focus on the antagonistic character of the prophet Comstock; the section will also discuss other points where the game clearly alludes to the religious symbolism of American Christianity, among other religious movements. Here, specific components of aesthetic depictions will be compared to symbols from religious history and, in so doing, their socio-cultural contexts will be explained.

2.1.1. The Motif of Exodus and the Chosen People

In the game, the player steers her avatar (the detective Booker DeWitt) around a city built in the style of 19th century federal architecture. It can be encountered in the form of smaller brick buildings as well as neoclassical examples of halls with white columns and domes. This style largely resembles prominent American buildings, such as the White House or the United States Capitol in

Washington, D.C., and is meant to point the player towards a historical frame of the early revolutionary and post-revolutionary United States. In the initial minutes of the game, the player is located in a building that could be described as a chapel or church and which is called the Welcome Center. It is filled with water on which small candles are floating. The lighting for the scene is dim, and rays of sunlight cut through the darkness illuminating specific spots of the setting. Within this backdrop, the player can observe several depictions of the prophet Comstock. For example, a stained-glass window shows a scene from the prophet's life. He is painted as a tall, elderly men with long white hair and an impressive white beard. His posture is straight, and he opens his both arms towards the viewer. His left hand is stretched out, towards the people who are surrounding and looking up to him. His right hand points up, to an array of golden clouds from which the roofs of some imposing buildings protrude. A banner is suspended over the whole arrangement, which reads: "And the Prophet shall lead the people to the New Eden".

In this scene, several signs invoke allusions to biblical stories and their American interpretations. First, in a scene in which a white-haired prophet leads a group of people (or even a people) to a heavenly or sky-based city, the banner specifically refers to this city as "the New Eden". The image of leading a people to a place called New Eden, which is situated in a heavenly environment, is an allusion to an intellectual movement associated with early colonial Puritanism and Congregationalist settlers during the late 17th and early 18th centuries (Jue 2008, p. 269). Following the initial phase of colonial settlement in New England, subsequent generations started to think of their ancestors in a quasi-mythological way. In the eyes of colonial theologians such as Increase Mather, Cotton Mather, and Edward Johnson, the actions of their forefathers to leave Great Britain resembled the book of Exodus, in which the Israelites fled from Egypt for a land promised to them by God (McKenna 2007, pp. 33–41; Hankins 2008, p. 4). This mythologization of the early settlers (who had never expressed an identification of their actions with those of the Israelites) had a lasting impact on following generations; for example, this ideology was further popularized by John F. Kennedy's or Ronald Reagan's invocation of John Winthrop's popular speech about "the city upon a hill" (Gaustad and Schmidt 2009, p. 65; Hodgson 2009, p. 2). The leading of a people towards a utopian place by means of a prophetic figure against the backdrop of American history, as it is depicted in the glass painting of the prophet Comstock, precisely conjures associations with popular conceptions of the mythical American past of the first colonies.

2.1.2. Comstock as Both Mosaic Figure and Cult Leader

Comstock's image appears throughout the game's unfolding story on posters, statues, cardboard cutouts, and paintings and features always the face of an elderly Caucasian male with long snow-white beard and hair. He is often crowned with a golden aureole that circles his head. This kind of golden halo can be also found on paintings and statues of Christian saints or also on images of other important figures from other religions, e.g., seen in Buddhist iconography. Some of those images show the words "Father Comstock. Our Prophet". The words "father" and "prophet" together with the aureole suggest a strong Christian framework. This is also true for his looks and hair that lean on popular images of the prophet Moses inscribed into popular discourse e.g., through the movie *The Ten Commandments* (1956).

The player first encounters Comstock through his image, which is displayed on a large canvas via a film projector. Several city guards kneel in front of his hugely projected face and have their heads bent in a submissive fashion. Comstock's role in the city is constructed as both a strong leader and religious figure who commands the absolute loyalty of his subordinates. The (white) populace of the city look up to him as to a father figure who led them to a newfound utopian place and who should be praised for his deeds. The unbreakable loyalty of his guards becomes evident in this scene if the player chooses to shoot these individuals; even when fired upon, the guards do not react but remain still. Such an action provokes a comment from Comstock, who explains to the player that when he commands his servants to kneel before his image, they do so without error. Comstock also addresses the player's character, Booker DeWitt, directly and scolds him with a booming and unearthly voice for having failed morally in his life by gambling and drinking.

Throughout the narrative of the game, Comstock is depicted as an unquestionable religious leader whose words are law. He is characterized as having prophetic abilities, which he uses to guide his people and to judge those who have failed in his eyes. In this way, *Infinite* encourages distinct associations with popular societal imagery, specifically, the discourse about so-called sects and cults. This narrative is strong in American culture but can be found generally throughout Western culture. It entails a certain uneasiness when it comes to religious groups which are led by a charismatic figure or which isolate themselves from general society. This fear of new and non-mainstream religious groups in America was largely sparked when non-Christian organizations, for example, Hinduist and New Age groups, arrived on American shores and gained greater popularity during the rise of the counterculture in the 1960s and 70s. Non-conventional religion was perceived to be a threat to established social norms; soon, rumors of so-called brainwashing and abuse of members of such groups surfaced. Although such fears were undeserved in many cases, anxiety about such groups grew to new heights in the 1990s in association with the prominent cases of murder and suicide within such new religious movements as the Solar Temple, Heaven's Gate, Aum Shinrikyo, and the Branch Davidians (Shupe et al. 2004, p. 198). Those tragedies strengthened the perception that non-conventional religions were often led by strong individuals who required their members submit to their power, even to the point of death. This stereotype has endured and continues to fuel cultural debates regarding certain non-mainstream religions. *Infinite* takes this stereotype and constructs Comstock's religious movement as a prototypical cliché of a zealous sect or cult. In an interview, Ken Levine also revealed that, in the early development stages for the first *Bioshock*, there were plans to feature a cult-deprogrammer who is tasked to extract a person from inside a cult group (Remo 2007). This may suggest that Levine is aware of the long-lasting debate regarding cults and that a part of this discussion was deliberately used as building material for *Infinite*'s narrative.

One of the last gameplay scenes in *Infinite* includes a final confrontation with Comstock. The prophet stands beside a small pool resembling a baptismal font; he appears as an elderly gentleman with a warm, soothing voice. He invites Elizabeth, the companion of the player throughout most of the game, to let him wash her dirty and bloodied hands. After an argument with the prophet, the player's character, Booker DeWitt, kills Comstock on the baptismal font whose last words are "It is finished". This can be interpreted as a reference to John 19:30 which states "So when Jesus had received the sour wine, He said, 'It is finished!' And bowing His head, He gave up His spirit" (New King James Version). This scene paints Comstock as a figure laden with references to the Christian tradition through his bearded Moses-like appearance, the baptismal font, and the reference to the last words of Jesus. The cult analogy is tied firmly to those Christian narratives and suggests to the player that she is confronted with a homicidal quasi-Christian sect.

2.1.3. Prophetic Visions

In a section of the game where the player witnesses a pageant, the life of Comstock is presented through oversized cutouts on a festival wagon. The pageant portrays Comstock's early life as a simple farmer. He is shown as being visited by an angel with white robes, who gives him a vision to build a city in the sky. Not only does this depiction point towards Comstock's prophetic and visionary powers but also to a specific part of American religious history. A popular account of a vision of an angel in early American religious history is that found in the Church of Jesus Christ of the Latter-day Saints (LDS), also known as Mormonism. In this story, Joseph Smith, the founder of the LDS, is said to have been visited by an angel in 1823; the angel told him the secret location of an undiscovered biblical text. Smith's religious community grew exponentially and is even today an influential part of the American religious landscape; however, the group remains controversial, particularly with regard to whether it ought to be described as a cult. (Whittaker 2010; Trepanier and Newswander 2012). It could be argued that Comstock's vision of an angel is to be understood as a direct reference to

Joseph Smith. The intersecting elements of angelic visions, prophetism, and Comstock as a charismatic leader emphasize to the player that she, as well as her avatar Booker, are faced with a non-conventional religious movement, one that is quickly framed as a non-conventional cult with many identifiable Christian elements.

2.2. Religious Themes in the Broader Narrative and Game World

This section investigates what the story and the overall world of the game tell the player about religion. Here, the perspective is broadened and more complex interwoven symbolic layers are discussed.

2.2.1. Millennialism and the Apocalypse

Comstock's religion is built upon his prophetic visions of a heavenly city for his people as well as the foretelling of the destruction of the world below this city. This apocalyptic worldview has appeared in different forms in religious history in the narrative of millennialism (also referred to as millenarianism). Since the initial settlement of the Puritans on the American continent, the motif of the end of the world remained an important theme in Puritan identity as well as in subsequent movements such as Congregationalism, Revivalism, and Evangelicalism. These end-times were conceived as a drastic but ultimately positive upheaval of the world, after which Jesus would install a divine rule over the people of the world. Several historical conflicts were interpreted by American Protestant contemporaries, such as Jonathan Edwards, as demonstrative of a violent world conflict that would pit good against evil and result in a utopian state (New 2012, p. 42; McKenna 2007, p. 67). The American War of Independence similarly was promoted as the ultimate confrontation between God and Satan's forces, as was the American Civil War eighty years later (McKenna 2007, p. 69).

In *Infinite*, Comstock not only waits for a final apocalyptic conflict that will lead to a divine period for his followers but is eager to actively destroy the world himself. In the game narrative, Comstock acquires a fictional technology through which he and his followers can lay waste to cities and lands which exist below the floating sky city. A dream sequence in the game depicts a devastating attack on New York. Comstock refers to this literal fire-and-brimstone apocalyptic destruction of the lands below the flying city as Judgement Day, which is another common Christian term for the imagined eschatological event in which God descends from heaven and separates the faithful from the sinners.

This image of the end-times is one of the cornerstones of classical evangelical fundamentalism. As a result of their increased marginalization from public discourse in the early 20th century, conservative Protestant Christians tried to regroup and find common ground to build a strong faith-based community. At the time, many of those conservatives agreed upon the so-called "five points of fundamentalism", which were common markers of their beliefs. One of those five fundamentals was the belief in the Second Coming of Christ on Judgement Day. This idea was made popular by Scottish missionary John Nelson Darby, who devoted himself to interpreting biblical accounts, such as those in the Book of Revelation. His interpretations had a major impact on how the end of the world and the coming reign of Jesus Christ were subsequently understood (New 2012, p. 109; Weber 2005, pp. 19–43). Today, this particular idea endures in evangelical beliefs and has become a frequent topic in popular culture, such as in the long-lasting and best-selling apocalyptic Christian novel series *Left Behind*, written by Tim LaHaye and Jerry Jenkins (Shuck 2005). But millennialism and an expectation of the end of the world was not only an evangelical narrative. Apocalypticism has also been connected with so-called doomsday cults and their reception by the general public. Several new religious movements who attracted media attention through mass-suicide, violent acts, or other tragic events were also firm believers in one or another form of the end of the world. It is interesting to note the differences in public opinion between the evangelical millennialist beliefs which are tolerated or at least not seen as worrisome and those which (rightly or not) are conceived as threatening.

2.2.2. Divinization of American History

Another part of American culture that *Infinite* prominently presents is the history of the United States. Through Comstock's biography, the player gets a glimpse into important parts of U.S. history as well as fictional adaptations of that history for the purposes of the game world. One cornerstone of the game's narrative is the founding of the United States and the individuals associated with it, i.e., the Founding Fathers, including George Washington, Benjamin Franklin, and Thomas Jefferson.

In an early section of the game, when the player and her avatar Booker leave the Welcome Center of the flying city, they encounter those three historical figures in the form of giant statues. At the bottom of the statues, several people kneel, fold their hands, and usher prayers, addressing the statues as, for example, "Father Jefferson". The statues are clad in wide robes, each holding a specific item: a key, a scroll, and a sword. In this scene, American historical figures are depicted in a style akin to that of Christian saints (who also are often equipped with specific symbolic attributes, i.e., keys for St. Peter) who are actively worshipped through prayer by their followers. The idea of American Civil Religion, a term coined by scholar Robert N. Bellah (Bellah 1967), is well known, demonstrative of how the American state and its idea are objects of practices and narratives that may be termed religious. However, the depiction of the Founding Fathers as saints goes a step further, by showing not only practices that are not merely analogous to religion but fundamentally are religious.

The topical thread of America and its idea as an object for religious practices and beliefs can be found throughout the game. Comstock and his followers are presented as fanatically devoted to the idea of the nation of America. The founding of the nation is presented more as a myth than as history. In the game's narrative, it is stated that an angel called Columbia originally showed the Founding Fathers a vision by which to construct the United States. Having successfully built this nation, everything went well until the American Civil War. The Civil War can be described as one of the most prominent secular myths of American history, with Abraham Lincoln as the great individual who accepted the risk of a war on American soil to abolish slavery. The game presents a different perspective on Lincoln. Here, Comstock and his followers paint the usually highly regarded 16th President of the United States as a demonic and devilish figure. He is shown as someone who led the nation astray, sowing discord among the citizens. Here, Lincoln's fight against slavery is a fight against the divine foundations of America. The player can observe two paintings in the game in which Lincoln and Washington are leading the armies of the Union and the Confederation, respectively, in the Civil War. Lincoln has horns, glowing red eyes, and a devil's tail (leading the Unionist army), whereas Washington (here, the figure leading the Confederation) wears a white robe and a golden aureole circles his head.

2.2.3. American Supremacy, Racism, and Its Ties to Religion

Slavery, or the mistreatment of people who are considered non-white, is an important narrative in the game. The economy of the city is built on the shoulders of black people, Asians, and Irish, whose workforce is exploited. These communities are tolerated but live in the lower depths of the city; they are considered as either moochers or savages who should be happy to be under the strict rule of Comstock. Occasional audio diaries or other clues that can be found in the game feature dialogue about the benefits of the slavery as a system that persisted until the end of the Civil War. It is presented as a just system and as one of the staples of the American nation. In the eyes of Comstock and his followers, America should be a nation of white people who embrace their destiny as supreme rulers over all other peoples in the world. Non-American and non-white people are subordinates who are a threat to the purity of the country. Such sentiments are expressed in the game on a mural where George Washington holds a bell and two stone tablets, an allusion to the Ten Commandments from the Old Testament, and is surrounded by dark and twisted depictions of black people, Jews, Native Americans, Irish, and Asians. On the side of the painting is written: "It is our holy duty to guard against the foreign hordes" as well as "for faith", "for purity", and "for god and country".

This master race ideology that is represented by Comstock and his followers is built in parts from the principles of the radical nationalistic and racist protestant group of the Ku Klux Klan. This group sought (and still seeks) to rid America from all which is considered foreign influence. The group was first established in the years following the Civil War but gained prominence in the 1920s, when its platforms included advocacy for "one hundred percent American" and stood against all influence from Jews, Catholics, black Americans, or other foreign groups (Lieven 2005, p. 132). This dichotomy between white American Protestantism and foreign non-Protestants which the Klan upheld is used in *Infinite* to construct Comstock's views on America. It is never clearly stated that Comstock believes in Protestant supremacy; however, the allusions to the ideology of the Klan or similar worldviews are abundant. There is even a radical branch of Comstock's followers who wear the same pointed hoods as the real-world Klan, although the game's rendition makes the hoods violet rather than the infamous white of the Klan.

2.2.4. Baptism and the "Born-Again" Experience

Another recurring theme in the game is the ritual of baptism (Bosman 2017). Before the player and her avatar Booker can enter the main stage of the game, i.e., the flying city of Columbia, the player undergoes this ritual of initiation into a religious fellowship. Here, the player is required to let a blind priest in black robes submerge Booker in water so that he might be reborn "in the sweet waters of baptism", as the priest proclaims. The theme of baptism, becoming somebody else, or general personal transformation is frequently mentioned at different occasions throughout the game.

Baptism is a fundamental ritual of Christianity, found within its many diverse traditions. However, *Infinite*'s setting and surrounding narrative suggest that the baptismal ritual mentioned or performed within the game are connected to a specific Protestant evangelical tradition in America. In the evangelical sphere, one of the key cornerstones of this broad denomination of American Protestantism is the individual's personal decision to accept Jesus Christ as one's savior. This narrative of turning willfully towards Jesus is referred to being "born again" and many Americans use this terminology to describe their religious orientation, e.g., labeling themselves as born-again Christians (Hankins 2008, p. 44). This emotional conversion from an individual who is "seeking" versus one who has "found" faith in Jesus was largely established as a narrative in American Protestantism during the First and Second Great Awakening at the end of the 18th and beginning of the 19th centuries. The converted or born-again individual does not necessarily have to be baptized; the extent of the action or ritual depends strongly on the evangelical group with which the individual identifies. However, baptism is a clear marker for this kind of conversion towards the faith evangelical groups promote. In the case of *Infinite*, a full-body submersion in water is the main depiction of this ritual practice and alludes to evangelical groups such as Baptists or Anabaptists; however, it may also be connected to more marginalized groups, such as the Mormons or Jehovah's Witnesses (which also largely baptize individuals by fully immersing them in water).

The player learns that Comstock also was once baptized and born again. From that moment, he sought to fulfil the prophecy that was sent to him by the angel Columbia: to build a utopian community for those who worship the Founding Fathers, believe in the supremacy of the white race, and want to be pure of foreign and un American influence.

2.3. Summary of Evangelical, Nationalist, Millennialist, and "Cultic" Elements

After having provided an overview of the most prominent points in *Infinite*'s depiction of religious motifs, I would like to summarize the game's overall construction.

Infinite's designers used images from a wide range of American Christianity to construct large sections of the game's aesthetics, narrative, and world. Examples of these general Christian motifs include the figure of the preacher, biblical stories like those in the Book of Exodus, and language that leans on the tone of the Bible. The player can hear gospel songs during gameplay and traverse church-like architecture. The ritual of baptism plays an important role in the game, an action involving being submerged in water, which is often connoted with being born again. Here, a more specific form of Christianity comes into play, where Evangelicalism relies heavily on the notion of being born again.

Gradually, this language of evangelical symbolism is transformed into an unusual religious setting. The predominant form of worship in *Infinite* is directed towards the Founding Fathers of America as well as the prophet Comstock, both of whom are depicted as stone statues or on posters with attributes of Christian saints. The history of the United States is extrapolated into a mythical experience in which the Founding Fathers and the prophet Comstock received a divine command from an angel to build a nation and a city in the sky, respectively.

This American nation is the beginning and the end of the game's predominant religious ideology and is largely defined as one that is exclusively inhabited and ruled by white people, to the exclusion of Jews, Irish, Asians, black people, Native Americans, and other "foreign hordes", as the game tells its player. This foundational belief of the Church of Comstock requires secession from everything considered antithetical to these supremacist values. The American Civil War is seen as the most outrageous treachery against those principles, because it was fought to abolish slavery and take away the white majority's god-given right to rule over non-whites. Here, the basis of evangelical symbolic language is further complemented by the established racist rhetoric of the Ku Klux Klan and other religious-political groups from throughout the history of the United States which have advocated a rule of whites only.

Lastly, this unbearable situation of the post-Civil War United States demanded a change in the eyes of Comstock and his followers. Accordingly, they fled from the (more or less) pluralistic, or at least less bigoted, status quo of the mainland into the clouds, where they built a society in accordance with their values. However, their exodus will only be complete when all else is eradicated in an apocalyptic fashion. Comstock dreams of a Judgement Day in which those who don't follow the doctrine of white supremacy are destroyed in flames. This millennialist expectation is a radical view which has been based on a cornerstone of evangelical belief. It has been transformed into a militant so-called doomsday cult which eagerly awaits the destruction of an evil world and also actively seeks to bring about that destruction.

3. Critique of Religion

In almost all cases, religion in *Infinite* is depicted as something dangerous and inhumane or at least unusual and strange. The player is confronted with followers of a charismatic leader actively preaching white supremacy and ultra-nationalism, ideas which they believe have been legitimized through the divine will of god. The prophet Comstock is painted as a bigoted and cruel antagonist who sends his followers to combat Booker. Both the prophet and his followers embody racist nationalistic and religious ideologies, those which most players probably find repulsive or which at least public discourse agrees to be highly unethical. The fight of the player is also a fight against those racist values that stand anathema to the cultural ideals of the context in which *Infinite* has been developed (i.e., western, liberal, multicultural).

By fighting the antagonists in the game, the player implicitly fights the kind of religious movement and ideology the followers of Comstock represent. In this game world, religious practice and ideas cannot be separated from Comstock's racist ideology. Accordingly, the question becomes in what way the game expresses a specific critique of religion and, if so, why it is present in the game.

3.1. Critique of What Exactly?

It has been shown that religion in *Infinite* is constructed as fundamentally linked to racist ideology. Both religion in general and, in particular American evangelical religion, are used as the basis for constructing a fictional religion that transports racist narratives and in and of itself represents an enemy against which the player fights. An initial interpretation of religion in the game could be that *Infinite* presents a critique of the specific religious movement of evangelical Christianity, which is presented as a medium for the promotion of racist ideas and deeds. Such a critique could be constructed as

Evangelicalism as a nurturer of racism. But this interpretation of *Infinite*'s perspective on religion is too limited. Through an analysis of religious motifs and narratives in the game, one also needs to emphasize what the designers chose not to show as well as themes they left untouched.

The game's inclusion of elements from evangelical Christianity are striking, inserted into the game to construct a religion in the game world that can be easily recognized as iconic touchstones of religion by its players. Baptism, worship, preachers, gospel songs, candles, discussion of god and angels, prophetic visions, and the punishments of the sinful—these iconic elements present a basic framework for the player to realize that she and her avatar have been put into a game world that relies heavily on religious themes. Although evangelical motifs can be found throughout the game, it is interesting which parts of Evangelicalism are absent in *Infinite*. Two most important parts of American evangelical Christianity are the Bible and the symbol of the cross (Hankins 2008, p. 1). The Evangelical Christians frame the Bible as the true word of God, a holy text which needs to be interpreted in the right way to give meaning for the practitioner's daily life. It is studied in bible classes, consulted to give spiritual guidance and inspiration, and its themes are discussed and disseminated through sermons at church or other religious events. In evangelical thought, the cross stands for the life, death, and resurrection of Jesus. It is not only a reminder of his deeds and his status as the Lord and son of God but also a hopeful sign for the coming end times in which the faithful will be rewarded.

Infinite relies on numerous evangelical motifs in the construction of its game world; however, neither the Bible nor the cross are clearly depicted in the game. There is no single character dialog, note, clue, or other aesthetic or narrative marker which mentions the Bible directly. The only hints to the Bible can be found in the books that lie around in the Welcome Center the player visits at the beginning of the game. But these texts do not display any symbols, such as a cross or the word "Bible" that could indicate its significance. One can find an emulation of a style of language that could stem from the King James Bible on the murals or banners adorning depictions of the prophet, but specific quotations from the Bible are noticeably absent. The only biblical reference is presented when Comstock dies with the words "It is finished". A similar observation can be made for the cross. It is only alluded to as a symbol on the garment of the faux-Ku Klux Klan in the game. The violet hoods are adorned with a long golden dagger which points downwards, resembling the icon of the Christian cross. Apart from this vague allusion, no sign of the cross motif is present in the game.

Another important part of Evangelical Christianity is the figure of Jesus Christ. The entire evangelical narrative landscape depends on his life, words, suffering on the cross, and his resurrection. The evangelical conversion of the born-again experience is a personal turning towards Jesus as one's savior. *Infinite* sidesteps the topic of Jesus by only mentioning god on select occasions. Terms such as Christ or Jesus are never mentioned, and the worship and prayers that are usually reserved for Jesus in Evangelical Christianity are, in the game, turned towards Comstock, the Founding Fathers, or a vague god figure.

3.2. Critique of Mainstream Religion as an Economic Risk Factor

Through a careful examination of the religious motifs that are absent from the construction of religion in *Infinite*, it appears that there is a deliberate omission of specific religious markers from a religion from which other symbols are easily extracted to build parts of the game world. The question is, why the designers chose not to include other markers, such as the Bible, the cross, and the figure of Christ into their otherwise critical construction of religion.

The interpretation proposed here points towards the economical foundations of the digital games industry, a highly capitalist venture, the mechanics of which are increasingly debated by gaming journalists and scholars (Dyer-Witheford and de Peuter 2009). The digital games industry is one of the highest grossing entertainment industries, with an estimated annual revenue of 26 billion dollars in the European, Middle-Eastern, and African market and 27 billion dollars in the North American market (McDonald 2017). Digital games that are produced for a mass audience tend to incur high development costs. There have been speculations as to *Infinite*'s development costs; industry analysts have estimated 100 million dollars (Goldberg 2013). Even if those specific numbers are incorrect, mass market games have frequently cost upwards of 50 million dollars to develop and often involve teams of hundreds who are responsible for the design of this entertainment product (Superannuation 2014). For example, *Infinite*'s design team consisted of over 200 employees (Plante 2014).

With those numbers in mind, it can be argued that a development studio and the publishing company which funds the development will do everything they can to ensure that the revenue of the sold product will surpass its production costs. For this production model to work, nothing in the development process can be left to chance. Game production must necessarily take into account what will appeal to players and critics as well as how to market a game to attract the largest possible audience. The higher the production costs, the bigger the target audience must be. An expensive game will be oriented towards a mainstream audience, one which comprises a range of tastes, social contexts, as well as political and religious backgrounds.

In the case of *Infinite*, the story of its long and arduous development indicates how important an above-average economic success was for the development studio. Journalistic coverage of the work at Irrational Games reported very high expectations from its publisher Take Two. Several industry commentators speculated that an overall sale of 11 million game copies would not be enough to fulfil investor expectations; subsequently, this was seen as a possible explanation behind the sudden closure of the development studio in 2014 (Alexander 2014; Handrahan 2015). From this perspective, it seems reasonable to assume that, in the five-year development period, those responsible for the game wanted to maximize the likelihood of a success and tailored the game accordingly to appeal to a broad consumer base, consciously avoiding any content that might offend potential customers. Accordingly, *Infinite* was obliged to cater to an audience which potentially included those who would take offense at the game's depiction of their religious beliefs as underpinning the narrative's antagonists. The evangelical landscape in America is vast. Roughly one quarter of the population of the United States considers themselves as born-again Christian (Hankins 2008, p. 44). From an economic standpoint, developers were unable to neglect this part of the population.

The analysis of *Infinite*'s construction of religion has demonstrated that, although evangelical symbols are used to denote religion in the game, the negative representation of religion does not focus exclusively on Evangelicalism. Negative and off-putting depictions of religion are largely centered on the Church of Comstock's cult-like aspects (in the popular sense of an allegedly dangerous, non-mainstream religion). The game presents no direct critique of a mainstream evangelical family which goes to church on Sundays, potentially are members in one of the big mega-churches and uses its social facilities, listens to Christian pop music, stands for mainstream conservative family values, and upholds a personal relationship with Jesus. The core beliefs of Evangelicals are left untouched by *Infinite*'s negative and stereotypical depiction of religion. When evangelical religious motifs are depicted in the game, they are often connected with the notion that they are being misused by the prophet Comstock and his followers. Mainstream conservative Evangelicals who play the game can observe that, even though familiar themes like baptism, worship, and god are invoked, their beliefs are not the target of ridicule. Mainstream conservatives can see the cultic followers of Comstock as appropriate enemies which need be stopped in their plan to destroy the world.

On the other hand, a more urban liberal demographic is also being catered to. Well known liberal critique and fear of conservative American Christianity nurturing racism and nationalism can still be applied while playing *Infinite*. Here the ultra-American jingoistic and xenophobic society of *Infinite*'s Columbia can easily be interpreted as a mirror of contemporary America when viewed through the eyes of those who are already highly suspicious of religiously conservatives. In more cynical words one could say that Irrational Games found a way to appeal to different tastes.

Infinite refrains from taking a critical stance on mainstream religion; it also is reluctant to position itself in the political debate it presents to the player. As mentioned above, the game depicts the workers' revolt against racist oppression as negatively as racist oppression itself, an attempt to withdraw from a political statement that could estrange either side of the argument (Alexander 2014; Smith 2016;

Pérez-Latorre and Oliva 2017). Religion is simply another cultural dimension which is openly depicted in the game but with an attitude that seeks to avoid any conflict with a possible audience.

Interestingly, *Infinite* is not the only example of a game which tackles the subject of motifs from American evangelical religion and the theme of dangerous cults. Recently, Ubisoft Montreal released the game *Far Cry 5* (2018) that also plays with themes of evangelical religion, putting the player in the setting of rural Montana in which a religious movement terrorizes the inhabitants of the fictional Hope County. This group, called Eden's Gate (an allusion to the already-mentioned so-called doomsday cult, Heaven's Gate), is depicted in association with iconic Christian symbols such as small-town churches, cardinal sins, and full-body baptism. Before the release of the game, discussions arose regarding the game as a commentary on current social-political events, such as the recent rise of nationalism and xenophobia in America, which has been partly attributed to the political activity of Evangelical Christians and other conservative groups. However, following its release, game journalists quickly determined that *Far Cry 5* was not a critique of American evangelical religion as a supporter of racism and bigotry but a stereotypical depiction of new religious (end-time) movements (Kuchera 2018). The game plays with clichés regarding brainwashing and lunatic doomsday cults which disturb and destroy local communities.

Simultaneously, *Infinite* uses recognizable evangelical motifs to establish a religious atmosphere for the player but avoids any critique of traditional evangelical religion. The ultra-nationalistic attitudes of Comstock and his army are not fostered by evangelical belief; rather, they are the doings of a cult which distorts American values and religion. The same could be said for *Far Cry 5*: motifs of rural churches and baptism as well as any potential association with violence and repression are not tied to a critique of evangelical values. Instead, they are presented within the game as a result of the teachings of a deviant cult that stands against conservative American Christian values.

As such, one can observe two examples of how prominent publishers of digital games have attempted to modulate their products to cater to stereotypes already understood by a large audience. Such games appear to criticize aspects of American culture and religion but only superficially. Instead of a commentary on any possible connections of evangelical or overall conservative Christian religion in America to contemporary societal problems, they present to the player the phenomenon of new religious movements, which have already been established in the popular discourse as something deviant and potentially threatening.

Certainly, it would be of use to analyze other mass-market games as to their usage and critique of religion or specific religious traditions to uncover additional or complementary mechanics of the depiction and non-depiction of mainstream religion. On the other hand, it could be also interesting to analyze if smaller studios, with a smaller audience and lower game production costs, use similar methods by which to treat religious topics or whether they have more leeway in the critical presentation of mainstream religious traditions.

Conflicts of Interest: The author declares no conflict of interest.

References

Alexander, Leigh. 2014. Irrational Games, Journalism, and Airing Dirty Laundry. *Gamasutra*, February 19. Available online: https://www.gamasutra.com/view/news/211139/Irrational_Games_journalism_and_airing_dirty_laundry.php (accessed on 30 March 2018).

Bellah, Robert N. 1967. Civil Religion in America. *Daedalus Journal of the American Academy of Arts and Sciences* 96: 1–21. [CrossRef]

Bissell, Tom. 2013. Does the Sneaker Have to Matter? An Interview with Ken Levine, the Mind behind BioShock. *Grantland*, March 26. Available online: http://grantland.com/features/tom-bissell-interviews-ken-levine-mind-bioshock/ (accessed on 30 March 2018).

Bosman, Frank. 2014. 'The Lamb of Comstock'. Dystopia and Religion in Video Games. *Online-Heidelberg Journal of Religions on the Internet* 5. [CrossRef]

Bosman, Frank. 2017. Accept your baptism, and die! Redemption, Death and Baptism in Bioshock Infinite. *Gamevironments* 6: 100–29.

Campbell, Heidi A., and Gregory Price Grieve. 2014. What Playing with Religion Offers Digital Game Studies. In *Playing With Religion in Digital Games*. Edited by Heidi A. Campbell and Gregory Price Grieve. Bloomington: Indiana University Press, pp. 1–21.

Clarkson, Michael. 2009. Critical Compilation. Bioshock. *Critical Distance*, May 12. Available online: https://www.critical-distance.com/2009/06/17/bioshock/ (accessed on 30 March 2018).

De Wildt, Lars, and Stef Aupers. 2017. Bibles and BioShock: Affording Religious Discussion on Video Game Forums. Paper presented at CHI PLAY '17 the Annual Symposium on Computer-Human Interaction in Play, Amsterdam, The Netherlands, November 15–18, pp. 463–75.

Dyer-Witheford, Nick, and Greig de Peuter. 2009. *Games of Empire. Global Capitalism and Video Games*. Minneapolis and London: University of Minnesota Press.

Gaustad, Edwin, and Leigh E. Schmidt. 2009. *The Religious History of America. The Heart of the American Story from Colonial Times to Today*, rev. ed. San Francisco: HarperOne.

Goldberg, Harold. 2013. The Nerd as Auteur in BioShock Infinite. *New York Times*, March 21. Available online: https://www.nytimes.com/2013/03/24/arts/video-games/the-nerd-as-auteur-in-bioshock-infinite.html?_r=0 (accessed on 30 March 2018).

Handrahan, Matthew. 2015. Bioshock Infinite Reaches 11 Million Sales. Take-Two CEO Strauss Zelnick Reiterates that Bioshock Is, "a Really Important Franchise for Us". Available online: https://www.gamesindustry.biz/articles/2015-06-01-bioshock-infinite-has-sold-11-million-units (accessed on 30 March 2018).

Hankins, Barry. 2008. *American Evangelicals: A Contemporary History of a Mainstream Religious Movement*. Lanham: Rowman & Littlefield.

Heidbrink, Simone, Tobias Knoll, and Jan Wysocki. 2014. Theorizing Religion in Digital Games. Perspectives and Approaches. *Online-Heidelberg Journal of Religions on the Internet* 5. [CrossRef]

Hodgson, Godfrey. 2009. *The Myth of American Exceptionalism*. New Haven: Yale University Press.

Jue, Jeffrey K. 2008. Puritan millenarianism in Old and New England. In *The Cambridge Companion to Puritanism*. Edited by John Coffrey and Paul C. H. Lim. Cambridge: Cambridge University Press.

Kuchera, Ben. 2018. Far Cry 5 Review. A Horrible Story Ruins an Enjoyable World. *Polygon*, March 27. Available online: https://www.polygon.com/2018/3/26/17164878/far-cry-5-review-ps4-pc-xbox-one (accessed on 30 March 2018).

Kuhn, Brittany. 2016. The Architecture of Bioshock as Metaphor for Ayn Rand's Objectivism. *Gamevironments* 5: 132–55.

Lieven, Anatol. 2005. *America Right or Wrong. An Anatomy of American Nationalism*. Oxford: Oxford University Press.

Lizardi, Ryan. 2014. Bioshock. Complex and Alternate Histories. Game Studies. Available online: http://gamestudies.org/1401/articles/lizardi (accessed on 30 March 2018).

McCutcheon, Russel T. 2007. *Studying Religion. An Introduction*. London: Equinox.

McDonald, Emma. 2017. The Global Games Market Will Reach $108.9 Billion in 2017 with Mobile Taking 42%. Available online: https://newzoo.com/insights/articles/the-global-games-market-will-reach-108-9-billion-in-2017-with-mobile-taking-42/ (accessed on 30 March 2018).

McKenna, George. 2007. *The Puritan Origin of American Patriotism*. New Haven: Yale University Press.

New, David S. 2012. *Christian Fundamentalism in America. A Cultural History*. Jefferson: McFarland.

Parker, Felan. 2017. Canonizing Bioshock. Cultural Value and the Prestige Game. *Games and Culture* 12: 739–63. [CrossRef]

Pérez-Latorre, Óliver, and Mercè Oliva. 2017. Video Games, Dystopia, and Neoliberalism. The Case of BioShock Infinite. *Games and Culture*. [CrossRef]

Plante, Chris. 2014. The Final Years of Irrational Games, According to Those Who Were There. *Polygon*, March 6. Available online: https://www.polygon.com/2014/3/6/5474722/why-did-irrational-close-bioshock-infinite (accessed on 30 March 2018).

Remo, Chris. 2007. Levine: BioShock Originally About Cult Deprogrammer. *Shack News*, August 30. Available online: http://www.shacknews.com/article/48731/levine-bioshock-originally-about-cult (accessed on 30 March 2018).

Smith, Ed. 2016. The Politics of 'BioShock Infinite' Are All the Worse When Revisited in a Heated Election Year. *Vice*, October 5. Available online: https://www.vice.com/en_us/article/exkvvk/the-politics-of-bioshock-infinite-are-all-the-worse-when-seen-in-a-heated-election-year-130 (accessed on 30 March 2018).

Shuck, Glenn. 2005. *Marks of the Beast. The Left behind Novels and the Struggle of Evangelical Identity.* New York: New York University Press.

Shupe, Anson, David G. Bromley, and Susan E. Darnell. 2004. The North American Anti-Cult Movement. Vicissitudes of Success and Failure. In *The Oxford Handbook of New Religious Movements.* Edited by James R. Lewis. Oxford: Oxford University Press, pp. 184–205.

Superannuation. 2014. How Much Does It Cost to Make a Big Video Game? Kotaku.com. Available online: http://kotaku.com/how-much-does-it-cost-to-make-a-big-video-game-1501413649 (accessed on 30 March 2018).

Trepanier, Lee, and Lynita K. Newswander. 2012. *LDS in the USA. Mormonism and the Making of American Culture.* Waco: Baylor University Press.

Weber, Timothy P. 2005. *On the Road to Armageddon. How Evangelicals Became Israel's Best Friend.* Grand Rapids: Baker Academic.

Whittaker, David J. 2010. Church of Jesus Christ of Latter-day Saints. In *The Blackwell Companion to Religion in America.* Edited by Philip Goff. Malden: Wiley-Blackwell (Blackwell Companions to Religion), pp. 508–26.

Article

Disenchanting Faith—Religion and Authority in the Dishonored Universe

Heidi Rautalahti

The Doctoral Programme in Theology and Religious Studies, University of Helsinki, Helsinki FI-00014, Finland; heidi.rautalahti@helsinki.fi

Received: 30 March 2018; Accepted: 27 April 2018; Published: 1 May 2018

Abstract: This game-immanent study approach and game content analysis focuses on the Dishonored video games series. The article examines how the topic of authority and religion are represented and discussed in the video game universe of the Dishonored games, where religion is referenced through explicit authority constructions. For comprehending the concept of authority and how it is created in the games, Max Weber's tripartite authority distinction is used as a comparison for understanding the authority image's legitimatisation in the game stories. The article explores how religion is reflected by the identified three authority ideals, and how the ideals are presented and constructed in the located main characters or agents. The Dishonored games can be interpreted as stories commenting and contesting societal authority models, asking who or what in which circumstances may have societal control and domination over others.

Keywords: game-immanent; video game; content analysis; Dishonored

---

1. Introduction

Mainstream video games today have reached, in design and mechanics, such cinematic proportions, that gameplay, narrative, and game aesthetics now portray extremely convincing new realities to explore. Not only video game systems and stories raise questions that correlate to real world issues (Bogost 2008), games hold an increasing economic and innovative status in society (Zeiler 2017). Traditionally, films have been described as mirroring the surrounding culture, as both representations, and offering self-reflection surfaces for the viewer (Pesonen 2016). This process may now be seen describing video game play. In this sense, video games have the ability to facilitate complex discussions, raise conversations, and comment on different societal themes, such as issues on religion. The focus of this article is to examine how the topic of authority and religion are represented and discussed in the video game universe of the Dishonored series, where religion is referenced through explicit authority constructions. For comprehending the concept of authority and how it is created in the games, I use Max Weber's tripartite authority distinction as a comparison for understanding the authority image's legitimatisation in the game universe (Weber [1922] 1978). I use the tripartite distinction as a model of how religious authorities can be located and discussed in the studied games. Regarded as one of the first early sociologists, Weber's legacy and relevance is still discussed and debated today (Hanke 2016; Ringer 2004). His concept of the tripartite distinction, which I use as an analytical application, rather than a focal point for theoretical critique, provides an interesting counter companion to discuss religion and authority models, and how they are represented in recent video game worlds.

This game-immanent study approach and game content analysis focuses on the Dishonored games: the first game "Dishonored" (Arkane Studios 2012), the second game "Dishonored 2" (Arkane Studios 2016), and the third game "Dishonored: Death of the Outsider" (Arkane Studios 2017). The shorter (length in play time) dlc games (downloadable content) "Dishonored: The Knife of Dunwall" (Arkane Studios 2013a), and "Dishonored: The Brigmore Witches" (Arkane Studios 2013b), are noticed as complementing the main story and characters. Altogether, the games vary in length, playthrough time, and how in-depth the main story is continued in each game. The main story is primarily forwarded in the actual games, but new characters may be introduced in the additional shorter downloadable games (dlc). For example, the main antagonist in Dishonored 2 is brought already as an acting character to the game universe in Dishonored: The Knife of Dunwall. In addition, the nature of one of the main characters, the Outsider, is reviled in story of the Dishonored: Death of the Outsider, the third Dishonored game.

The article's games represent religion through conflict with varying authority types, and therefore, the games problematise different constructs of legitimisations of power. For this reason, the Dishonored video game universe has been chosen for closer analysis. The analysis' focus is especially mainly on antagonist characters, the story villains, as they represent the opposing powers that are to be fought against in gameplay. Following Weber's definition of the three ideals of authority; charismatic, traditional, and legal, (Weber [1922] 1978), religious authority in the games can be identified within these ideals. The article asks how religion is reflected by the identified three authority ideals in the Dishonored universe, and how the ideals are presented and constructed in the characters.

The key characters or agents which I define in the games, who legitimate their status through religion, are The Outsider, the order of The Abbey of the Everyman, and Delilah Copperspoon. These operators are the focus of the analysis, while through them, the authority models which relate to religion are carried on in the game narratives. Religion in this article is understood as how the game stories present the concept in character building and game story.

I will also reference on depictions of members and followers of the located religious authorities, and how authority positions are reflected by the followers. A definition by Émile Durkheim for identifying religions is to acknowledge the followers, the collective's position, as formulating the religion itself (Durkheim [1912] 1995). In the Dishonored games, I see the followers of the religious authorities reflecting the leader's positions of domination, as well as creating a community. The explicitly named and organised religion-related groups consisting of members in the games are The Overseers, The Oracular sisters, The Eyeless gang, and The Cult of the Outsider. The antagonist-counter partners, the protagonist, and main player characters (the characters which the player has the option to play in the main games), Corvo Attano, Emily Kaldwin, and Billie Lurk, reflect the authority legitimisations, as well.

Mainstream video games may encompass varying cultural material, where religion is one theme among many others. Cultural values and beliefs are reflected widely in popular culture, where video games are not an exception (Love 2010; Oswalt 2003). Video games do not shy away from controversial topics in game stories or moral explorations in gameplay. Including themes on sexuality, gender or killing, religion has been and is a "hot potato" among video games and video game culture, which has stirred debates of appropriateness. So-called moral entrepreneurs or religious groups have criticised video game contents as not portraying their faith properly (Zeiler 2014). Popular games, such as the BioShock-series, Horizon Zero Dawn (Guerilla Games 2017), or The Witcher 3: Wild Hunt (CD Projekt Red 2015) also deal with, among other themes, issues concerning religion, whether it is linked to authority images or it represents a way of discussing belief conventions. In a critical sense, video games can be seen joining popular culture conversations on religion criticism by also making explicit claims on issues concerning religions, such as Dishonored games do, concerning ideas about religious authority and its legitimisation.

Religious authority images may be argued to have had overall problematic representations in popular culture stories. Philip Jenkins argues that the Catholic Church, as a historical religious authority, has, in Western popular culture film and television, been treated in a negative way. Church leaders have been associated with conspiracy and violence, including resemblances to organised crime (Jenkins 2003). As a story discourse the anti-Catholic narrative conventions can be seen continued in video game depictions of organised religions and authorities, as the Dishonored games show. Religion, concerning its institutionalised stereotypical form in video games, has previously been, as well, linked as a motivator for violence and conflict in the video game stories (Perreault 2012). The video game narrative of criticising religious authorities is, however, closely tied to gameplay and the procedural nature of the game system and story conventions, and how narrative is forwarded in the games.

2. Game-Immanent Study Approach and the Dishonored Universe

Whether we comprehend video games as programmed processes the player learns to follow, or approach games only as stories where the player is seen as a reader, the active element of play cannot be surpassed. The play experience is a multimodal interactive experience influenced by game design, the game world, and the player's subjective reception (Salen and Zimmerman 2004). In general, Heidbrink et al. (2014) suggest that religious elements can be studied in "game narratives", "game aesthetics", "game worlds", "gameplay", and "gaming culture". To analyse game content is to acknowledge the researcher subjects' limitations, but also position oneself in a research framework. The recently established approaches have been the game-immanent and actor-centred study approach (Heidbrink et al. 2014, 2016). The game-immanent frame comprehends research questions that focuses on the game content itself, gameplay and narrative, as the actor-centred approach stresses receptive experiences (Heidbrink et al. 2014). These naturally overlapping approaches can also be seen defining the researcher's position towards their study material, which is the case in this article. In this study, I understand the utilised game-immanent approach also as a close reading of the game "text", a process which is sometimes used to describe a game content analysis (Bizzocchi and Tanenbaum 2011). Information of the story and characters I explicate in the following analysis are forwarded and to be found in the Dishonored games' main story events, gameplay actions, game character dialogue, video scenes, and game world lore, which may be discovered in various documents from letters to books, and heard from "audiographs" situated the game world. In this chapter, I also demonstrate the games' story for comprehension, where and how the tripartite distinctions may be compared and read.

However, the Dishonored games challenge a general game content reading, while gameplay (play strategies and styles used to proceed in the game), is tied to different narrative outcomes. The game reading of the Dishonored games is heavily influenced by subjective play while the altering narrative options, and ultimately, game endings are determined through the player's individual choices. Although the main narrative ending outcomes are limited only to two different main endings, a positive or negative ending (varying slightly in a third ending if certain characters were killed), and the final video scenes may vary based on the actions of the player during the game (Dishonored Wiki 2018). Choices in the game narrative outcomes and options are, today, popular traits in video games (Boyan et al. 2015), while they are seen pleasurable and empowering to the player (Eichner 2014).

The first Dishonored games motif: "Revenge Solves Everything" can be seen as a question defining gameplay for the player—does, indeed, revenge solve everything? The Dishonored games represent a style of branching video game stories, which means that the narratives alter along different gameplay paths that are chosen by the player (Lebowitz and Klug 2011). In the Dishonored games, the player may choose to use a low-chaos or high-chaos gameplay path, meaning that the game presents options for killing hostile characters or to find other ways of proceeding in the game story. These taken paths affect the amount of reoccurring hostile characters or environmental hazards in the game worlds, where low-chaos results in a less hostile world, and high-chaos in a hostile one. The chaos count also affects how the ending story unfolds, altering from an unhappy to a positive one. This means that on the high-chaos path, the ending video scenes depict the protagonist to be a revengeful and aggressive victor, as the low-chaos result describes a merciful and just protagonist. The games motif, the preliminary question, can therefore, in a reflective sense, have different answers concerning how the games are played and what choices the player makes. The player may self-reflect, while playing, if revenge is the gameplay option of choice, or is a more altruistic, non-lethal path possible.

In genre, which in video games can describe gameplay features or storytelling conventions, the Dishonored games situate as first-person shooters and stealth games, where hiding, using the environment, or assassinations are strategical traits used to proceed in the games. The aesthetical environment of the Dishonored games situate them to a retro future genre, a more technically developed historical environment than their assumed age (Bosman 2014). Even though the game worlds are situated at the end of 1800, they are enhanced with futuristic steam and metal innovations regarding weaponry, means of transportation, and architectural housing infrastructures. The game environments give the impression of a culturally and temporally European Victorian style harbour city milieu, but with some distinct advances from factual historical portrayals. Dishonored has been referenced as "neo-Victorian" in visual style (Hanson 2016).

The whole main story of Dishonored is tied to protagonist and player characters Corvo Attano and Emily Kaldwin, beginning from the grey harbour city of Dunwall in the first Dishonored game. In the rat plague-infested city of Dunwall, common people live in misery, as the city elite wine and dine. Brick walls and street corners are garnished by catchphrase graffiti that underline the societal segregation such as "Send us Food not Bullets". Organised crime gangs control the city's black market, handling smuggling and extortion. A religious militant order, called The Abbey of the Everyman, upholds the law and marches the streets, observing and disciplining anyone using or worshipping unorthodox magic, especially magic originating from the deity Outsider. In the world of Dishonored, magical forces or deities are not framed strictly as supernatural phenomena, although there is only one worshipped deity, the Outsider. The story of the Outsider or his origins are not explicated in the first game, while there he is mainly referenced among the common people as a mystical saviour who is the object of folk beliefs. The Outsider is, though, a major factor in helping chosen individuals in their lives by giving them the "the Outsider's mark", and granting magical abilities, which is where the protagonist characters Corvo and Emily receive their powers.

In the first game's story, the player character is Corvo, a bodyguard for the Royal Empress of Dunwall Jessamina Kaldwin. The game begins with the assassination of the Empress, and Corvo is framed for her death. Corvo's goal is to escape his accusers, find out who is really behind the assassination, and save the kidnapped Empress's daughter Emily. During the events The Abbey of the Everyman's leader, the Lord Regent has taken reign over Dunwall, which tightens the orders' religious soldiers, and The Overseers' activity in the streets. In the beginning, Corvo encounters the Outsider, who sees Corvo as an interesting subject to help. The varying aiding supernatural powers that Corvo receives are, for example, the Blink action. With this function, Corvo is able to move fast over long distances or heights. From time to time, the Outsider returns to look over Corvo narrating, in the video cutscenes, the previous gameplay options, whether they were chosen towards low-chaos or high-chaos options—killing enemies or proceeding in stealth.

During the first game and its following chronological dlc-games Dishonored: The Knife of Dunwall, andDishonored: The Brigmore Witches , it is reviled that the Outsider has granted magical abilities to many others. The so called "Knife of Dunwall", the assassin leader Daud, had been bestowed these abilities as well, but chose to use them for his own benefit. The Brigmore witch leader Delilah Copperspoon, was rewarded these abilities too, but turned them into her own brutal campaign to become the next sovereign. The second Dishonored game, Dishonored 2, centres on Delilah's endeavour, while the protagonist aims to stop her plans.

The second game takes place in the same Dishonored universe, but mainly in another harbour city in the south of the Empire called Karnaca on the Island of Serkonos, and 15 years later from the first games' events. The sandy and windy city of Karnaca is built similarly as Dunwall, having the same elements portraying miserable life for the common folk and a more glamorous one for the city elite. Graffiti texts on the walls tell the same story of mistrust in city officials: "No one will keep us from death". The Overseers and soldiers watch the streets, and more fighting gangs lurk in alley corners. The rat plague is now the bloodfly infestation, and more people are shown homeless, but the presence of the Outsider is less essential.

In Dishonored 2, the player has the gameplay option of not choosing The Outsider's gift of supernatural abilities into the game. In this case, the gameplay would be executed without the extra abilities, making the gameplay very different, using only weapons and the protagonist's physical skills.

In the game, the player has also now the choice of playing with Corvo as the player character or to choose his daughter, who has now grown to be the Empress Emily Kaldwin. The events begin again by a coup, in which according to the player's choice, Corvo or Emily, is imprisoned and the one must save the other and stop the coup—stop the antagonist character Delilah. Now, the game motif stands: "Take Back What's Yours." The player has, again, the option of low-chaos or high-chaos gameplay, resulting in an according story outcome in similar branching paths.

Whether playing Emily or Corvo, the characters enter Karnaca with awe when they see the state of the city. They talk in game dialogue: how could have they been so blind as not to realise the poor conditions of people and how local leaders have misused their power? This retrospective viewpoint emphasises the game's ways of building authority images through societal tensions. Authority is pinned with responsibility, or the lack of it, where I see the image of religious authority is also placed for discussion.

Compared to the first game, in Dishonored 2, The Overseers and The Abbey of Everyman are referred to in game dialogue as bringing order to people's lives in a positive manner. The orders—dogmatic scriptures called "The Seven Strictures"—are even said, in game dialogue, to bring comfort to some. Dishonored 2 expands, also, on the story of the orders' presence in the game worlds, while now a sisterhood, The Oracular sisters' division is said to reside in the Island area. In the second Dishonored game, the antagonist characters are not only hostile Overseers, but consisting of a new group of all female witches led by the coup leader Delilah Copperspoon. As the game's main antagonist, Delilah's plan is to become an immortal sovereign for all to worship eternally. The player character has the option in the game finale to kill Delilah in a hostile way, or to find a non-lethal solution for her.

The third Dishonored game, Dishonored: Death of the Outsider, is a sequel to Dishonored 2, continuing the main narrative by expanding and focusing on the Outsider's story. Events, which occur a few months after Dishonored 2's ending, are shown through the previous supporting character (now protagonist) and player character, Billie Lurk. Billie is reviled already in Dishonored 2 as the pseudonym Megan Foster, and to have been a part of Daud's assassination group while the Empress mother was killed in the first Dishonored game. Now Billie tries to atone her past by beginning a mission to save Daud, who has been in hiding for many years. After finding Daud, he asks for one last favour—to kill the Outsider. Daud is convinced that the Outsider deity, in his words, "the black-eyed bastard", is the reason for all the previous havoc and chaos in the Empire which needs to stop, and Billie feels obliged to help. Even though she is not granted the Outsider's mark, Billie finds magical artefacts which make her supernaturally powerful. She begins investigating different locations for clues where the Outsider could be in Karnaca, where the events take place. She finds out that a criminal gang called The Eyeless, who as well as running a private club, manufacture bonecharms, a sort of talisman for magical purposes. She also finds out that the gang is actually an organisation for the lowest members of a religious cult that was formed around the deity itself. Billie sets out to find the location of The Cult, since they could lead her to the Outsider. The Cult, as referenced in the game, is not only interested in the deity, and are more focused in a supposed other realm called the Void. The Cult believes that the Void is a supernatural and magical plane which is inhabited by the dead, but where the living may visit or draw powers from. As magic is considered a plausible force in the Dishonored universe, the Void's essence and powers are shown studied and "theologically", investigated by the cultists in the third game. When Billie reaches the cultist's hideout, blackboards, a vast library, and school desks are to be found in the environment. The Cult is convinced that magical properties and eternal life can be harnessed from the forces of the Void, where the Outsider is also believed to have originated from. During the game, Billie may, in gameplay, react to the world in stealth or in a lethal way, but the story finale—killing the Outsider or to deal with him in a non-lethal way—may be chosen at the very end, as Billie reaches the Void itself (Thielenhaus 2017).

3. Tripartite Ideals of Authority and the Characters of Dishonored

The story of the Dishonored games circulates around power struggles in a societal scale; who can dominate, and how is it justified. Especially in the formulation of the main located agents, The Outsider, the order of The Abbey of the Everyman, and Delilah Copperspoon, the authority ideals concerning religious authority are carried on in the games. The tripartite authority model by Max Weber may be used to examine the construction of these characters, and locate depictions of religious authorities.

Max Weber (1864–1920) a German historian and social scientist, is considered as a classic in the fields of sociology and sociology of religion. He is most known for his understanding approach in humanities, and his pioneering work on examining societal structures, authorities, work ethics, and religion in society. Weber argued that religion is not merely a representation of humanity, but a force and action of its own, causing societal changes and developments. Especially his work on Calvinist Protestantism led to the conclusion that its ethics of individualism, obedience to hard work, and obedience to authorities paved the basis for Western capitalism. His idea was that religion and individual motives would reside in a dynamic relation with social constructions, which may, in time, lead to societal changes (Bowie 2008; Davie 2008). Even though the plausibility of this framework can be regarded today as applicable, Weber's thoughts on the advancements of Western capitalism and rationalism may be debated (Ringer 2004).

His notable work consisted of concepts explaining social and economy structures, where the three-part model was formulated, explaining how authority is legitimised in societies. The three ideal types of authority, which may be found in Weber's "Economy and Society", were built on Weber's understandings of historical authority depictions. According to Kieran Allen, Weber was not, in fact, as much interested in how domination and power were achieved, as how power was maintained. According to Weber, the use of power became visible in the dynamics of the one in command and the one being ruled, where a natural desired contract of obedience was formed. The followers of the one leading would obey the contract as a "valid norm", which Allen points out to be the most acclaimed definition on the formulations of authority legitimations in Weber's work. Even though, according to Allen, Weber did not focus on the aspect of economic necessity and domination, and he assumed that in time, domination generates legitimacy. The aspect of survival may also be seen cultivating authorising positions, when tied to distribution of economic resources (Allen 2004).

Authority and domination, by Weber, was understood as regarding the structural governance of economic resources, such as the positions of banks or the distribution of natural resources, as Allen explains. On the other hand, domination meant also an official governance and distribution of non-economic resources, such as referenced to armies and state officials, which Weber concentrates on in the tripartite distinction—the three ideals. The ideal types of authority; traditional, charismatic, and legal, reflect societal structures of authority divisions. The traditional ideal of authority derives from cultural customs and age-old conventions founded on the continual belief in them. Allen references that Weber's traditional authority ideal may be found in the description of a tribal chief or feudal leader. The charismatic authority ideal may be found in the domination of a heroic persona or appealing, "charismatic" figure. This may manifest in the positions of a warrior, a prophet, or for example, a religious leader, according to Allen. Weber himself describes the charismatic authority, also defining through "supernatural" or "superhuman" qualities (Weber [1922] 1978). The legal authority ideal references that domination is gained from trust in official rules, which appear among state offices and bureaucrats (Allen 2004).

In the Dishonored universe, authority can be located in similar distinctions. Authority is seen in the city images, where the divide is visible in the examples of how the protagonist characters, common people, the elite, state soldiers, and religious leaders react to one another. The games contest the three ideals in creating conflict and power struggles between these actors mentioned above, especially among the protagonist and antagonist characters. The game story of conflict; the fight against these authorities, mark the antagonist characters—the authority that demands resistance as a premise for the story. By these contested authority legitimisations, the games raise the question of what can be plausible grounds for domination, especially regarding religious authority. The games may be seen asking, are these authority ideals worth the obedience and given legitimisations, or should the conventional norms of domination be challenged? The contest of these authority ideals is rooted in the main story events, as previously discussed, where dilemmas of good leadership and taking responsibility of the ones being ruled also arise. The authority ideals are contested mainly by the antagonist characters or agents, which I examine here further, reflecting on the previously discussed game story.

3.1. The Abbey of the Everyman; Tradition and Legality as Authorities

The organized, state empowered religion of the Dishonored universe The Abbey of the Everyman begins, in the first game, as an ultimate evil and fanatically-led religious group, who watches and controls common people by denying religious plurality, and endorsing the order's own ways. The order's status is shown in The Overseer brothers' assignments to hunt magical artefacts or monitor citizens' lives, if they are seen as heretic, as referenced in the games. All beliefs or rituals connected to the Outsider are seen as foul. In game dialogue, the Overseers might even comment on the player character's heretic ways, as they bare The Outsiders' mark. In the first game, the player learns that for repelling heresy, The Overseers have developed a technical musical device to block the use of supernatural powers. The device resembles an organ grinder, while the sound prevents the player character's actions if they are too close to the device. In addition, The Overseers outfits' consist of an armoury and weapons, emphasizing their militant image. The atmosphere towards The Abbey, as it is sometimes shortly referenced in the Dishonored games, changes though in the second game, while another more powerful antagonist is set as the main target for the player character's fight. In the second game, now, the reigning Empress, Emily Kaldwin, is shown to have worked together with The Abbey to bring stability and protection to the common people after the first game's events, and has now defeated the rat plague. In game dialogue, it may be heard The Overseers' reference to The Abbey as something to be "served", or The Abbey may be hoped to "give blessings" to someone. Although the second game consists of Emily trying to gain back her reign and fighting against the hostile Overseers, she (if chosen as the player character) contemplates in game dialogue The Abbey bringing at least peace to people when Delilah's actions are seen even more monstrous.

The third game expands on The Abbey of the Everyman's position and actions in the Empire. During Billie's movements in the city, public announcements may be heard where it is reminded that citizens should regularly attend The Abbey's sermons for moral guidance. The announcements also notify that neighbourly vigilance is preferable, and all unordinary activities are to be reported. These public notices may be seen as mediating a sense of fear and worry in the city among people. In the third game, it is also revealed that The Oracular sisters and Overseer brothers do not converse with one another, and the sisters are depicted to live more isolated from city life. The sisters, who tie their eyes with cloth to be more intuitively immersed with their surroundings, declare prophecies, which are nevertheless seen as an ultimate authority within The Abbey.

The Abbey's existence is at least shown as controversial in the Dishonored games, while from hostile beginnings, The Abbey's depiction changes and broadens to be shown including aims to stabilise the society after disastrous events. In the third game, The Oracular sisters and The Overseers join forces and work together to investigate and purge the remaining heresy, as they call the mess that Delilah and her witches made in Karnaca during the second game's events. However, the investigations are far from merciful, regarding the captured witches. The inquisition like research methods, resemble torture. In one of the third game's side stories, a captured witch may be found in one of The Overseer's torture cellars. She begs Billie for her life, and the player may choose how to deal with the situation, to set her free or leave her be.

The Abbey more or less defines itself through depictions of what they are not. They do not console with magic attributed to the Outsider, as game lore documents reveal, but they watch strictly over people's lives, and place importance on the Empire's future. Billie explains, in one cut scene in the third game, that The Abbey teaches the Void to be the "source of doubt, heresy, and suffering". The authority ideals that The Abbey of the Everyman reflects in the previously-described game events are legitimatised as the traditional and legal ideal. The orders status is legitimatised through tradition, the Empire's trust in them, and in the legal role of protecting the ruled; to uphold the belief that they will protect the cities from heretical forces. The Overseers' traditional authority legitimisation is, however, questioned in the story, and also in the game milieu's graffiti texts, where their protective watching is referenced as "butchering" (graffiti found in the third game).

3.2. Delilah Copperspoon and a Charismatic Domination

Delilah Copperspoon's life, up to her violent self-proclaimed reign, had been miserable. She was born as the Emperors' illegitimate child at the same time Emily's mother had been born. Delilah was, however, denied her birth rights, and in time, banished to face the Dunwall streets. Later, Delilah became interested in the occult and witchcraft, and studied natural philosophy and the structures of the world. The Outsider took an interest in the scholarly gifted Delilah, and granted her supernatural abilities, but Delilah obsessed over revenge. Her first plans to take over the reign resulted in her imprisonment inside an oil painting, a story that is told in the dlc game Dishonored: The Brigmore Witches. During Dishonored 2, the player finds out that certain individuals let, in a séance, Delilah out of the painting, and she came back as a supernatural being, residing in between the Void and the world of the living.

Compared to the traditional and societal depiction of a religious authority of The Abbey of the Everyman in the first Dishonored game, Delilah's image is a more fantastic one. In the second Dishonored game, she acts as a supernatural and magical figure, reaching deity-like attributes, but still depending on her earthly followers and believers to gain authority. Delilah's converted followers and minions consist of women who she shares her powers with, but who blindly follow Delilah in her plans. The player character may find letters and documents, where Delilah's supporters scheme systematically to convert the Oracular sisters to join Delilah's cause. The witches are shown as magical hostile characters, who are also depicted as chanting, make potions, studying magical properties, but fearing their leader.

Delilah can be interpreted to claim a charismatic ideal of domination. Her persona and supernatural powers also underline this legitimisation. Her own aim is to be obeyed and worshipped forever, as she reveals in the ending scenes of the second game. This may be also seen as aiming towards gaining traditional domination; as a ruler, she demands loyalty from her subjects. However, in the end, most of Delilah's followers perish alongside her after her final defeat, as peace is restored in the ending of Dishonored 2. In the third game, some of the defeated witches are shown to have joined The Eyeless gang as a last consolation to access spiritual powers. In the third game, some witches can be heard to comment in game dialogue on The Eyeless being only "pseudo-spiritual" in their aims of gaining supernatural powers. The idea of an orthodox way of conducting religion or supernatural abilities are present in the game worlds, also in the witches' statements. If religion in the first Dishonored game is built to reflect negative connotations of a traditional religious authority, the second Dishonored game builds a charismatic religious authority to be extremist, mindless, and fanatic.

3.3. The Outsider as a Charistmatic Authority

While the Outsider is not a straightforward antagonist character to be fought against in the Dishonored games, he represents a contested authority that may be located as a religious authority reflecting on the tripartite ideals of domination. The Outsider receives his authority in a charismatic authority legitimation, while the model of a deity or a god can be interpreted linking to the charismatic ideal of domination, in Weber's distinction (Allen 2004). The Outsider's mystery, persona, and ancient origins are shown to fascinate people, especially because of his powers and the continuing possibility to be gifted by his mark.

Throughout the games, the Outsider acts as an independent, supporting character, who appears from time to time to reflect in cutscenes on the player character's actions and choices, simultaneously living in the in-between world, the Void. In general, the Outsider is shown as an ambiguous trickster deity, whose intentions are not clear, but enjoys being a spectator of human life. In the third Dishonored game, the player learns that the Outsider is not originally a deity, but a man who had been purposefully trapped and ritually sacrificed by ancient cultists to the Void to act as a resource beacon distributing the powers of the Void to the human realm and to The Cult. Since his tragic birth, the origins of the Outsider had remained hidden, and he became the source of inspiration to new generations of cultists and folk beliefs.

The Outsider's domination constructs also from the people and followers who believe in his mystery. The Outsider is considered as a saving deity for common folk, while, for example, graffiti stating: "The Outsider is watching", can be found around the city in the first game. In the third game, The Eyeless gang and the more scientifically-oriented cult investigates the enigma of the Outsider and the Void. The final story, however, reduces this mystery of the deity and the belief in him to secular origins. The Outsider is stripped away from his mystical god-like status, and replaced with a humanised explanation. In the end, the Outsider was only a man, who was a victim of other men. The authority image, which was built around the deity's charismatic attributes, shifts dramatically in the third game.

The authority image of the Outsider is also contested in one of the last scenes in the third Dishonored game. The assassin, Daud, contemplates, in game dialogue, how the Outsiders' mark, the granted magical abilities, are a gift that is bestowed only onto selected few. "All the bitterness, hatred, and fear—and the Outsider gets to choose who wields his black magic, and who cowers in the dark. That's something no one should decide." he says to Billie during his last days. Daud reflects on the dilemma of the deity's authority: who or what can be in a position of domination and decide for others. Billie, however, replies by reminding that their own or other people's actions cannot all be blamed entirely on the Outsider, but Daud stays determined. Daud assumes the Outsider as the perpetrator for all misfortune in the Empire, while Billie sees responsibility in their own doings. The conversation between Billie and Daud underlines a dilemma that is increasingly highlighted from the second Dishonored to the third game: how does the sense of responsibility, and religious authority and domination combine?

After the Outsider is released back to the world, whether the player chooses the lethal or non-lethal ending option, Billie narrates equally in the ending scenes on the future of the Empire. She points out that even though the influence of the Outsider is now gone, the magic of the Void continues to exist in the world and affect people in unknown ways.

4. Discussions

The Dishonored games can be interpreted as stories commenting on the located authority models asking who or what in which circumstances may have societal control over others, and what would that control or domination require from that authority. As previously discussed, Weber did not focus, in his work, on the aspect of how authority positions were gained, as much as on the explanations on authority distinctions. Allen argues that Weber did not explicate on "contradictory motives" why people become ruled, or comparing how entire nations might have overthrown their once legitimate leaders (Allen 2004). The Dishonored games definitely brush on the aspect of individuals overpowering displeasing authorities. The displeasing ruler is shown, composed of several qualities that sum up to the ideal that an authority should express a sense of responsibility. A ruler's negligence is depicted in the lack of care for common people, which is visible in the city milieus of Dunwall and Karnaca. It is visible in the actions, status, and the strict religious control of The Abbey of the Everyman, which is actualised in the Overseers' and the Oracular sisters' work. The antagonist Delilah's dictatorship, and treating followers as subordinates, reflects a negative authority image as well. In the third game, the Outsider's assumed authorising position, of an otherworldly caring deity, is challenged and taken apart. All that is left is the subjective authority of the protagonist. The subjective authority is gained as a separation and othering process, detaching the protagonist from the displeasing located religious authorities. In the games, the protagonist becomes their own authority, where religious authorities or the idea of deities as authorities are dismissed.

The Dishonored games may be viewed as accommodating different models of legitimisations of authority. In each game, the models are tried on in constructing a religious authority, but discarded in the end, as a resolution of the protagonists' fight against the story antagonists. On the other hand, the games, regarding their temporal situation in the late 19th century, can be seen as stories contesting today's postmodern individual player, by placing them in conflict with "historical" authorising models of domination and control relating to religion.

The religious criticism the games can be argued to partake in, is, however, situated in a traditional frame. William James makes the distinction that religious criticism should be directed separately onto the individual believer or the religious institution (James [1909–1921] 1999). The Dishonored games may be seen continuing similar distinctions in its criticism, while the story of contested religious authorities is forwarded between the protagonist characters, "the individual believers", and the located religious authorities, "the religious institutions". The criticism is placed in between these actors' problematised dynamics.

The relationship connecting the protagonist characters' and the located contested authorities also provides contemplation on how politics and power are represented and debated in video games and popular culture narratives. Tim Nieguth argues that popular culture products "challenge socio-political realities", and would then provide a plausible arena for research, also within political sciences, whether focused on narratives, conceptual discussions, or processes constructing popular culture production (Nieguth 2015). The examination of Weber's conceptual ideals on authority and religion regarding images of social or societal power in the Dishonored games, as a research application, would then provide very topical possibilities to be expanded to other genres of popular culture products.

The Dishonored games can be, therefore, summarised to ask, who has and who should have control and authority in society—a religion, a god, or human beings? The tripartite authority distinction can be seen compared between the games, forwarded and carried from character to character, where each game and additional game concludes in defeating the authority legitimisation ideals.

5. Conclusions

Religious authority in the Dishonored universe can be located and reflected by Weber's tripartite authority ideals. The ideals can be argued to be presented through a criticising frame in the depiction of the game's religious authorities. The religious authorities are shown as poor models sustaining peace and care, and taking responsibility for the ruled, as the game stories or character constructions depict.

The religious authorities, based on the three ideals of domination, are contested in the first Dishonored game by displaying the negative sides of the traditional and legal religious authority represented by The Abbey of the Everyman. The order is shown as threatening to common folk, denying people's freedom of religion and choice. In the second Dishonored game, the charismatic religious authority, Delilah Copperspoon, rules as a fanatic individual and dictator, oppressing all to her will.

The critical argument the first game begins with, is continued and strengthened in the second game; religious authorities in their domination become dictating authorities. The third game, however, approaches this statement differently. The defeated deity Outsider, as a charismatic authority, is portrayed as ambivalent and ambiguous. The humanisation the deity undergoes, contests a charismatic authority, which resembles nihilistic reflections, where demystified gods become obsolete authorities. The only leading authority that remains after each game's end is the individual subject, the player protagonist.

The Dishonored game's different depictions contesting religious authorities, and especially the fights against them, can be argued as reflecting negotiations of religious authorities' placements in today's society. The video game narrative of criticising religious authorities, as discussed above, does relate to anti-Catholic stereotypes, but moves to focus more on the individual's relation to authority. The individual's choice to obey an authority, the legitimisation of the three ideals, seems not to be sufficient reasons for domination, according to the games. As the games contest the religious authority ideals, they leave room for speculation of what would, then, an adequate religious authority be, or should there be one at all? The sense of responsibility, at least, would be one acquired notion the games make on preferred authority. All in all, the games build the image of religious authorities, or faiths, as disappointing and disenchanting.

Funding: This research received no external funding.

Conflicts of Interest: The author declares no conflict of interest.

References

Allen, Kieran. 2004. *Max Weber: A Critical Introduction*. London: Pluto Press, pp. 97–116.

Arkane Studios. 2012. *Dishonored*. Video Game. Rockville: Bethesda Softworks.

Arkane Studios. 2013a. *Dishonored: The Knife of Dunwall*. Dlc. Rockville: Bethesda Softworks.

Arkane Studios. 2013b. *Dishonored: The Brigmore Witches*. Dlc. Rockville: Bethesda Softworks.

Arkane Studios. 2016. *Dishonored 2*. Video Game. Rockville: Bethesda Softworks.

Arkane Studios. 2017. *Dishonored: Death of the Outsider*. Video Game. Rockville: Bethesda Softworks.

Bizzocchi, Jim, and Joshua Tanenbaum. 2011. *Well Read: Applying Close Reading Techniques to Gameplay Experiences*. Edited by Drew Davidson. Well Played 3.0 Video Games, Value and Meaning. Halifax: ETC Press, pp. 289–90.

Bogost, Ian. 2008. The Rhetoric of Video Games. In *The Ecology of Games: Connecting Youth, Games, and Learning*. Edited by Katie Salen. The John D. and Catherine T. MacArthur Foundation Series on Digital Media and Learning. Cambridge: The MIT Press, p. 121.

Bosman, Frank G. 2014. The Lamb of Comstock. Dystopia and Religion in Video Games. *Online-Heidelberg Journal for Religions on the Internet* 5: 162–82.

Boyan, Andy, MAtthew GrizzArd, and Nicholas Bowman. 2015. A massively moral game? Mass Effect as a case study to understand the influence of players' moral intuitions on adherence to hero or antihero play styles. *Journal of Gaming & Virtual Worlds* 7: 41–57.

Bowie, Fiona. 2008. *The Anthropology of Religion. An Introduction*, 2nd ed. Hoboken: Blackwell Publishing, pp. 68–69.

CD Projekt Red. 2015. *The Witcher 3: Wild Hunt*. Video Game. Warsaw: CD Projekt RED.

Davie, Grace. 2008. *The Sociology of Religion*. London: SAGE, pp. 28–29–40–42.

Dishonored Wiki. Available online: http://dishonored.wikia.com/wiki/Dishonored_Wiki (accessed on 12 February 2018).

Durkheim, Émile. 1995. *The Elementary Forms of Religious Life*. Translated by Karen E. Fields. New York: The Free Press (Simon & Schuster), pp. 39–44. First published 1912.

Eichner, Susanne. 2014. *Agency and Media Reception. Experiencing Video Games, Film, and Television*. Berlin: Springer, pp. 11–12.

Guerilla Games. 2017. *Horizon Zero Dawn*. Video Game. San Mateo: Sony Interactive Entertainment.

Hanke, Edith. 2016. Max Weber worldwide: The reception of a classic in times of change. *Max Weber Studies* 16: 70–88. [CrossRef]

Hanson, Ben. 2016. Inside Dishonored 2's Exaggerated Art Direction. Available online: http://www.gameinformer.com/b/features/archive/2016/05/23/oppression-opulence-and-decay-inside-dishonored-2s-bold-art-direction.aspx (accessed on 12 February 2018).

Heidbrink, Simone, Tobias Knoll, and Jan Wysocki. 2014. Theorizing Religion in Digital Games Perspectives and Approaches. *Online-Heidelberg Journal for Religions on the Internet* 5: 5–51.

Heidbrink, Simone, Tobias Knoll, and Jan Wysocki. 2016. *Digital Methodologies in the Sociology of Religion*. Edited by Sariya Cheruvallil-Contractor and Suha Shakkour. Digital Methodologies in the Sociology of Religion. London: Bloomsbury, pp. 159–71.

James, William. 1999. *The Varieties of Religious Experience, A Study in Human Nature, Being the Gifford Lectures on Natural Religion Delivered at Edinburgh in 1909–1902*. New York: The Modern Library, pp. 34–36. First published 1909–1921.

Jenkins, Philip. 2003. *The New Anti-Catholicism: The Last Acceptable Prejudice*. New York: Oxford University Press, pp. 157–76.

Lebowitz, Josiah, and Chris Klug. 2011. *Interactive Storytelling for Video Games A Player Centred Approach to Creating Memorable Characters and Stories*. New York: Elsevier, pp. 203–4.

Love, Mark C. 2010. Not-So-Sacred Quests: Religion Intertextuality and Ethics in Video Games. *Religious Studies and Theology* 29: 191–213.

Nieguth, Tim. 2015. Culture and Politics Revisited: The Political Science of Popular Culture. Edited by Nieguth, Tim. In *Politics of Popular Culture: Negotiating Power, Identity, and Place*. Montreal: MQUPT, pp. 181–91.

Oswalt, Conrad. 2003. *Secular Steeples. Popular Culture and the Religious Imagination*. Harrisburg: Trinity Press International, p. 154.

Perreault, Gregory. 2012. Holy Sins: Depictions of Violent Religion in Contemporary Console Games. Paper presented at 2012 Conference on Digital Religion Center for Religion, Media and Culture, Boulder, CO, USA, January 12–15.

Pesonen, Heikki. 2016. *Mad Sisters and Evil Mothers: Representations of Nuns and Convents in Western Films*. Edited by Hämäläinen Riku, Pesonen Heikki and Utriainen Terhi. Helsinki Study of Religions, Publication Series of the Study of Religions in Helsinki. Helsinki: Helsinki University, p. 388.

Ringer, Fritz K. 2004. *Max Weber: An Intellectual Biography*. Chicago: University of Chicago Press, pp. 252–55.

Salen, Katie, and Eric Zimmerman. 2004. *Rules of Play Game Design Fundamentals*. Cambridge: The MIT Press, pp. 314–17.

Thielenhaus, Kevin. 2017. Dishonored: Death of the Outsider—How to Get the Best (& Worst) Endings. Available online: http://gameranx.com/features/id/120883/article/dishonored-death-of-the-outsider-how-to-get-the-best-worst-endings/ (accessed on 12 February 2018).

Weber, Max. 1978. *Economy and Society, based on the German*, 4th ed. Berkeley: University of California Press, pp. 241–44. First published 1922.

Zeiler, Xenia. 2014. The Global Medialization of Hinduism through Digital Games: Representation versus Simulation in Hanuman: Boy Warrior. In *Playing with Religion in Digital Games*. Edited by Heidi Campbell and Gregory P. Grieve. Bloomington: Indiana University Press.

Zeiler, Xenia. 2017. Introduction. In *Methods for Studying Video Games and Religion*. Edited by Vit Šisler, Kerstin Radde-Antweiler and Xenia Zeiler. Abingdon-on-Thames: Routledge, pp. 3–4.

Article

Contemplation, Subcreation, and Video Games

Mark J. P. Wolf

Communication Department, Concordia University Wisconsin, Mequon, WI 53097, USA; mark.wolf@cuw.edu;
Tel.: +1-262-243-4262

Received: 2 March 2018; Accepted: 16 April 2018; Published: 26 April 2018

Abstract: This essay asks how religion and theological ideas might be made manifest in video games, and particularly the creation of video games as a religious activity, looking at contemplative experiences in video games, and the creation and world-building of game worlds as a form of Tolkienian subcreation, which itself leads to contemplation regarding the creation of worlds.

Keywords: video games; contemplation; subcreation; imaginary worlds; religion; world-building

---

1. Contemplation, Subcreation, and Video Games

At first glance, video games and religion may seem to have little to do with each other; perhaps they even seem at odds, the latter regarding what is serious and holy, while the former appears to be frivolous entertainment. But like any other medium, video games encompass a wide variety of content, which is both used and abused; and just as we would not reject the use of film or television for religious purposes, neither should the video game be rejected. Even painting and the idea of religious imagery itself was initially questioned. To answer this, during the Seventh Session of the Second Council of Nicaea, on 13 October, 787, the church fathers issued a declaration concerning the use of holy images:

> As the sacred and life-giving cross is everywhere set up as a symbol, so also should the images of Jesus Christ, the Virgin Mary, the holy angels, as well as those of the saints and other pious and holy men be embodied in the manufacture of sacred vessels, tapestries, vestments, etc., and exhibited on the walls of churches, in the homes, and in all conspicuous places, by the roadside and everywhere, to be revered by all who might see them. For the more they are contemplated, the more they move to fervent memory of their prototypes. Therefore, it is proper to accord to them a fervent and reverent adoration, not, however, the veritable worship which, according to our faith, belongs to the Divine Being alone—for the honor accorded to the image passes over to its prototype, and whoever venerate the image venerate in it the reality of what is there represented. (Tanabe et al. 2015)

We have moved from the painted image, to the photographic image, to the moving image, and now, with video games, to the interactive moving image.

Religious and theological ideas can be made manifest in video games, including the appearance of religion and religious iconography within video games and through the playing of video games as a potentially religious activity, especially contemplative ones that vicariously place the player in a different environment, as found in games like Cyan's *Myst* (1993) and *Riven* (1997), Bill Viola's *The Night Journey* (2007), Jenova Chen's *Journey* (2012), or David OReilly's *Everything* (2017).

2. Video Games and Contemplation

When Cyan's *Myst* was released in 1993, it was noted not only for its beautiful graphics but also for its relatively unusual style of gameplay; during the opening sequence, the player's character (the game is always from a first-person perspective, so the player's avatar is only implied) is left on a lonely island without being given any objective or goal. The player then wanders the island, discovering messages, objects, machines, and locations, and must figure what to make of it all. Not only that, but the various places encountered each are quiet and still, with only ambient sounds (and occasionally ominous music enhancing the mood) and very little movement visually (only a few animated details, like a turning windmill or a flitting butterfly, to keep the visuals from seeming frozen). As a puzzle game, *Myst* is a very contemplative experience, though the player's thoughts will likely be about exploring the various locations, learning how to operate simple machines, and listening to occasional messages from non-player characters. Even so, the game promotes a thoughtful, quiet, careful approach to life that could easily be applied to areas of one's life outside the game. *Myst* became the best-selling computer game of all time, a title it held until 2002, demonstrating that contemplative games can be as popular as action-based games.

Other games have also been designed to create a contemplative mood and experience for players, such as video artist Bill Viola's *The Night Journey*, which has been touring as a part of art exhibitions in museums since its appearance at SIGGRAPH in 2007, and it has only recently been made commercially available in 2018. *The Night Journey* has grayscale imagery of a computer-generated landscape that is softened and filtered into a murky and motion-blurred slow-moving hypnotic experience (a 10-min trailer including gameplay video of *The Night Journey* can be seen at https://www.youtube.com/watch?v=zL1_twK2NDc). According to the game's website, the game's purpose is "to tell the universal story of an individual's journey towards enlightenment," and the following description is given:

> The game begins in the center of a mysterious landscape on which darkness is falling. There is no one path to take, no single goal to achieve, but the player's actions will reflect on themselves and the world, transforming and changing them both. If they are able, they may slow down time itself and forestall the fall of darkness. If not, there is always another chance; the darkness will bring dreams that enlighten future journeys.

> The interactive design of The Night Journey evokes a sense of the archetypal journey of enlightenment through the mechanics of the game experience—i.e., the choices and actions of the player during the game. The game design explores a challenging question: what is the game mechanic of enlightenment? How can we model such an intensely personal yet archetypal experience in a game? (https://www.thenightjourney.com/)

While Bill Viola is primarily a video artist, not a game designer, there are more commercial games that also deal with such experiences. Jenova Chen, a co-founder of Thatgamecompany, is known for more contemplative games and has lead the team that created *Cloud* (2005), *flOw* (2006), *Flower* (2009), and *Journey* (2012). *Cloud* is about a boy in a hospital bed who dreams of flying. Players manipulate clouds while flying through the sky. As the game's webpage describes it, "Cloud is a game designed to remind the player of the natural beauty ignored in their daily life. A cup of sparkling water, waving leaves under the sun, blue gradient in the sky, infinite forms of clouds. It is a unique game; a relaxing, non-stressful, meditative experience" (https://www.jenovachen.com/flowingames/cloud.htm). In *flOw*, players steer a simple geometric organism, which can devour other smaller organisms and objects, enlarging it as it adds material to itself (or loses it). Due the abstract nature of the graphics, the actions are not violent or even aggressive but rather promote a quiet contemplative state, similar to that of viewing fish in a fish tank. *Flower*, a spiritual successor to *flOw*, has the player controlling the wind to blow flower petals around a meadow and was designed more with the player's emotional experience in mind than any objective or goal. Finally, *Journey* is about a lonely journey through a desert and to the top of a mountain and the spiritual growth that occurs along the way. Just as thatgamecompany was going bankrupt after releasing *Journey*, the game became the best-selling PlayStation Network game of all time (Takahashi 2013). Chen says he has received many notes of appreciation from players, and one, from Sophia, a 15-year-old girl who lost her father to illness, explained how it affected her:

Your game practically changed my life. . . . It was the most fun I had with him since he had been diagnosed. . . . My father passed in the spring of 2012, only a few months after his diagnosis.

Weeks after his death, I could finally return myself to playing video games. I tried to play Journey, and I could barely get past the title screen without breaking down into tears. In my dad's and in my own experience with Journey, it was about him, and his journey to the ultimate end, and I believe we encountered your game at the most perfect time.

I want to thank you for the game that changed my life, the game whose beauty brings tears to my eyes. Journey is quite possibly the best game I have ever played. I continue to play it, always remembering what joy it brought, and the joy it continues to bring.

I am Sophia, I am 15, and your game changed my life for the better. (Takahashi 2013)

Another contemplative game set in an expansive world is David OReilly's *Everything* (2017), which was designed to encourage the player to consider the connectedness of the universe. Players can "become" anything in the game, from plants and animals roaming the wilderness, down to bugs and even microbes at the microscopic end of the scale, as well as landmasses, planets, stars, and galaxies at the macroscopic end of the scale. As OReilly describes it, "*Everything* is a game about the things we see, their relationships, and their points of view. In this context, things are how we separate reality so we can understand it and talk about it with each other" (Muncy 2016).

While most of the contemplative games mentioned so far have been non-narrative ones, story-based games can also be designed to encourage contemplation, like Cyan's *Myst* (1993) and *Riven: The Sequel to Myst* (1997). In addition to being a quiet, atmospheric game of navigation and exploration, *Riven* is also the story about Gehn, a builder of worlds who has made a religion for the primitive islanders who live on his island and uses it to subjugate them and rule over them. The player, of course, knows nothing of this upon arriving at the island with only the scantest of directions as to what to do. Much of the realizations of Gehn's megalomania, his religion, and the situation of the islanders is left for the player to discover and gradually piece together as the player finds temples, equipment, machinery, and other clues as to what has been happening on the island. *Riven* is part of the larger story and world behind the *Myst* series of games, which includes the subject of world-building itself, or what author J. R. R. Tolkien referred to as "subcreation."

3. Subcreation and Video Game Worlds

Writing about authors and their making of imaginary worlds, Tolkien coined the term "subcreation" in order to make a distinction between the kind of *ex nihilo* ("from nothing") creation that only God can do and the creation done by human authors and artists, in which imaginary worlds are made using materials and concepts that are inevitably taken from the world we know, which Tolkien referred to as the Primary World (imaginary worlds are then referred to as "secondary worlds"). The term "subcreation" literally means "creating under," which refers to its reliance on Primary World. Subcreators can take existing concepts and ideas and rearrange their elements to create new creatures, beings, locations, objects, and ultimately, entire imaginary worlds.

The characters in the Myst franchise (which has extended to books, games, soundtracks, and beyond) are from the fictional D'ni culture, who write Descriptive Books that can describe a world and connected Linking Books that can allow a person to go into the world described in the Descriptive Book for that world. The world of Riven, for example, was written by the character Gehn, who feels entitled to rule the world. The games involve characters, and the player's implied character, going back and forth between these worlds, called Ages, as well as to D'ni, the name of the great underground cavern in the Primary World where the D'ni live (or lived, as the cavern is in ruin as the story begins). The Art of Writing, as the book-writing is called, is something that is guarded and carefully taught, since the worlds described in the books need to be consistent, stable, and hospitable to human life before anyone can safely visit them. Worlds which are hastily written or flawed can collapse, taking all their inhabitants with them. Despite all the precautions, of course, these powers are inevitably abused by those who see this as an opportunity to dominate and control worlds.

Interestingly, the creators of the Myst franchise, Rand and Robyn Miller, who founded the company Cyan Worlds, are Christians and, like Tolkien, grew more concerned about the theological aspects of their world as it grew and developed. Early on, the Descriptive Books were said to create the worlds that were described in them, but the brothers realized that this seemed to result in *ex nihilo* creation, so they changed their mythology so that the worlds all already existed somewhere, and that the precise description of a world written into a Descriptive Book allowed it to connect with that world that matched its description, without actually causing the creation of that world. Thus, the writing of different Ages, or worlds, could still occur as it had in all their stories, but the explanation and theology behind it all would not contradict Christian theology.

The act of writing a description of a world and opening a portal that allows one to enter into that world is rather analogous to the very act of writing a video game, especially one which has an elaborate world that the player enters vicariously. In the games, players use a cursor shaped like a hand to click on an image in a linking book to enter an Age, and the very acting of pointing and clicking happens not just diegetically, but nondiegetically, as the player performs a similar action to "enter" the world of the game itself. Likewise, programmers who write video games must have code that produces a stable world that will run without errors destroying the player's experience of the world. Thus, the making of video games is itself a form of world-building and a subcreative activity that can be used to reflect on the nature of the nature of what it means to create a world or for players to inhabit one.

Some games, like *SimCity* (1989) and other sandbox-style games like *Minecraft* (2011), involve world-building, inviting players to build cities, countries, or even worlds. In the genre of "god games," players are given a godlike control over various events and processes; for example, in *Spore* (2008), the player controls the development and growth of species of creatures. Although these kinds of game experiences may sometimes only tenuously connect to what we normally may think of as religious content in games, a wide range of games either overtly or covertly use content, concepts, ideas, or situations that encourage contemplation and reflection on themes that are religious or spiritual in nature, and make players more aware of their role in the world, or of Creation itself. While novels and films can perform a similar function in one's life, the interactivity found in video games creates a unique experience in which players can directly see the consequences of their actions, as they are forced to make decisions and contemplate outcomes. Due to their interactive nature, and the way decisions lead to consequences that can in turn lead to further decision-making, video games are an ideal medium for moral training, and can be written to demonstrate the difficulties faced in moral dilemmas, even limiting the time given to come to a decision.

In "The Incarnated Gamer: The Theophoric Quality of Games, Gaming, and Gamers," Frank G. Bosman identifies five levels on which religion can be found in video games (Bosman 2017). There is the material level, the referential level, the reflexive level, ritual (an in-game behavior associated with religion), and the meta level, in which the experience of gaming is identified as religious. To these one could add a sixth level, the subcreational level, which is the experience of actually designing and creating a video game; this extends beyond the meta level insofar as it goes beyond the playing of a game to the making of a game. Some games, like the genre of "god games," give the player control over a world, while others, such as the aforementioned "sandbox" games *SimCity* (1988) and *Minecraft* (2009), come even closer in what they allow players to do, actively allowing them to build and construct the worlds within the games, but these still do so according to templates and the fixed categories of objects and building materials already present in the game; the actual creation of games and game worlds themselves, without such preconceived infrastructures, is closest to true subcreation. While the average gamer does not get involved with video games to this extent, the availability of game creation software, player-created modding, and even the design stage that may or may not lead to the actual instantiation of a game itself, represents an experience in which a designer encounters a number of fundamental questions about the design of a game world, which is also another form of subcreation.

First, the creation of a video game world is similar to that of imaginary worlds found in other media; it is called into being with words, like Creation itself. The computer code that makes up a video game world goes beyond the words of novel-based worlds in that the computer code that calls them into being does so through the algorithmic means provided by the computer rather than merely relying on the audience's imagination. Like literary worlds made of words and audiovisual worlds like those of film and television, video game worlds are accessible only indirectly, though video game worlds allow a degree of interaction that extends beyond merely imagining, watching, and listening, since it requires actions and decisions from the player. While all the same decisions found in the making of other imaginary worlds can be found in the making of video games, such as the geography of the world, its layout and design, the appearance and behavior of its flora, fauna, architecture, and other creatures and objects, and so forth. But the decisions and participation of the game world subcreator extend far beyond the involvement and participation mentioned in Bosman's fourth and fifth levels because the restrictions placed on the player by an already-existing game are absent from the game design process; the designer is free to begin to subcreate a world in whatever direction is desired.

The idea that human beings as subcreators imitate God's acts of Creation, as a way in which human beings are created in the image of God, is described in Tolkien's writings on subcreation (Tolkien [1939] 1964), and appears before Tolkien's work in Nikolai Berdyaev's *The Destiny of Man* (1931), in which he wrote, "God created man in his own image and likeness, i.e., made him a creator too, calling him to free spontaneous activity and not to formal obedience to His power. Free creativeness is the creature's answer to the great call of its creator." (Berdiyaev [1931] 2009). While human creativity occurs in all the arts (and in industry as well), subcreation, the building of imaginary worlds, which includes video game worlds, is perhaps closest in kind to God's creation of the world, despite the inevitable incompleteness and relatively tiny stature of human-made imaginary worlds. Though they lack the scale or complexity of the real world, the subcreator's creative ambition can still be that of the making of an entire world, and an interactive one at that.

As a game world is built, the subcreator must decide to what extent the world will reflect an existing religious tradition, if it will reflect one at all. This reflection is embedded within the game engine and the world in subtle ways that may not be immediately obvious to players but only gradually emerge during the course of gameplay, as different actions and behaviors are carried out and lead to their respective consequences. How actions are connected to consequences are one way that a game's outlook is revealed and can describe an embedded ethics that inherently condemns or condones behaviors, leading to rewards or punishments. Consequences can also be short-term or long-term in nature, just as selfishness may seem to help an individual in the short term but become detrimental over the long term. The overarching powers behind the world, which oversee players' behaviors, enforce rules, and reward outcomes, may also be overt, in the forms of godlike characters (who may even be in the form of the player character), or simply a set of inherent rules that remain unpersonified, leaving them as a part of the background of a game world, where they are to be gradually learned through inference and deduction.

Designing a world as an exercise also makes a subcreator more conscious of the decisions that go into the design of a world; the way these decisions must balance and coexist with each other, and how they will collectively determine the experiences of the players who vicariously enter the game world. Even in a relatively simple form of a world, for example, the two-dimensional, low-resolution worlds of the games created for the Atari 2600, there are still many decisions to be made and many existing conventions that designers may choose to follow or to actively resist using. Most games, for example, have their difficulty level set ideally within the "flow" corridor of mental enjoyment between anxiety and boredom, as described by Mihaly Csikszentmihalyi (1990) and used in video game theories (see Juul 2005, p. 113), so that players will be challenged but will ultimately be able to prevail, mirroring the Christian belief, derived mainly from 1 Corinthians 10:13, that God will not permit us to be tempted or suffer beyond what we are capable of enduring. Likewise, game designers populate their worlds with non-player-characters (NPCs), some of which hinder players while others help them, but neither of which remove the player's ability to make the free will choices which are necessary to gameplay; in cases when this is violated, for example, in the forced baptism scene in *Bioshock Infinite* (2013), there are complaints from players, both religious and nonreligious alike (see Hernandez 2013).

Finally, even the smallest details of a world, which include the designs of the artifacts of the world's cultures, can reveal much of the backstory of a world, and together, such details imply the outlook and developmental journey of the non-player-characters that inhabit a world along with the players' characters. Like other imaginary worlds, video game worlds are built with a past, a history, already in mind; we see the results of that history in ruins, buildings, cultures, legends, characters, and the overall situation in which the player-character finds himself or herself when the game begins. In the imaginary world tradition, often the main character is a savior figure who is given the job of "saving the world," and video games continue to carry on this tradition as it becomes especially appropriate in an interactive medium (Wolf 2017, pp. 51–55). The world designer, then, is designing a fallen world, one where the consequences of sin have become manifest, similar to our own world. Even if the main character's saving of the world is one of military victory rather than moral renewal, the battle is almost always framed in terms of sides that are clearly those of good versus evil. Thus, the same challenges and crucibles that make our lives and deeds have merit and meaning are the same requirements for interesting video game narratives.

As game designers explore video game design possibilities, especially now that a number of contemplative games have proven that they can even be successful commercially, perhaps we will see more games exploring themes and issues that relate to spirituality and religion. And games involving world-building, as well as commercially-available software that allow players to create their own games and game worlds, will also serve to aid reflection and contemplation of the world we live in and what lies beyond it. For some time, imaginary worlds have been a mainstay of popular culture, and an interest in world-building continues to grow. As stated in my book, *Building Imaginary Worlds: The Theory and History of Subcreation* (2012),

> Subcreation is not just a desire, but a need and a right; it renews our vision and gives us new perspective and insight into ontological questions that might otherwise escape our notice within the default assumptions we make about reality. Subcreated worlds also direct our attention beyond themselves, moving us beyond the quotidian and the material, increasing our awareness of how we conceptualize, understand, and imagine the Primary World. And the more aware we are of it, the better we can appreciate the Divine design of Creation itself and our place in it. (Wolf 2012, p. 287)

Video games, then, can be used to convey religious ideas and convey religious experiences, encouraging contemplation and reflection, provided they are designed with such goals in mind; and, of course, they can also be used to devalue these things, and promote negative attitudes towards them. Although they have come a long way in only a few decades, video games are still a relatively young medium compared to books, paintings, sculpture, and other media, many of which have long histories in the conveyance of religious content and ideas. Whatever one presently thinks of video games, and their increasingly prominent position in popular culture, they have a great potential to influence the minds of those who play them, for good or for ill. The relationship between religion and video games continues to evolve and needs to be explored in greater detail, especially by game designers who desire to create experiences for their players that will help them become better human beings who will, in turn, desire to build a better world.

Conflicts of Interest: The author declares no conflict of interest.

References and Notes

Berdiyaev, Nikolai. 2009. *The Destiny of Man*. Brooklyn: Angelico Press. First published 1931.

Bosman, Frank G. 2017. The Incarnated Gamer: The Theophoric Quality of Games, Gaming, and Gamers. In *Boundaries of Self and Reality Online: Implications of Digitally Constructed Realities*. Edited by Jayne Gackenbach and Johnathan Bown. London: Ebevier Inc., pp. 187–204.

Csikszentmihalyi, Mihaly. 1990. *Flow: The Psychology of Optimal Experience*. New York: Harper Perrenial.

Hernandez, Patricia. 2013. Some Don't Like *BioShock*'s Forced Baptism. Enough to Ask for a Refund. Kotaku.com, April 16.

Juul, Jesper. 2005. *Half-Real: Video Games between Real Rules and Fictional Worlds*. Cambridge: The MIT Press.

Muncy, Jake. 2016. In the New Game *Everything*, You Can Be, Well, Everything. *Wired*, March 10. Available online: https://www.wired.com/2016/03/everything-announcement/ (accessed on 1 March 2018).

Takahashi, Dean. 2013. An Interview with Jenova Chen: How Journey's Creator Went Bankrupt and Won Game of the Year. VentureBeat.com, February 8. Available online: https://venturebeat.com/2013/02/08/an-interview-with-jenova-chen-how-journeys-creator-went-bankrupt-and-won-game-of-the-year/ (accessed on 1 March 2018).

Tanabe, Rosie, and et al. 2015. Second Council of Nicaea. *New World Encyclopedia*. Available online: http://www.newworldencyclopedia.org/p/index.php?title=Second_Council_of_Nicaea&oldid=990288 (accessed on 1 March 2018).

Tolkien, J. R. R. 1964. On Fairy-Stories. In *Tree and Leaf*. London: George Allen & Unwin Ltd. First published 1939.

Wolf, Mark J. P. 2012. *Building Imaginary Worlds: The Theory and History of Subcreation*. New York: Routledge.

Wolf, Mark J. P., ed. 2017. *The Routledge Companion to Imaginary Worlds*. New York: Routledge.

Article

The Paranormal in Jane Jensen's "Gray Matter"

Pavel Nosachev

Department of Culture Studies, National Research University Higher School of Economics, Moscow 101000, Russia; pnosachev@hse.ru

Received: 28 March 2018; Accepted: 16 April 2018; Published: 17 April 2018

Abstract: The main research issue of this article is to determine the extent to which Western esotericism influences the formation of computer game plots. The methodological framework is the occultural bricolage theory (C. Partridge). This article looks at how the paranormal is represented in the game "Gray Matter", created by J. Jensen. Jensen has always used occult bricolage as the main method for creating her games, but in "Gray Matter" this method is perfected. Although the game plot is built around paranormal events, they are not given any unambiguous interpretation; their status is the main question of the game. There are three answers to this question. The first answer is the beliefs of Sam Everett, a girl magician who does not believe in the supernatural. The second answer is the research of Dr. Styles, a neurobiologist convinced that the mind is an energy that can be objectified after death. The third answer is the theory of Dr. Ramusskin, a psi-phenomena specialist, who believes that super-abilities are real, and that spirits and the afterlife exist. It is the last answer that Jensen promotes in creating the game. The basis of "Gray matter" is a bricolage of Stephen King, the works of the Society for Psychical Research, works on parapsychology and the debates around psi-phenomena in neuropsychology.

Keywords: Western esotericism; religious studies; game studies; paranormal; society for psychical research; sacred; secular; occulture

1. Introduction

The theme of the sacred in computer games is complicated and diverse. In addition to the obvious play with well-known Christian ideas and myths, and appeal to images of Eastern religions (Hinduism, Islam, Buddhism), images and myths, syncretic by nature, that are unrelated to specific religious traditions are often used in games. How, for example, to evaluate such popular games as those about vampires or werewolves; do they use classical mythological religious plots, or refer to their modified forms? How can the usage of myths about Atlantis and other lost civilizations, so popular in many games, be categorized? These questions require us turn to the field of research into Western esotericism, which has been actively developing over the past three decades. Indeed, all these plots refer to a special type of world perception that is not directly related to world religions. Western esotericism (Hanegraaff 2013), as a generator of syncretic religiosity, has become an invaluable depository for screenwriters and game designers since the birth of computer games. This is not surprising: its images are vivid and memorable, they always sound familiar due to wide popularity in the media, and they provide the consumer with an inexhaustible sense of secrecy, because the very term esotericism in the mass consciousness is associated with something inexplicable. This is why it is more popular than well-known, and in some ways boring, religious mythology. In addition, the esoteric mythologemes are so diverse that their combination gives authors an inexhaustible source of ideas for new plots. Therefore, it is rational to consider the specifics of the role of Western esotericism in computer games with reference to a concrete example.

The best and most developed framework for analyzing these manifestations in popular culture is the theory of Christopher Partridge. Partridge proposed the concept of *occulture* in his dilogy,

The Re-Enchantment of the West (Partridge 2005, 2006). According to Partridge, *occulture* originated from *occultism*; this term has been often used and had a very broad meaning. According to Partridge, occultism:

> ... can be described as a subculture of various secret societies and 'enlightened' teachers involved in disciplines concerned with the acquisition of arcane, salvific knowledge (gnosis and theosophia), the experience of 'illumination', the understanding of esoteric symbolism (often related to occult interpretations of the Kabbalah), the practice of secret rituals and initiatory rites, and particularly the quest for aprisca theologia, philosophia occulta or philosophia perennis—a tradition of divine gnosis communicated, it is believed, through a line of significant individuals, including Moses, Zoroaster (Zarathustra), Hermes Trismegistus (the mythical author of the Hermeticd), Plato, Orpheus, and the Sibyls. (Partridge 2005, p. 69)

In the twentieth century this subculture has gradually emerged from the underground and became one of the sources of modern mass culture. In this way, occulture appeared.

> Occulture includes a range of 'deviant' ideas and practices ... including magick (as devised by Aleister Crowley), extreme rightwing religio-politics, radical environmentalism and deep ecology, angels, spirit guides and channeled messages, astral projection, crystals, dream therapy, human potential spiritualities, the spiritual significance of ancient and mythical civilizations, astrology, healing, earth mysteries, tarot, numerology, Kabbalah, feng shut, prophecies (e.g., Nostradamus), Arthurian legends, the Holy Grail, Druidry, Wicca, Heathenism, palmistry, shamanism, goddess spirituality, Gaia spirituality and eco-spirituality, alternative science, esoteric Christianity, UFOs, alien abduction, and so on. (Partridge 2005, p. 70)

Modern society was imbued with these themes, they became an integral part both of its private and public spheres. The widespread popularity of occultural mythologemes led Partridge to the idea that occulture is not simply a subculture. It is 'culture' more broadly conceived, concerned with esoteric, paranormal, and occult themes, which is primarily disseminated within popular culture (Partridge 2016). The bricoleur is the constitutive element of the occulture. In Partridge's theory, a bricoleur was a tailor sewing a patchwork of religiosity from pieces of occultism. Partridge supposed in his works that occultural bricolage was one of the most popular ways of creativity in modern culture. If this is true, then it would be interesting to trace the role that it plays in the creation of computer games.[1] We will now turn to the work of the writer and successful game designer Jane Jensen, in order to consider the specificity of occultural bricolage in computer games, using her work as an example. For further analysis I will use game reading combined with intertextual analysis of popular culture.

2. The Way of the Bricoleur

Jensen has worked on adventure games throughout her life. The role of this genre is significant for the development of the whole industry. This genre is almost of the same age as modern personal computers, so its history repeats the history of the development of the PC in many respects (Salter 2014). It should be noted that, according to the very specifics of the games, this genre should have a serious connection with the occulture. One reviewer described this genre as follows: "The very word *adventure* conjures images of exploring strange and dangerous environments, venturing into uncharted realms,

---

[1] Partridge only outlines an approach to the analysis of computer games, limiting his study to movies, music and subcultural currents. This is how Partridge describe the possibility of occulture game studies: "For example, much might have been made of the video game genre, which, replete with occultural baggage, puts the elusive powers sought by occultists virtually into the hands of the player. The individual enters the occultural matrix and acquires occultural-like knowledge and skills in order to manipulate supernatural forces" (Partridge 2005, p. 183).

foiling the diabolical plans of archetypal enemies, solving mysteries and having unusual experiences. The entire graphic adventure genre is ill led with detailed plots and fascinating settings and characters. Sometimes, the adventure milieu is handled in a very serious fashion" (Computer Gaming World 1994, p. 53). The first computer puzzle games appeared in the mid-70s and represented text narrations in which a player, using a set of commands entered from the keyboard, could solve puzzles and move further along the plot. The first such game was the *Colossal Cave Adventure* of 1976. Four years later, Ken and Roberta Williams founded the *Sierra On-Line* company that became one of the genre industry leaders. It was this company that produced the first quest, *Mystery House*, which used graphic drawings and in many respects made the genre of adventure one of the most successful for computer games in the late 1980s and the first half of the 1990s. Jane Jensen began her career at this company. Her debut game was *Gabriel Knight: Sins of the Fathers*, which immediately gained public attention and popularity. According to critics, this game brought the genre of adventure games to a new level, proving for the first time that the computer game can be frightening (Wilson 1993, p. 14), in that the plot can compete with the thrillers of Stephen King (Ardai 1994, p. 32), and by design can be an interactive movie (Ardai 1994, p. 32). Critics also noted that Jensen's game occupied the almost empty niche of computer horror. This reception led to the recognition of *Gabriel Knight: Sins of the Fathers* as the best adventure game of 1994, according to two large computer game magazines (Computer Gaming World 1994, p. 53). It should be noted that critics saw an occult basis in the game, and one of the reviewers noted that "*Gabriel Knight* throws the player convincingly into the world of Satanism and live sacrifice, of seedy and lecherous New Orleans" (Ardai 1994, p. 36). Such characteristics were not accidental; it was an indication of the direction of all further Jensen's creativity, her games were an illustrative example of occultural bricolage.[2] Jensen's first success made her continue the story of Gabriel in her next two games, each of which was based on an occultural plot. The first part of the series used the history of ritual murders related to Voodoo magic. The plot of the second part built around the investigation of crimes committed by werewolves, and the third part was based on the search for the grail combined with the theme of secret societies and vampires. Jensen carried out research for the creation of each game. For example the last game of the Gabriel trilogy, *Gabriel Knight 3: Blood of the Sacred, Blood of the Damned*, came out in 1999. To a large extent its plot was based on the famous book by Michael Baigent, Richard Leigh and Henry Lincoln, *The Holy Blood and the Holy Grail* (Baigent et al. 1983). The game used all the main "findings" of these authors: a story with the genealogy of Christ, a story with His descendants, an extensive interpretation of the grail, etc. Thus, four years before Dan Brown's *The Da Vinci Code*, the ideas of Baigent and Lincoln were embodied in this computer game. Jensen unmistakably found the attraction of the idea of *Sacred Blood and the Holy Grail* for the consumer, this was later confirmed by the stunning success of *The Da Vinci Code*. However, the format of the adventure computer game, created in poor quality 3D, did not allow her to realize her findings on the same high level as Brown. From the perspective of the theory of occulture, the most curious of Jensen's games is *Gray Matter*, released in 2010 by her own *Pinkerton Road Studio*. Firstly, this is the most ordinary of all of Jensen's games compared to the Gabriel series, or her last game *Moebius: Empire Rising*, it contains almost no supernatural phenomena. Secondly, the whole plot of the game is built around the status of paranormal phenomena. The main intrigue is the answer to the question: is there really anything outside the bounds of modern scientific knowledge about the world? Thirdly, *Gray Matter* is the best example for the demonstration of the work of occultural mythologemes in computer games. Let us now turn to these themes one-by-one.

---

2   The fact that Jensen is a typical occultural bricoleur is undoubted. All of her big games and books are based on a complex cocktail of occultural mythologemes and ideas. Thus, her most famous novel, *Dante's Equation* (Jensen 2003), which was even nominated for the Ph. Dick Award, is based on the idea of the fifth dimension popular in New Age Science and Kabbalistic gematria; the stylized Kabbalistic tree of Sefirot is even placed on its cover.

3. The World of *Gray Matter*

To begin, it is better to say a few words about the plot. The game is built around the story of Sam Everett, a girl who has accidentally gained entry to the house of the famous neuroscientist, David Styles, and is posing as his new assistant. In this role, Sam recruits a group of students for a series of experiments to visualize physical exercises and their possible influence on the physical condition and health. These experiments immediately become mysteriously connected with inexplicable events occurring on the campus of Oxford University and coincide chronologically with Styles' experiments. The game has two protagonists, Sam Everett and Dr. Styles, each of whom has their own goals. There are four tasks for the player: to enter the professional magicians club, *Daedalus*, and find the answer to the inexplicable phenomena on the campus in the role of Sam; to define if communication with the spirit of the doctor's deceased wife is possible, and to find the causes of events on the campus in the role of Dr. Styles. The main antagonist in the game is not known from the beginning, the whole intrigue is built around its definition. In the end, it turns out that Angela Mulholland, one of the participants in Styles' experiments, is endowed with paranormal abilities.

We have already established that despite the fact that the main theme of the game is paranormal phenomena, this game is very typical of Jensen's work. It is easy to compare the plot of *Gray Matter* with the plots of other Jensen games. The first shortcut of *Gabriel Knight: Sins of the Fathers*, showing the hero's dream, immediately hints at magical rituals related to human sacrifices. In the next interactive scene after the shortcut, in the dialogue between the protagonist and his assistant Grace, it becomes clear that Gabriel is writing a horror book about voodoo magic (a typical occultural element), and there are ritual murders (another occultural stamp) in the city. By the middle of the game (in the third chapter) Gabriel knows that he is a descendant of a German family of so-called *Schattenjäger*, who at all times have fought with evil forces and defended the world. In this way, by the middle of the game, the whole plotline passes completely into the realities of occulture, with the occultural realities in the game considered as normal. The second part, *Gabriel Knight 2: The Beast Within* begins with a shortcut in which residents of the town come to Gabriel's German castle with a request to protect them from werewolves. The third part, *Gabriel Knight: Blood of the Sacred, Blood of the Damned* begins with the story of a child of a noble family who needs to be protected from the persecution of vampires. Thus, the occultural component is not simply given to the player at once, it is introduced as an evident element, a part of everyday life. The world of the Gabriel trilogy is a place where voodoo magic rituals are real, where werewolves and fighters with evil spirits live, powerful secret societies operate, and where the religious history is only a facade for the hidden realities of esoteric practices. A similar situation is found in Jensen's previous game *Moebius: Empire Rising*, where all political events are subject to the Moebius law and are only an echo of past events.

The world of *Gray Matter* is completely different. There are regular references to occultural mythologemes and stereotypes in the aesthetics of the game from the very beginning. The first shortcut shows an old English mansion in the pouring rain, lit by lightning flashes.[3] This mansion makes a frightening impression on the girl sent to be an assistant to Dr. Styles and, in addition, a strange shadow banishes her. The place frightens her so much that she leaves without trying to cross the threshold of the house. Sam Everett, the main character, a post-goth girl, is not shy, she is a magician and lover of English literature, she has *Frankenstein* by Shelley in her bag, which is why the house does not make any unpleasant impression on her.

The image of the house owner—Dr. Styles—has been created to embody all the figures of the mad scientists known to literature (it is not insignificant that Sam has Shelley's novel in her bag). He is a loner, does not leave the house, wears a mask on his face, is very rich, and carries out strange experiments in the basement. This effect is further enhanced by Sam's comparison of Styles to Dracula

---

[3] An obvious and direct reference to clichéd images from literature (E.A. Poe, H.P. Lovecraft), films and games on the occultural theme (*Darkseed*, *Black Mirror*).

when none of the Oxford students are willing to participate in his experiments. The first meeting between Sam and the doctor deliberately develops the player's anxiety through increasing suspense. However, the most interesting thing in *Gray Matter* is that all these classic methods are used only to make the player feel surprise. Styles turns out to be a high-quality neurobiologist, depressed after the tragic death of his wife, his mask covers the burn marks that he received trying to save her, and the experiments in the basement are aimed at studying the possibility of brain functioning; they help to understand the degree to which visualization can affect the entire body. Thus, almost all the indications of occultural mythologemes turn out to be fake by the beginning of the second part of the game. Even when, in the third part, Styles' private laboratory with an isolation tank and random number generator for contact with deceased people, are shown, the player sees only a scientist who has experienced a grievous loss and who is trying to find an opportunity to overcome the death of a loved one by means of his science. It is already clear at this moment that the main issue of the game is the status of paranormal phenomena.

4. Three Shades of Gray

In the game, there are three ways of understanding the paranormal. Samantha Everett, the main character, represents the first. She is a young girl with an unstable psyche and a difficult past, and does not have an education. Sam is a magician and she sees her future in this occupation. If anything unusual is possible for her, then it is only what is created by the illusion of a skillful manipulator. Therefore, for the whole game she tries to find and expose the villain who is arranging the strange events in Oxford. Her reluctance to believe in the supernatural is so stubborn that even when evidence of the inexplicability of the events becomes apparent, she still continues to suspect a clever fraudster, a "master illusionist, one of the best in the world" (*Gray Matter*, chp. 6). Her way of thinking is described very accurately in the words of her magician mentor, Mephistopheles, which are spoken before Sam finds out about the existence of real super-abilities: "magicians in general don't believe—anyone else might be capable of the real thing" (*Gray Matter*, chp. 8). Sam finally recognizes the possibility of the paranormal explanation of events only in the last scenes of the game. A similar position is also taken by Styles' friend, Dr. Hellborn, who suspects Styles of insanity caused by depression and sleep deprivation.

The second way of understanding the paranormal is represented by the figure of another protagonist—Dr. Styles. Styles leads the *Center for Cognitive Abnormality Research*. His specialty is the study of abnormalities in the development of the brain. Styles' scientific career before his wife's accident (reconstructed in the game according to archival data from newspapers and magazines) was built around studying the possibilities of human potential. He became especially famous as a result of an article on the reality of the existence of super-powers of the brain, for which he was severely criticized by his colleagues and was noticed by parapsychologists, who appreciated his ideas. Styles' theories are a borderline between occulture and recognized science. In Styles' ideas many clichés common to so-called new age science (Hanegraaff 1997, pp. 113–81)[4] are represented: the idea of the potential hidden in the unused part of the brain; the image of the brain as a television like a transmitter of information; the concept of consciousness as energy, which only the brain can hold for a while; and the idea that the brain can project consciousness into the past and the future. Styles believes in the possibility of the existence of his wife's consciousness after death. Everything that he does in the first parts of the game is aimed at the objectification of her consciousness in tangible form. Styles also appears to be a typical new age scientist due to certain practices, using the isolation tank and activating his abilities to visualize the past by stimulating all the sense organs. In one of the dialogues, Styles

---

4   It should be noted that some of these clichés (for example, that we only use 10 percent of our brains) are the property of pop culture and do not relate to real science. Here one can see the intertextuality of popular culture, as "10 percent of the brain" is a common trope that is sometimes found in films, tv-series or games, and is embedded in "the encyclopedia of knowledge" of modern man.

emphasizes that our reality is our perception (another New Age cliché), he "chose the reality to keep his wife alive" (*Gray Matter*, chp. 5), but he has been shocked by the inexplicable events in the house that indicate that his deceased wife Laura could indeed return. Such an attitude to events indicates that Styles is also a skeptic, who shares a number of considerations from the New Age sphere, but does not believe in the reality they suppose at all.

The third way of understanding the paranormal is represented by Dr. Ramuskin, who appears in the game in only one scene, but the understanding of the world that he expresses is at the same time the disclosure of all the mysteries of the game and an indication of the origins of Jensen's bricolage. Characters like Ramuskin are Jensen's visiting card. They perform a *deus ex machina* role, appearing somewhere in the middle of the narrative, and their explanations shed light on all the ambiguities of the game and provide the hero with an end to Ariadne's thread, with which it is possible to find a way out of the maze of the plot. The brightest example of such a hero is Professor Hartridge from the first part of *Gabriel Knight*,[5] whose lecture about voodoo clarifies everything in the plot. Ramuskin plays the same role in *Gray Matter*. His first time appearance is as the author of a book on parapsychology, from which Styles takes instructions for his experiments contact the consciousness of his deceased wife. Later Styles visits the scientist in his house. The appearance of Ramuskin's house is interesting. Obviously, he is much poorer than Styles: there are oscilloscopes for measuring paranormal activity on the table in his house, there are images of Buddha and Parvati on the wall, there is a dancing Shiva and Indian elephants on the fireplace. Ramuskin is represented intentionally as a marginal scientist, a typical example of the occulture.[6] His ideas are typical. He explains all the strange phenomena in Styles' house through the spirit of the deceased wife. For some reason (possibly a trauma at the time of death or an unresolved problem) her spirit cannot accept death—cannot enter the afterlife. Here, classical considerations regarding the spirits of the dead are shown, dating back to the history of spiritualism in the second half of the 19th century (Guttierez 2015, pp. 48–274). All forms of Styles' work (contact through the RNG, messages during visualization) are considered by Ramuskin as classic messages from the world of spirits. He interprets the incidents in Styles' house and during experiments related to the case at the university as the classic manifestations of telekinesis, i.e., the super-abilities of living people. In addition, he talks about cases of similar superpowers in humans, in particular, the story of a shaman who had the gift of producing electricity with such intensity and strength that it led to fires and whose pyrokinetic abilities did not work when he was wet. In conversation with Styles, Ramuskin mentions the Society of Psychical Research, an organization created in the 19th century, whose goal was to study unusual and unexplained phenomena from a scientific point of view. The cases investigated by the SPR, according to Ramuskin, are similar to the Styles case. Ramuskin indicates directly that the story of the shaman was investigated by the Society of Psychical Research in 1900.[7] Thus, Ramuskin appears as a typical exponent of occulture, popularizing its classic ideas.

In addition to the three forms of reflection on paranormal phenomena, the source of these phenomena is also present in the game—in the secondary character, Angela Mulholland.[8] It is clear from the player's first acquaintance with her that Angela is inclined to genuinely believe in real magic and fairies. Later the player discovers that Angela's father was a magician and pub owner who died in his pub during a fire. According to Style's experiments, Angela's brain was active as if in the phase of sleep in the unexplored part of the brain. Angela herself believes that all of her abilities come from

---

[5]   There are similar situations in other games. For example in the last game, *Moebius,* this role is performed by the teacher of the main character, Professor Reed. After a brief conversation with the Professor, a file revealing the meaning of the whole theory of *Moebius* appears on the main character's computer.

[6]   For more information about the marginal position of researchers of the paranormal see Hansen (2001). It is interesting that, according to Hansen, the paranormal is an antistructure, it is always associated with destruction, a transition, a violation of the established order, a paradox, or an ambiguity; it blurs the boundaries. That is why the paranormal manifests in moments of serious social shock and changes, or during periods of personal crisis (for example, as in this case, the loss of a lover).

[7]   One of the rare cases where the game makes a direct reference to the source from which its images have been taken. This is almost the same as making an academic footnote in a fiction book.

[8]   Her surname is especially interesting in that it refers to the famous David Lynch film.

fairies who turn out to be bad, because they hurt her father. Thus, the case of Angela in the game also does not have a definite solution, it is only clear that she has some special abilities.

5. Components of Occultural Bricolage

As we have already noted, *Gray Matter*, is unlike most computer games on the occultural theme, as it does not deal directly with the reality of another world and its related forces, but places all unexplained phenomena on the verge between mental illusions and the reality of another world. Here, Jensen's game follows a special tradition in the literature of horror that developed at the beginning of the 20th century. Unlike classics of this weird and new weird genre (Cowan 2015, pp. 469–77), for example H.P. Lovecraft or E. Lee, writers such as A. Blackwood, G. Meyrink, and S. Grabiński left the reader with an uncertain sensation of the possible reality of another world, placing the fact of its existence on the verge between a psychological illusion and reality. Following this tradition, *Gray Matter* deliberately does not directly answer key questions, even at the very end of the game. This uncertainty is best expressed in the final words of Dr. Styles: " . . . I don't have proof of anything . . . lots of research is needed" (*Gray Matter*, Final shortcut). It can be said that the game is deliberately built around a secret that does not have a direct solution, so that the player, who has reached the end, feels a sense of dissatisfaction and will wait for the second part, in which, according to the teaser, the answers will be provided.

However, it seems that mysterious things are only attractive when the secret conceals some reality in itself, therefore, the answers to unresolved questions should be provided in the game directly. It is possible to find them if we apply the explanations to the plot suggested by Dr. Ramuskin, the main occultural character in the game. According to him, there are two forces in the game: Angela, gifted with telepathic abilities from childhood and seeking an alliance with Styles by any means, and the spirit of Laura, Styles' wife, who tries to tell her husband about the threat from Angela and the causes of her death. This theory is confirmed completely by a number of game events: the spirit of Laura tells Styles about the threat from Angela twice (the first time in the isolation tank, when she asks about the state of the car in which Laura died, and the second time on the lake, when she reminds Styles about a student who came to him on the day of the disaster), and the random number generator finally completely reproduces the message from the spirit in the final stages of the game—the word "imposter", unambiguously indicating Angela, who is trying to impersonate Laura. At the end of the game, Angela behaves exactly the same as the shaman from the SPR study who was described by Ramuskin—the characters push her into the water to neutralize her, after which she cannot make fire. Thus, all the secrets of the game are built around the exploitation of classic mythologemes and images of occulture, but Jensen deliberately does not show them directly. This is unprecedented for Jensen, since all of her previous games were completed without defaults and understatement. Moreover, this is a unique case for the whole genre, in which every game has been viewed as the finished product.

Let us now return to the roots of Jensen's bricolage. It is obvious that the novels of Stephen King were one of the main sources for *Gray Matter*. The image of the main antagonist, Angela Mulholland, is a combination of King's *Carrie* and *The Firestarter*. Angela's main psi-ability—pyrokinesis, inherited from her parents (from her father, in Angela's case)—and the story about the experiments of the scientist at the university, who was considered to be insane, are taken from *The Firestarter*. Angela's psychological shape, her strange behavior that is caused by the knowledge of her psi-abilities, as well as her asociality, unsociability and religiosity are all taken from *Carrie*.

All explanations of the activity of Laura's spirit, as well as the forms of this activity, fit into the general patterns of the spiritualism of the second half of the 20th century. The use of an RNG-generator is also a common practice in parapsychological studies. In addition, Jensen used real discussions on the status of parapsychology that were present in neuropsychology at the beginning of the 21st century (Shermer 2003; Moulton and Kosslyn 2008). To tell the truth, the majority of neuropsychologists consider all phenomena of a parapsychological nature to be poorly substantiated and unprovable, whereas Dr. Styles joins Jensen in this debate from the standpoint of neurobiology, defending the reality of these phenomena.

The whole story with the scientific explanation of the parapsychological phenomena (telekinesis, pyrokinesis, etc.) is directly related to the Society of Psychical Research, some examples that are given by Ramuskin are taken from the works of this society. Maybe the whole game is a deep echo of this society's activity. It would be better to remind ourselves that the activity of SPR was focused on verifying the inexplicable and strange phenomena of spiritualism, telepathy and telekinesis with the help of modern scientific tools.[9] As an elite society that united in its circle a lot of outstanding figures of modern scientific knowledge,[10] the society seriously engaged in the study of a mass of cases recognized as being the result of superstition and charlatanry by mainstream science. It was this society that gave rise to the parapsychological research of the 20th century. Egil Asprem characterizes its ideology as follows: "the possible reality of spiritualism and other occult phenomena would not constitute a break with a naturalistic worldview, but rather indicate that our picture of the natural world had to be radically expanded" (Asprem 2015, p. 267). According to Jeffrey Kripal, members of SPR "embraced science as a method that could throw new light on old religious questions" (Kripal 2015, p. 262). It is interesting that members of the society, in spite of the denunciations made,[11] were religious and sometimes believed that they had experienced the paranormal. Thus, one of the founders of the society, Frederic Myers, was convinced that, with the help of a medium, he communicated with the deceased wife of his cousin, whom he loved. Myers in his life had a passion for Greek paganism, Christianity and agnosticism, and discovered that the theory of Darwin synthesized his personal religious credo. Myers believed that there are only three apparent facts: the reality of life after death, the imprint of every past thought and action in the universe, and that there is progressive infinite moral evolution to an absolute goal (Kripal 2010, pp. 36–90). Some of his colleagues had similar beliefs (McCorristine 2010, pp. 103–38). All these ideas are central themes of the game. It can be said that Styles' ideas are similar to the principles of Myers, and the central idea for the SPR, namely to expand the boundaries of science, is reflected in all of Styles' activities.

It is interesting that both the psi-ability of Angela and the appearance of Laura's spirit are used as the basis of the plot of the game at the same time. In fact, this blurs the boundaries of scientific explanation in favor of a crypto-religious explanation. It is worth remembering that the whole idea of studying paranormal things began from the phenomenon of the poltergeist, originally considered to be an evil restless creature from the spiritual world, or the ghost of a deceased person that showed itself in extravagant and dangerous forms. The term *paranormal* replaced the term *supernatural*, which was theologically-burdened and colored by skepticism. The focus was gradually shifted from the world of spirits to human abilities in the study of paranormal events. The idea was simple, while it was not possible to discuss the reality of the spirits of dead people, it was entirely possible to scientifically study a person's special and unexplained abilities. According to Jeffrey Kripal, it is thanks to the study of the paranormal that the poltergeist became "not an angry ghost but the ghost of anger" (Kripal 2014, p. 244). Destroying this scientific tradition, the spirits of the dead and psi-abilities coexist in *Gray Matter*.

6. Conclusions

Now let us ask ourselves: what does the story of *Gray Matter* contribute to the general theme of this issue, "The Sacred and the Digital"? First of all, it is obvious that religion in modern computer games has become the space for bricolage. In the Jensen's case, this is a bricolage that plays with

---

[9] Six committees were officially created in the society from the moment of its organization in 1882: reading of thoughts, mesmerism, the Reichenbach phenomenon, the phenomena of spirits and houses with ghosts, psychic phenomena and a literary committee (McCorristine 2010, p. 114).

[10] According to Shane McCorristine "With members such as William E. Gladstone, Arthur Balfour, Lord Tennyson, Arthur Conan Doyle, Robert Louis Stevenson, William James, William McDougall, Henri Bergson, Charles Richet, Sigmund Freud and Carl Gustav Jung, the SPR resembled a Who's Who of the fin-de-siecle" (McCorristine 2010, p. 104).

[11] Spiritualists later called SPR a 'Sadducean' organization (McCorristine 2010, p. 112).

themes and images from the sphere of Western esotericism. Jane Jensen is a typical occultural bricoleur, mixing elements from different esoteric teachings, near-scientific theories and fiction to create the plot of her games. The players—the consumers of Jensen's product—are also bricoleurs. The use in the game of commonplaces from occultural mythology (psi-abilities, contact with spirits, the possibility of life after death, etc.) is an indication that all these occultural plots are included in "the encyclopedia of knowledge" (Eco 1986, pp. 46–86) of the modern player; they are easily identified by him and are considered either as a norm or as a generally accepted fantastical assumption. Here again we return to Partridge's idea that occulture has become ordinary, and has determined much of the specifics of modern mass culture. Moreover, the commercial success in the sphere of computer games (especially games built on fantasy or sci-fi) is often associated with the exploitation of occultural images, where they have become the norm and recognizable.

Perhaps the game under consideration indicates one more interesting trend. Reductive models that lead to the explanation of strange phenomena by means of natural causes do not satisfy the target audience of games like *Gray Matter*. After all, Jensen deliberately refuses to explain the strange phenomena as only a special type of human ability, she adds the reality of life after death and the existence of spirits as facts. The modern player still wants to repeat Tennyson's verses "And may there be no sadness of farewell/When I embark;/For though from out our bourne of Time and Place/The flood may bear me far,/I hope to see my Pilot face to face/When I have crossed the bar". The reality of this being beyond the bar, even without meeting with its pilot, still remains an attractive alternative to the modern reductive explanation of the spiritual world. Parareligious plots show the desire of the modern man to create his own religion, in which the reality of the sacred still occupies a central place.

Conflicts of Interest: The author declares no conflict of interest.

References

Ardai, Charles. 1994. *Voices in the Knight*. San Francisco: IGN, pp. 32–36.

Asprem, Egil. 2015. The Society for Psychical Research. In *The Occult World*. Edited by Christopher Partridge. New York: Routledge, pp. 266–74.

Baigent, Michael, Richard Leogh, and Henry Lincoln. 1983. *Holy Blood, Holy Grail*. London: Jonathan Cape.

Announcing the New Premier Awards. San Francisco: IGN, pp. 51–58.

Cowan, Douglas E. 2015. The Occult and the Modern Horror Fiction. In *The Occult World*. Edited by Christopher Partridge. London: Routledge, pp. 469–77.

Eco, Umberto. 1986. *Semiotics and the Philosophy of Language*, reprint ed. Bloomington: Indiana University Press.

Guttierez, Cathy. 2015. *Handbook of Spiritualism and Channeling, XVIII*, index ed. Leiden and Boston: Brill.

Hanegraaff, Wouter J. 1997. *New Age Religion and Western Culture: Esotericism in the Mirror of Secular Thought*. Albany: State University of New York Press.

Hanegraaff, Wouter J. 2013. *Western Esotericism: A Guide for the Perplexed*. London and New York: Bloomsbury Academic.

Hansen, George P. 2001. *The Trickster and the Paranormal*, 1st ed. Philadelphia: Xlibris, Corp.

Jensen, Jane. 2003. *Dante's Equation*. New York: Del Rey.

Kripal, Jeffrey J. 2010 *Authors of the Impossible: The Paranormal and the Sacred*. Chicago: University of Chicago Press.

Kripal, Jeffrey J. 2014. *Comparing Religions*. Oxford: John Wiley & Sons.

Kripal, Jeffrey J. 2015. Frederic W. H. Myers. In *The Occult World*. Edited by Christopher Partridge. New York: Routledge, pp. 260–65.

McCorristine, Shane. 2010. *Spectres of the Self: Thinking about Ghosts and Ghost-Seeing in England, 1750–1920*. Cambridge: Cambridge University Press.

Moulton, Samuel T., and Stephen M. Kosslyn. 2008. Using Neuroimaging to Resolve the Psi Debate. *Journal of Cognitive Neuroscience* 20: 182–92. [CrossRef] [PubMed]

Partridge, Christopher. 2005. *The Re-Enchantment of the West: Volume 1 Alternative Spiritualities, Sacralization, Popular Culture and Occulture*, 1st ed. London and New York: T&T Clark.

Partridge, Christopher. 2006. *The Re-Enchantment of the West, Vol. 2: Alternative Spiritualities, Sacralization, Popular Culture and Occulture*. London: T&T Clark.

Partridge, Christopher. 2016. Occulture and Everyday Enchantment. In *The Oxford Handbook of New Religious Movements*. Oxford: Oxford University Press, vol. 2.

Salter, Anastasia. 2014. *What Is Your Quest?: From Adventure Games to Interactive Books*, 1st ed. Iowa City: University of Iowa Press.

Shermer, Michael. 2003. Psychic Drift. Why Most Scientists Do Not Believe in ESP and Psi Phenomena. *Scientific American* 288: 31. [CrossRef] [PubMed]

Wilson, Johnny L. 1993. *Between Dark And Daylight/Gabriel Knight Explores the Shades of Gray*. San Francisco: IGN, pp. 14–15.

Article

I Have Faith in Thee, Lord: Criticism of Religion and Child Abuse in the Video Game the Binding of Isaac

Frank G. Bosman [1,*] and Archibald L. H. M. van Wieringen [2]

1   Department of Systematic Theology and Philosophy, Tilburg University, 5037 AB Tilburg, The Netherlands
2   Department of Biblical Sciences and Church History, Tilburg University, 5037 AB Tilburg, The Netherlands;
    A.L.H.M.vanWieringen@TilburgUniversity.edu
*   Correspondence: F.G.Bosman@uvt.nl or A.L.H.M.vanWieringen@uvt.nl

Received: 26 March 2018; Accepted: 12 April 2018; Published: 16 April 2018

Abstract: The game The Binding of Isaac is an excellent example of a game that incorporates criticism of religion. Isaac is a roguelike dungeon crawler with randomly generated dungeons. Both from the perspective of narrative and of game design, McMillen built The Binding of Isaac around the Biblical story of Genesis 22:1-19, which has the same name in Jewish and Christian tradition, but he placed it in a modern-day setting in which a young boy is endangered by a mentally disturbed mother who hears "voices from above" that instruct her to sacrifice her only child. Multiple critical references to Christianity can be found in addition to the narrative: hostile embodiments of the seven deadly sins, rosaries, Bibles, and crucifixes, and unlockable characters, such as Mary Magdalene, Judas Iscariot, Samson, and Cain, who are all depicted negatively in both Jewish and Christian traditions. McMillen's inspiration came from his own experiences with his family, which was made up of both Catholics and born-again Christians. The game describes both the dark creativity and the mental and physical abuse associated with religion. In this article, we analyse the narrative of The Binding of Isaac by performing an intertextual comparison with the Biblical narrative of Genesis 22:1-19. We then analyse the three-fold narrative structure of the game which enhances and nuances the criticism the game directs at religion.

Keywords: studies; Bible; theology; Isaac; Catholicism; criticism of religion; child abuse

---

> "To prove your love and devotion, I require a sacrifice. Your son Isaac will be this sacrifice. Go into his room and end his life as an offering to me, to prove that you love me above all else!"

The quotation above is not taken from the book of Genesis, as careful readers will already have understood, but it resembles Gen 22:2 very closely. "Take your son, your only son Isaac, whom you love, and go to the land of Moriah; and offer him there as a burnt offering … " The verse is part of the larger narrative on Abraham, who seems willing to offer his only son to God without asking any questions, simply because God asked him to do so. The passage, known in the three monotheistic religions as "the Binding of Isaac" (Caspi and Greene 2007), has been heavily debated in many theological contexts, but has also been used to bluntly criticise the supposedly inherently violent nature of institutionalised religion in general, and of monotheism in particular. In his *God Delusion* (Dawkins 2006, p. 242), Richard Dawkins put it as follows:

> A modern moralist cannot help but wonder how a child could ever recover from such psychological trauma. By the standards of modern morality, this disgraceful story is an example simultaneously of child abuse, bullying in two asymmetrical power relationships, and the first recorded use of the Nuremberg defence: 'I was only obeying orders.' Yet the legend is one of the great foundational myths of all three monotheistic religions.

The opening quote of this article is not taken from Genesis, but from the prologue of *The Binding of Isaac*, a digital game by independent game developer Edmund McMillen (2011). Both the game itself and its prologue/epilogue depend strongly on Catholicism in general and on the Biblical story of the binding of Isaac in particular. The abundant use of rosaries, Bibles, crucifixes, holy water, and the like suggests this, as does the prologue/epilogue that closely resembles the Biblical narrative, but deviates from it on a number of key points, even apart from the contemporary staging.

In the game, Isaac's mother is presented as a theomanic single mom, who hears "voices from above" urging her to "save" her young son Isaac who has become "corrupted by sin". Ultimately, the voice from above commands her to kill her son to "prove that you love me above all else" an injunction which the mother immediately prepares to carry out. Isaac, seeing his mother's madness, flees into an unknown "abyss" he discovers under a rug in his bedroom.

The game shows what Isaac finds in this abyss—innumerable dangers, insects, and abominations—until he succeeds in killing the "Heart of Mother". Victory brings the player back to the epilogue, where his mother's deadly blow is stopped by a Bible that falls onto her head from a shelf. However, multiple alternative endings found throughout the game suggest that Isaac did not meet with a happy end, pointing as they do to several forms of child abuse, many of them interlaced with religious symbols and notions.

In this article, we examine McMillen's game by establishing the intertextual relationship (Kristeva 1980) between the Genesis narrative (the arche-text) and the game *The Binding of Isaac* (the feno-text). Intertextuality is a synchronic approach, focussing on the characteristics texts have in common. To establish this relationship, we discuss both texts, first the Biblical text (Section 1), then the game text (Section 2), from a synchronic point of view, with special attention to their semantics and to the various roles of the characters and the text-immanent author and reader. In the description and interpretation of the Bible text, we differentiate between the semantics of the text and the communication in the text.

In the description and interpretation of the game text, we differentiate among five different narratological levels: the "pre-text" of McMillen's religious inspiration (Section 2.1); the prologue/epilogue (Section 2.2); the game in the strict sense, which takes place between the prologue and epilogue (Section 2.3); the post-prologue/epilogue (Section 2.4); and the multiple endings found throughout the game (Section 2.5). Finally, we propose a reconstruction of the "real" story of *The Binding of Isaac*, incorporating the different intertextual relationships between the two texts (Section 3).

We regard games as "digital (interactive), playable (narrative) texts" (Bosman 2016) in this article. As text, a video game is an object of interpretation. As narrative, it communicates meaning. As game, it is playable. As digital medium, it is interactive. Treating video games as playable texts and using a gamer-immanent approach (Heidbrink et al. 2015), we have performed a close reading of the video game, including its remake (called *Rebirth*) and its two expansion packs (*Afterbirth* and *Afterbirth+*), by playing the game and all its versions ourselves several times.

1. The Arche-Text: The Genesis Narrative

Genesis 22:1-19 tells the story of God who tests Abraham. God asks Abraham to sacrifice his son Isaac. Obeying God's command, Abraham goes to the mountains of Moriah. Isaac goes with him. On the mountain, Abraham builds an altar and prepares everything for the sacrifice. However, at the very moment he is about to kill Isaac with a knife, God's angel intervenes. Instead of the son, he sacrifices a ram. The mountain becomes a sign about the mountain of the Lord. God's angel acts for a second time. He praises Abraham and promises him numerous offspring. The story concludes with Abraham returning from the mountain.

The narrative text of Genesis 22:1-19 has been discussed extensively over the centuries. The diachronic exegetical discussion, e.g., concerning the Yahwistic source as an older edition of the text (see especially: Westermann 1981, pp. 429–47), is not important for our research into the intertextual, i.e., synchronic, relationship between the biblical text (arche-text) and the video game (feno-text). Therefore, we focus on a synchronic analysis first.

The narrative contains two semantic themes (Van Wieringen 1995, pp. 293–99). The first is about testing, expressed mainly with the verb *to test* (נסה), the second is about the cult, expressed by using a set of three verbs: *to take* (לקח), *to go* (הלך), and *to sacrifice* (עלה לעלה). These two semantic themes are intertwined.

The narrative opens with the first semantic theme. After these things, God tested Abraham (verse 1). This test appears to consist of a threefold instruction (verse 2). Abraham appears to be very willing to implement it, because the first thing he does, early in the morning, is to saddle his donkey (verse 3), something one normally does at the moment of departure. However, the text of the narrative mentions the first two elements of the instruction three times, but does not mention the third element, to sacrifice.

In verse 3, Abraham *takes* Isaac and Abraham *goes*. However, instead of sacrificing, verse 4 has Abraham *seeing*. Abraham's eyes are focused on the place of the sacrifice, i.e., the cultic location. In verse 6, Abraham *takes* the wood required for the sacrifice, and places it upon Isaac. He also *takes* the fire and the knife in his own hand, and he *goes* with Isaac. There is no reference to sacrificing.

The activities of taking and going are mentioned again in the verses 8b–10. Abraham and Isaac are *going* to the place of the sacrifice. When they have reached this place, Abraham *takes* the knife, instead of Isaac. This activity of taking the knife, which did not appear in God's instruction, is recounted in slow motion. Again, the activity of sacrificing is absent. Instead of sacrificing, Abraham is about to cut Isaac's throat, which was not part of God's instruction either. Fortunately, the angel of the Lord intervenes to prevent Isaac from being killed (the verses 11–12).

Verses 11–12 not only stop Abraham from improperly implementing the instruction, but also reintroduce the theme of the test. The angel of the Lord solemnly declares that Abraham has passed the test.

Verses 13–14a take up the semantic theme of the sacrifice again and mention two aspects. First, the Lord's command is properly implemented. Abraham *goes*, he *takes* the ram, instead of his son, and *sacrifices* it. Second, in addition to this set of three activities, the activity of seeing, which was already present in the text as a substitute for the activity of sacrificing, is mentioned twice as an inclusion: Abraham *sees* the ram (verse 13a) and, unto this very day, people say that the Lord *sees*.

The theme of the test is mentioned one last time before the final verse 19. Once again, the angel observes that Abraham has passed the test, but this time several future promises accompany the statement.

The semantic theme of the test predominates in the reception of Genesis 22:1-19 (Agus 1988; Rowley 2015). The test is interpreted as inviting unquestioning obedience to God. Just do what God asks you, even if he asks you to sacrifice your own son.

However, the complex semantic themes in the text demonstrate that this interpretation is restrictive, and the complex communicative structure makes it clear that it is inadequate (Van Wieringen 1995, pp. 300–4). In verse 5, Abraham says to his servants that "we", i.e., Abraham and Isaac, will return from the mountain. Was Abraham telling a white lie? Or did he already know that Isaac would not be sacrificed? Verse 8 contains the same communicative tension. Abraham says to his son that God will provide the ram for the sacrifice. Was Abraham telling a white lie again? Or did he already know that Isaac would not be sacrificed? Ultimately, Isaac is not sacrificed.

According to the text of the narrative, there must have been a communication between the Lord and Abraham which is not mentioned in the text itself. In verse 2, the Lord says that he will point out the mountain of the sacrifice to Abraham, and in verse 4 Abraham actually sees this mountain. If this information really was about the mountain of the sacrifice, it may have been more than just information of a location.

What about Isaac? In verse 7, he asks his father a question about the sacrifice. The question expresses his surprise that everything they need for the sacrifice is there except the ram. However, Isaac does not mention the knife in his question. The knife seems to be absent in Isaac's perception—even when Abraham takes the knife to cut his throat. The final verse 19 is surprising. It says that Abraham returns to the servants, but does not mention Isaac. Where is Isaac, who has been given away to God? Is he still on the mountain? These questions are (and remain) unanswered by the text.

One aspect of the diachronic analyses of Genesis 22:1-19 might be of importance here. As the *Sitz im Leben*, many exegetes used to believe that the text was discussing child sacrifices in ancient Canaan. The narration's purpose would be to make clear that child sacrifices should be rejected. God seems to ask for it, but in fact he does not: he opens the religious form of obedience and cult instead. In fact, we now know that child sacrifices were not common in ancient Canaan, and perhaps only in situations of severe hostile threat. In the modern reception of Genesis 22:1-19, the idea of the God of Israel not asking for child sacrifices, in contrast to the idols of Canaan, is still present (see the recent discussion in (Bauer 2017). This view on child sacrifices probably inspired McMillen for this video game in which child abuse is central, as we will explain in detail below.

The reception of Genesis 22:1-19 in the Jewish and Christian tradition is very complex (see also: Lenzen 2003). For our intertextual examination of the arche- and feno-text, it is important to notice that both traditions have their own specific accent as expressed in the name of this biblical passage. In the Jewish, i.e., Rabbinic, tradition, the narrative is known as "the Binding of Isaac", in Hebrew עֲקֵידַת יִצְחָק the *Aqedat Yitzhaq*, or in short the *Aqedah*. This implies that Isaac is the main character. He is in focus. In the Christian tradition, the narrative is known as the Sacrifice of Abraham, which implies that Abraham is the main character. In *the Binding of Isaac*, Isaac is the main character, whereas the character of Abraham is not prominent, which implies that, in its reception of the arche-text, *the Binding of Isaac* is closer to the Jewish than the Christian tradition.

2. The Feno-Text: The Game Narrative

The Binding of Isaac is a roguelike top-down dungeon crawler, designed by Edmund McMillen (designer) and Florian Himsl (programmer). Directly inspired by the classic 1986 NES game *The Legend of Zelda* (McMillen 2012), the game connects chamber to chamber, incorporating procedurally-generated levels that particularly enhance and stimulate multiple playthroughs, for which the player is rewarded by unlockable characters, passive items, or achievements. The gamer must first defeat all the monsters in a given chamber before he can enter the next. The player controls a naked figure, Isaac, whose primary weapon is his ability to "shoot" tears at his enemies. Helpful items can be found and active and passive abilities can be unlocked during the game to add to Isaac's armoury. When Isaac's life reaches zero, the player is forced to restart the game from the beginning.

The original *The Binding of Isaac* (BoI) was released in 2011 for Windows, and later ported to OS X and Linux. In 2012, the first expansion pack was released, entitled *Wrath of the Lamb*, a reference to the biblical book of Revelation (see especially: Rev 6: 16). In 2014, a remake of the original BoI was released, dubbed *Rebirth*, developed and published by Nicalis for Windows, OSX, Linux, PlayStation 4, and PlayStation Vita, and later also for Wii U, New Nintendo 3DS and Switch, Xbox One, and iOS (McMillen 2014). In 2015, two new expansions were released, *Afterbirth* (McMillen 2015a) and *Afterbirth+* (McMillen 2015b), introducing new items, enemies, bosses, and endings. The game was applauded by critics and fans alike, obtaining a score of 84 on Metacritic.com. A list of all versions and expansions is listed below (Table 1).

Table 1. Versions of *the Binding of Isaac*.

Ab.	Games	Expansions	Release
BoI	The Binding of Isaac		2011
WoL		Wrath of the Lamb	2012
BoR	The Binding of Isaac: Rebirth		2014
BoA		Afterbirth	2015
BoA+		Afterbirth+	2015

Caption text: The various versions of *The Binding of Isaac*, including expansion packs.

Five different narratological levels can be distinguished in *The Binding of Isaac*: (1) McMillen's inspiration; (2) the prologue/epilogue; (3) the game in the strict sense, which takes place between prologue and epilogue; (4) the post-prologue/epilogue; and (5) the various endings of the game.

2.1. Pre-Text: McMillan's Inspiration

In various online articles and interviews, the designer McMillen has quite clearly articulated the religious inspiration for *The Binding of Isaac* (Holmes 2011; Jagielski 2011; Smith 2011; McMillen 2012). He describes his religious upbringing as a hybrid between Roman Catholicism and born-again Christianity, both sides contributing to the creation of *The Binding of Isaac*:

> I grew up in a religious family. My mom's side is Catholic, and my dad's side is born-again Christians. The Catholic side had this very ritualistic belief system: My grandma could essentially cast spells of safe passage if we went on trips, for example, and we would light candles and pray for loved ones to find their way out of purgatory, and drink and eat the body and blood of our saviour to be abolished of mortal sin. As a child growing up with this, I honestly thought it was very neat, very creative and inspiring. It's not hard to look at my work and see that most of the themes of violence actually come from my Catholic upbringing, and in a lot of ways I loved that aspect of our religion. Sadly, the other side of my family was a bit more harsh in their views on the Bible; I was many times told I was going to hell for playing *Dungeons & Dragons* and *Magic: The Gathering* (in fact, they took my MtG cards away from me), and generally condemned me for my sins. (McMillen 2012)

McMillen includes dark and adult content most other game developers would rather avoid or neglect.

> A lot of the content in Isaac is extremely dark and adult. It touches on aspects of child abuse, gender identity, infanticide, neglect, suicide, abortion, and how religion might negatively affect a child, which are topics most games would avoid. (McMillen 2012)

BoI's major theme was indeed inspired by the Biblical narrative of the same name.

> The games story was inspired heavily from a story in the bible called the Binding of Isaac, where God asks Abraham to sacrifice his son Isaac to Him to prove his devotion. (Jagielski 2011)

McMillen wanted to reflect his own dualistic experience of religion, in showing both its positive and negative effects. On the one hand, the self-hatred and isolation McMillen experienced in his youth, but on the other also the creative openness that biblical passages have that allow their readers to interpret them each in their own way. The multiple endings that players can reach in BoI are a reference to this openness:

> The Bible is a very good, creatively written book, and one of my favourite aspects of it is how so many people can find different meanings in one passage. I wanted Isaac to have this in its story as well, which is why the game's final ending(s) have many possible interpretations. (McMillen 2012)

McMillen's heavy use of religious phrases, artefacts, items, and images is, therefore, not accidental to the game, but expresses the developer's inspiration and intentions. Every interpretation of the game's content should take this religious inspiration into consideration.

2.2. The Prologue/Epilogue Narratives

The prologue and epilogue appear as simple pencil drawings on a desk (later identified as Isaac's). The tip of a small finger is seen in the bottom left corner of the screen (also later identified as Isaac's) next to a half-visible pencil. A fly can be seen hovering over the pictures, one of the main simple enemies the player will encounter in the game. The title, "The Binding of Isaac", appears in handwritten letters together with a small simplified version of Isaac drawn below.

Isaac and his mother are introduced to the gamer as they stand beside each other and smile. Isaac is small compared to his mother, indicating he is still in pre-puberty. Their names are written beside them: "Isaac" and "Mom". The narrator recounts:

> Isaac and his mother lived alone in a small house on a hill. Isaac kept to himself, drawing pictures and playing with his toys as his mom watched Christian broadcasts on the television. Life was simple, and they were both happy. That was, until the day Isaac's mom heard a voice from above.

We see a drawing that shows a simple house as drawn by a young child: one door, one window, and a tree and bushes beside it. Isaac is shown sitting on the floor beside mom's couch. He is surrounded by two dolls (in silhouette) and is working on two separate drawings with undistinguishable lines and figures. Isaac's mother smiles as she watches over him from the couch. She holds the television remote control in her right hand, the television itself stands before her. Then she suddenly appears shocked by something only she notices. Lines blinking from above indicate that a voice is coming "from above". The narrator says,

> "Your son has become corrupted by sin! He needs to be saved!"—"I will do my best to save him, my Lord," Isaac's mother replied rushing into Isaac's room removing all that was evil from his life.

We see Isaac's mother dashing into Isaac's room, tearing down a poster from the wall, and stuffing Isaac's belongings into a box she holds under her arm. She has a frantic expression. Isaac is shown with a doll and a handheld computer in his hands, which both disappear as a sign of his mother's rigorous devotion to the assignment she has been given. Eventually, even his clothes disappear, and Isaac is naked. Again, we see Isaac's mother on the couch, the remote control in her hand, but Isaac is standing naked and without toys. The narrator recounts,

> Again, the voice called to her: "Isaac's soul is still corrupt! He needs to be cut off from all that is evil in this world and confess his sins."—"I will follow your instructions, Lord. I have faith in thee," Isaac's mother replied as she locked Isaac away in his room, away from the evils of the world.

We see how Isaac is thrown into his own room. The door closes behind him and Isaac lies naked on the ground. Again, we see Isaac's mother on the couch, but now with a crazy look on her face: one eye is larger than the other one and there is a contorted smile on her mouth. For the third time a voice rings out from above, which only she can apparently hear. Her old smile returns when she replies to the voice,

> One last time, Isaac's mom heard the voice of God calling to her: "You have done as I asked, but I still question your devotion to me. To prove your faith, I will ask one more thing of you."—"Yes, Lord. Anything," Isaac's mother begged. "To prove your love and devotion, I require a sacrifice. Your son Isaac will be this sacrifice. Go into his room and end his life as an offering to me, to prove that you love me above all else!"—"Yes, Lord," she replied grabbing a butcher's knife from the kitchen.

Isaac's mother is seen with a butcher's knife in her hand, looking grimly at the closed door of Isaac's room. Isaac is looking through a crack in the door, sees what his mother is doing, and understands the consequences it will have for him. We see Isaac sitting on the floor, shaking with fear. He tries to find a way out of his room, but the door is locked and iron bars block his only window.

> "Isaac, watching through a crack in the door trembled in fear. Scrambling around his room to find a hiding place he noticed a trapdoor to the basement, hidden under his rug."

Isaac finds a hidden trapdoor under the rug in his room. Neither the rug, nor the trapdoor were visible in earlier scenes, as if they did not exist then. He opens the hatch, while Isaac's mother bursts through the door, brandishing the knife in her hand.

> "Without hesitation, he flung open the hatch just as his mother burst through his door and threw himself down into the unknown depths below."

Isaac jumps through the hatch and lands in an unknown room, while light from above shines on him. There is no further trace of his mother.

Although this is not the end of the prologue, we leave the scene for the time being and return to it in Section 2.5. Isaac and his mother are living together in their home. Whereas everything is all right at the beginning, things quickly get out of hand when Isaac's mother starts to "hear voices". As we have seen before, McMillen is undoubtedly referring to the mother's madness, not her possible piety. Isaac's theomanic mother wants to kill her son because she thinks she has received a divine commandment that she must do so, and Isaac is barely able to escape by entering a previously unknown doorway that leads to a space under the house.

The epilogue takes the narrative almost directly from where the prologue ends. Isaac is still in his room, standing fearfully in a corner as he tries—in vain—to escape his murderous mother. The narrator:

> Isaac was cornered. His mother, fuelled with the desire to serve her god, was bearing down on Isaac. "I will do as I'm told, my lord. I love you above all else", Isaac's mother repeated to herself.

Isaac's mother is towering above him, her knife ready to strike. The look on her face is totally manic. Isaac is lying on the ground, his eyes closed, with his arms around his legs, in the foetal position. His mother is ready to strike. We can now see a bookshelf with a book and a vase on it that were not there in earlier scenes.

> "This was the end of the line for Isaac, his mother was far too strong for him. But just as he accepted his fate, god intervened, sending an angel down from above to stop his mother's hand. And just like that, it was over."

The book on the shelf suddenly becomes adorned with the Christian sign of the cross, indicating that it is a Bible. As soon as the narrator speaks about God's intervention, the book mysteriously falls or is thrown onto the mother's head, knocking her out. As she lies stretched out on the floor, either dead or unconscious, Isaac jumps onto her body, holding up his hands in the air in a victory pose.

Although this is not the end of the epilogue, we will stop at this point to better interpret the prologue and epilogue as a (wondrous) tale about a young son and his theomanic mother, whom he defeats with the help of divine intervention. However, the end of the prologue and the beginning of the epilogue do not match each other perfectly: the prologue ends with Isaac jumping down "into the depth" and it gives way narratologically to the beginning of the game itself, while the epilogue seems to be unaware of Isaac's successful escape attempt. Ultimately, Isaac is triumphant: he defeats his mother and saves his own life. However, this rather simplistic but religion-critical interpretation is challenged by the other narratological levels, which we discuss below.

2.3. The Game Narrative

The game itself (excluding for the moment the (post)prologue/epilogue and the various alternative endings) is littered with references to the Christian tradition in general and Roman Catholicism in particular. Ludologically, the player's only goal is to work his or her way through different levels in six different chapters. Narratologically, the player—Isaac—delves deeper and deeper into the abyss under the rug in his bedroom, until he is finally able to slay his deranged mother, who is depicted in a dehumanized form, as a real monster who needs to be defeated. The different chapters—Basement/Cellar, Caves/Catacombs, Depths/Necropolis, Cathedral/Sheol, and Chest/Dark Room—evoke the idea of descent in general, and in particular the psychological notion of descending into one's own soul in the search for deeper personal understanding, in combination with the Christian notion of hell and the underworld (the Hebrew/Jewish *sheol*) as a place where the wicked are punished.

As Isaac flees his theomanic mother, who is clearly inspired by the figure of Abraham in the Genesis narrative, we see numerous references to Christian lore. It is not necessary to give an exhaustive list of all items and entities that contain religious references; a few examples will suffice. The category of "active collectibles" (items that can be activated for bonuses) contains Christian objects like the Bible (which instantly kills the Mother Monster at the end of the game), the Book of Revelation (increases chance of finding special devil/angel rooms in the chapters), and the Dead Sea Scrolls (randomly activated item).

However, there are also numerous references to satanic lore, another one of McMillen's (2012) sources of inspiration. The designer has spoken about the "witch hunt" by conservative Christians in the 1980s against everything considered non-Christian, and the categorical labelling of such elements as "Satanist". Thus, there is the *Book of Belial* (the third book of The Satanic Bible by Anton LaVey, 1969), the *Book of Secrets* (a compilation of technical and medical recipes and magical formulas used in Wiccan circles), the *Book of Shadows* (ditto), the *Necronomicon* (H.P. Lovecraft's fictional grimoire), and the *Book of Sin*.

The category of "passive collectibles" (items that provide automatically applied bonuses) also contains the same two sources of inspiration. On the one hand, there is the "Blood of the Martyr" (a crown of thorns worn by Jesus according to the Biblical narratives), a "cat-o-nine-tails" (an implement similar to that used to flog Jesus), a "halo" (with which Catholic saints are traditionally depicted), "Guardian Angel", "Seraphim" (a certain group of angels from Christian lore), the "Eucharist", "Jacob's ladder" (from Gen. 28:12), a "rosary", "holy water", Longinus" spear (also known as the "Spear of Destiny") and a "Holy Grail". On the other hand, we find "Abaddon" (a pentagram), a "Ouija board", "Judas' Shadow", "leprosy", "Lord of the Pit" (inverted cross), "Succubus" (male demon) and the "Eye of Belial" (demon from the Old Testament).

These references can be found even in the major bosses that the player encounters. Thus, there are the seven deadly sins—Envy, Gluttony, Wrath, Pride, Lust, Greed, and Sloth—which take the form of Isaac himself, indicating the psychological nature of these sins. We find "the Harbingers" from the Book of Revelation, in multiple variations: Famine, Pestilence, War, Death, Conquest, and "the Headless Horseman". Other bosses are clearly physically inspired by medieval demons, including horns and inverted crosses, called "the Dark One", "the Adversary" (from the Biblical book of Job), "The Fallen", and "the Duke of Flies" (a reference to the figure of *Beelzebub*, a Philistine deity from the Old Testament, dismissed by Jesus in the New Testament as "the Lord of the Flies").

Finally, there are the unlockable characters (see Table 2), who are either devils, or "unlucky figures" from the Old and New Testament narratives, unjustly condemned in the Christian tradition.

Table 2. Unlockable characters in *The Binding of Isaac*.

Character	BoI/BoR	BoA	BoA+
???	X		
Azazel	X		
Cain	X		
Eden	X		
Eve	X		
Isaac	X		
Judas	X		
Lazarus	X		
Lost, the	X		
Magdalene	X		
Samson	X		
Keeper		X	
Lilith		X	
Apollyon			X

Caption text: An overview of unlockable characters in various versions of the *Binding of Isaac* (see also Table 1). <???> indicates the name of an unlockable character in the game.

Unlockable characters can be used by the player to replay the game in another avatar, which usually not only differs aesthetically from the standard one, but is usually granted a number of perks or disadvantages.

Most of the unlockable characters are derived from the Bible. Together with his brother Abel, Cain is the main character in the story of Gen 4:1-16. Cain is the villain who kills his brother. Sacrifice plays an important role in this story. God accepts Abel's sacrifice, but rejects that of Cain. The dominant interpretation in the reception of this biblical narrative is that Cain did not sacrifice the best of his flock, whereas Abel offered God the best fruits of the land. Because Cain did not offer the best he had God does not love him, and Abel falls victim to the ensuing quarrel between God and Cain. However, this idea is not mentioned in the text at all. The narratological plot of the biblical account points in a different direction: the problem is that there is no communication with Abel. Cain does not speak to his brother. By denying him all communication, Cain has already killed Abel, as it were, before the actual murder. In the Jewish Testament of Abraham (1st/2nd century), Abel is portrayed as a sun-like angel (Van der Toorn et al. 1999, p. 2).

The unlockable character Eden is named after the Garden of Eden, the décor of the biblical stories of Genesis 2–3. God entrusts the newly created humans with the care of the garden. They are free to do anything they want, except to eat from the tree of good and evil. They nevertheless do just that and suddenly becomes aware of their nakedness. The reception of these stories has more often than not held the woman responsible for eating from the forbidden tree (Tischler 2009, pp. 13–23). This could be the reason that Eden is a female unlockable character. In the Romantic area, the loss of innocence was seen as the loss of childlike innocence. In the videogame, Isaac is naked on all narratological levels. Child abuse can be regarded as a loss of innocence. This loss is not caused by the child's own sins. It is caused by the sins of his parents. In a way, the child is the victim of the primordial sin, i.e., a sin committed by a parent—or by his first forefathers in the Garden of Eden in Genesis 3.

Eve is regarded as the first human who disobeyed God (Gen 3). Mary Magdalene, although she was the first human witness of the risen Christ (John 20), is erroneously regarded in the Christian tradition as a converted prostitute (John 8) who was possessed by "seven demons" (Mark 16:9). Judas, of course, is the discipline who betrayed Jesus for thirty pieces of silver (Mat 26:15), after which he was overcome by guilt and committed suicide (Mat 27:5), thus burdening his soul even more. Samson is the main character in Judges 13–16. He is famous because of his strength: he tears a lion to pieces and defeats an entire army of enemies on his own. He falls in love with Delilah, who overpowers him by discovering his secret. In certain Christian traditions, Delilah is interpreted as Satan, who tests Samson (Caesarius of Arles, 5th/6th century).

Lazarus is a New Testament figure, a friend of Jesus. After Lazarus's death, Jesus comes to Bethany, the place where Lazarus lived, and raises him from the dead by telling him to come out of the grave. After his resurrection, Lazarus led a Christian life. In the Eastern tradition he became the first bishop of Kition (Larnaka) on Cyprus; in the Western tradition he became the first bishop of Marseille in France. Some traditions say that Lazarus never once smiled or laughed during the first thirty years after being raised from the dead, because he had seen the unredeemed souls in the netherworld.

The unlockable character Azazel evokes the biblical figure of Azazel. Azazel is only mentioned in Leviticus 16:8.10.26. The majority of the Old Testament exegetes interpret Azazel as a kind of demon, but there is no consensus about his origins: Azazel could be a nomadic, Egyptian, Anatolian, or Syrian demon (Van der Toorn et al. 1999, p. 129). What is clear, is that Azazel is related to the rite of Yom Kippur, when a sacrifice is made to effect reconciliation between God and men. The he-goat offered in sacrifice is not killed, however, but sent away into the desert, to Azazel.

Apollyon is the Greek name for the Hebrew Abaddon. In the Bible, the name Abaddon is used as a synonym of Sheol, i.e., the netherworld, in Proverbs 15:11; 27:20; Job 26:6, or of the grave in Psalm 88: 12. In Job 26:5–6, Abaddon seems to denote more than a place, namely a demon of deadly destruction (Van der Toorn et al. 1999, p. 1). Lilith is the name of a fearsome she-devil associated, in both Judaism and Christianity, with child abduction and involuntary nocturnal emissions (Bosman and Poorthuis 2015).

The narratological level of the game seems to confirm the narratological levels of the prologue/epilogue and of McMillen's religious inspiration. Isaac is confronted with a theomanic mother figure who wants to kill him because she has heard a voice from on high commanding her to do so, which is a criticism of Abraham's blind obedience in the Genesis narrative. In both narratives, however, Isaac is rescued by "divine intervention". In Genesis, Abraham is the hero who is praised for his obedience by God's messenger, while in the game Isaac takes the role of the hero by triumphing over his crazy mother.

2.4. The Post-Prologue/Epilogue Narratives

The story of *The Binding of Isaac* could just have stopped here. McMillen would have made his main points: religion should be criticised for fostering blind obedience instead of critical thinking, and children especially risk becoming the primary victims of the religious zeal of their parents. In this perspective, religion appears as a form of legally and socially accepted child abuse. However, the prologue/epilogue and the game are only the first two of a total of four narratological layers.

As has been seen, both the prologue and epilogue have alternative endings, which we have so far ignored to avoid confusion. The prologue consists only of primitively hand-drawn pictures, probably done by Isaac himself. This intuition is fed by the real ending of the prologue, in which we see Isaac—in full colour instead of the black and white rendering of the previous drawings—as he laughs in the middle of his room. He holds a white sheet of paper in his hand, and he folds this before disappearing. We see other drawings hanging on his wall in the background. Again, a fly hovers before the camera.

The epilogue also has a kind of double ending. Initially, it seems that Isaac has defeated his mother by means of the Bible which falls on top of her. However, we then see Isaac again, depicted in full-colour, as he stands in his room, a fly hovering next to him. The door of his room is flung open and a silhouette appears in the doorway, resembling Isaac's mother, including a raised butcher's knife. The screen fades to black, without showing what happens next.

His "post-prologue" and "post-epilogue" deliver a new interpretive layer to BoI's narrative. Everything we have seen in the prologue/epilogue, including the game in between, seems to be the product of Isaac's imagination, as drawn on sheets of paper in his bedroom. Everything the player has encountered, including the hours of gameplay, could be reinterpreted as Isaac's psychological attempt to come to terms with an apparently abusive mother who wants to hurt him badly.

If this is indeed the case and it is true that everything stems from Isaac's imagination, then the whole idea of his mother's motivation for her abusive behaviour may also have been invented by Isaac. Confronted with an evil mother, Isaac looks for a rationale to *understand*—only up to a certain point of course—her behaviour towards him. As Isaac and his family are familiar with Christianity, Isaac may have chosen a biblical story, well known to him, that mirrors his own situation. By altering the traditional plot of the biblical "binding", a story that includes a "hero" with whom he shares his name, Isaac can construct a fantasy in which he not only provides a "sensible context" for his mother's behaviour, but also makes sure that he comes out on top.

This would mean that "the voice from above" his mother hears exists only in Isaac's fantasy, just as his own supposed sinfulness and the corresponding double punishment of the removal of his belongings and his isolation. Even the divine intervention, the Bible that falls on his mother's head, is an expression of Isaac's hope that his terrible situation will end in a satisfying way.

Seen in this light, BoI not only contains criticism of religion, but is also a psychological coping strategy in which Isaac tries to come to terms with living with an abusive mother. In this context, religion is not the cause of the abuse, but the narrative form in which the coping mechanism can take place. While the prologue/epilogue and the game itself appear to end with the victory of Isaac, the post-prologue and, especially, the epilogue seem to suggest the opposite: Isaac cannot stop his mother with his fantasies and is at his mother's mercy. Even though we are not shown what his mother does to him, we do not have to think long to understand that Isaac shares the fate of his Biblical name-giver, but without reprieve through divine intervention.

2.5. The Ending Narratives

When the player has successfully defeated the Mother Monster in the game, he reaches the epilogue (and post-epilogue) discussed above. However, BoI is a game that strongly stimulates multiple playthroughs, thanks to the randomly generated dungeons and the high number of unlockables. Once the player has succeeded in beating the game again, twenty different endings can be found. These endings can be unlocked by defeating certain enemies who function as end bosses. Some endings provide ludological bonuses, e.g., passive items or unlockable characters (see Table 3).

Table 3. Various endings of *The Binding of Isaac*.

Endings	Name	Source	Unlocked by	Description		Effect
Epilogue	Epilogue	BoI/BoR	Defeating Mom for the 1st time.	Isaac's mother is struck down by a Bible.		<no effect>
1	Eden	BoI/BoR	Defeating Mom again.	Isaac is swallowed by chest, emerges as Eden.	UC	Eden
2	Glue	BoI/BoR	Defeating Mom again.	Isaac finds rubber cement in the chest, uses it.	PI	Rubber cement
3	Noose	BoI/BoR	Defeating Mom again.	Isaac finds a noose in the chest, hangs himself.	PI	Transcendence
4	Hanger	BoI/BoR	Defeating Mom again.	Isaac finds a wire coat hanger, jams it into his own head.	PI	Wire coat hanger
5	Mother	BoI/BoR	Defeating Mom again.	Mother's arm reaches from inside the chest, grabs Isaac.	A	Everything is terrible
6	Vomit	BoI/BoR	Defeating Mom again.	Isaac opens chest, vomits into the chest, causing explosions.	PI	Ipecac
7	Syringe	BoI/BoR	Defeating Mom again.	Isaac finds syringe in the chest, (apparently uses drugs).	PI	Experimental treatment
8	Quarter	BoI/BoR	Defeating Mom again.	Isaac finds a quarter (coin) in the chest.	PI	Quarter
9	Fetus	BoI/BoR	Defeating Mom again.	Isaac finds Dr. Fetus in the chest, wearing top hat and monocle.	PI	Dr. Fetus
10	???	BoI/BoR	Defeating Mom again.	Isaac finds ??? lying in the chest, who sits up and smiles.	UC	??? (= unlockable character)
11	Heart	BoI/BoR	Defeating Mom again.	Isaac finds "It Lives" in the chest, growling and smiling.	UB	It Lives
12	Light	BoI/BoR	Defeating Sheol chapter.	A bright light shines on Isaac from the chest, switches to different characters, Isaac steps into the chest.	...	...
13	Bible	BoI/BoR	Defeating the Cathedral chapter.	Isaac reads the Bible, looks into mirror, which shows Isaac with red eyes and black skin.	...	...
14	Pictures	BoI/BoR	Defeating the Chest chapter.	Various pictures of Isaac's life are shown, "the end".	...	...
15	Poster	BoI/BoR	Defeating the Dark Room chapter.	A missing persons poster is shown on a pole, Isaac's mother can be seen in the background.	...	...
16	Crying	BoI/BoR	Defeating Mega Satan.	Isaac lies crying inside the chest, assumes demon form.	...	...
17	Skeleton	BoA	Defeating Hush.	Ending #15, mother opens chest, flies and spiders, ghastly landscape, Isaac pops out of red chest, large shadow bends over him.	...	...
18	Cave 1	BoA	Defeating Ultra Greed in Greed Mode.	Isaac is shown in a small cave, the entrance collapses, rotting shopkeeper who looks suddenly in the camera.	...	...
19	Cave 2	BoA+	Defeating Ultra Greed in Greedier Mode.	As #18, but the shopkeeper's head falls off, spewing geyser of spiders.	...	...
20	Final	BoA+	Defeating Delirium.	A combination of multiple endings and unique material.	...	...

Caption text: Overview of the endings in various versions of the *Binding of Isaac*, how to unlock them, and their ludological effects (see also Table 1): A = Achievement; PI = Passive item; UB = Unlockable boss; and UC = Unlockable character. <???> is the name of an unlockable character in the game.

Narratologically, however, they provide numerous possible endings to Isaac's story, just as McMillen himself stated (2012). When all 21 endings are considered, including that of the (post-) epilogue, a new interpretation proposes itself concerning Isaac's "real story", even if major uncertainties have to be accepted. We examine them more closely below, while trying to fit them into the larger narrative of BoI.

Endings 1–11 present Isaac finding a chest, which he opens to find something (or someone) inside. Endings 12–20 present Isaac in different settings, some of which feature chests, while others do not. In the majority of cases, the ending represents danger to or death for Isaac, contrasting with the "happy" outcome of the main game and its epilogue.

Endings #2 (glue) and #7 (syringe) show Isaac picking up either rubber cement or a syringe from the chest, followed by a visibly deranged Isaac who is clearly under the influence of an intoxicating substance. Endings #3 (noose) and #4 (hanger) suggest either suicide or murder. We see Isaac hanged or with a twisted hanger driven through his head. The noose in ending #3 is reminiscent of Judas (Iscariot), whom we also encountered earlier as an unlockable character. According to Matthew 27:3–10, Judas committed suicide by hanging himself after betraying Jesus. However, in contrast to Judas, the Isaac of the video game is not a traitor. He commits suicide—something he should not do.

It is remarkable that the player of the video game cannot see Isaac's face in the video game. He sees him from behind only. This implies that there is no possibility of face-to-face-contact. The way in which the child hangs in the noose is an expression of the impossibility of any communication. In this way, the Isaac of the video game is more like Abel than Judas Iscariot. In the version of Acts 1:18–19, however, Judas dies because his belly bursts open and his intestines fall out.

Ending #5 (mother) is about a hand—seemingly Isaac's mother's—which comes from inside the chest, grabs Isaac, and pulls him in, while demonic laughter is heard. In the biblical narrative, the hand of Abraham plays a role in the slow motion just before the slaughter of Isaac. While Abraham's hand stretches out and grabs a knife, the hand in ending #5, which must be Isaac's mother's hand, stretches out and grabs her son. While Abraham's hand is stayed, the mother's hand is not.

Ending #6 (vomit) shows Isaac throwing up into the chest as he sees something inside it, followed by explosions, so that Isaac's fate remains unknown. Ending #8 (quarter) is one of the few endings that produce a good outcome for Isaac: he is rewarded with a quarter (coin) that gives the player a financial head-start at the beginning of every run-through.

Endings #18 (cave 1) and #19 (cave 2) show Isaac getting trapped inside a cave because of falling rocks that block the only entrance. When the debris is cleared, apparently after a very long time, we see a zombie-like Isaac smiling at the camera. These two endings can be interpreted as a reverse Lazarus story (John 11:1–54). Whereas Lazarus is inside the grave, and the stone that closes the grave is removed so that he is able to come out, the child goes the opposite way: he enters the grave and is trapped inside by a multitude of stones at the entrance of the grave.

The Endings #9 (foetus), #10 (???) and #11 (heart) are all connected to infanticide. While the "Dr. Fetus" from Ending #9 is also a reference to McMillen's earlier game *Super Meat Boy* (McMillen 2010), the foetus-in-a-jar is a reference to abortion. In Ending #10, Isaac finds a blue doll that resembles himself, with two crosses for eyes (just like the defeated mother from the epilogue). The blue colour could be a reference to "blue baby syndrome" that leads to cyanosis in infants because of heart failure. Ending #11 shows Isaac looking into the chest only to see something that scares him terribly. Behind him a heart is shown in the form of Isaac himself, shouting loudly. The music played while defeating this unlocked boss (dubbed "It Lives" in the game) is called "ventricide", a made-up word denoting either "killing of the heart" (English "ventricle" + Latin *caedo*, "to kill") or "killing of the womb" (Latin *ventus*, "womb" + *caedo*).

In Ending #12 (light), Cain, Mary Magdalene, Judas Iscariot, Eve, and Azazel appear (all unlockable characters). The Isaac of the video game is placed in the company of these "bad guys", these "losers" in the biblical narratives. He joins them voluntary. The décor in which the Old Testament figures of Cain and Eve appear consists of large intestines. Are they a reference to the intestines of the big fish in which Jonah stayed for three days and nights? Jonah experienced a rebirth by emerging from the fish's intestines. This could imply that joining the group of unlockable characters is a form of rebirth for the Isaac of the video game too.

Ending #13 (Bible) sticks to the Biblical setting. Isaac reads the Bible and looks into a mirror. Mirrors are rarely mentioned in the Bible. 1 Cor 13:12 uses the image of a mirror to explain that we cannot yet see the final salvation because we currently see in the dark, but that, when salvation will be fully realised, we will no longer see any vague reflection, but salvation itself. The child appears to gain some kind of knowledge or insight from reading the Bible. The insight in question could be two things. (1) Isaac comes to think in the same way his mother does, implying consent to being sacrificed. The devilish version of himself in the mirror perhaps points to this interpretation. Isaac agrees with his mother that he is sinful and must be sacrificed, thus mixing his mother's first two "motivations" in the prologue with the third one (proof of loyalty to God). (2) Isaac believes the exact opposite: he disagrees with his mother, which in fact would be in accordance with the biblical story in Genesis 22:1-19. The ending gives no clues as to which option it is. The simple fact of reading the Bible does not in itself give any information about someone's faith. It is not about the act reading the Bible as such, but about how the act of reading the Bible is performed.

Ending #16 (crying) also incorporates a kind of self-identification of Isaac. Isaac is lying in the chest, again in a foetal position, just as in the epilogue. He is crying silently, but his breathing becomes louder, indicating a lack of oxygen in the chest. Then, he is changed into a demon, who smiles frantically into the camera.

Endings #15 (missing) and #17 (skeleton) both indicate that Isaac has run away from home, #17 that Isaac has hidden himself in the chest in his room. In #15, we see a missing persons poster nailed to a pole beside Isaac's house. Isaac's mother can be seen standing on the other side, apparently looking for her son. After the missing persons poster of Ending #15, in #17 we see an unknown figure, probably Isaac's mother, opening the chest and finding Isaac's bones, covered in cobwebs, indicating that he has been there for a very long time. Ending #17 continues with Isaac opening the chest in an unknown, ghoulish, grey countryside. His shadow grows into a vampire-like figure that screeches at Isaac.

Without a doubt, the most insightful endings are Endings #14 (pictures) and #20 (final). Both endings feature polaroid pictures with their distinctive white passe-partout. In Ending #14 we see a stack of pictures disappearing in the distance, with a typical dungeon from the game in the background, although there is nothing in it. The fact that the pictures disappear makes it increasingly difficult to see the details of the subsequent pictures. We see the following scenes. (a) Mother, Isaac (fully dressed) and a male figure, probably Isaac's father, who is not seen or heard anywhere else in the game. (b) Isaac's mother with an unknown female child, who is not seen or heard anywhere else in the game either.

(c) A naked Isaac in his room with a devilish, dark figure in the corner in the back, who resembles Isaac's silhouette with the hanger through his head (Ending #4). (d) Isaac's mother and father smiling at each other as they hold hands. (e) Isaac (dressed) outside, alone. (f) A naked Isaac crying, sitting beside a closed chest. (g) Isaac's mother holding a knife in her hand as she did in the prologue, epilogue, and post-epilogue. However, we cannot see who she is threatening with the knife: Isaac, Isaac's father/her husband, or someone else? (h) Isaac and his mother look through a window at an unidentified person outside, perhaps his father. (i) The text "the end" appears.

The final Ending #20 is the most elaborate, in which various other endings re-appear and are recontextualised. We see the following scenes. (a) A naked Isaac lies in a chest, breathing heavily (cf. Ending #16). (b) A naked Isaac smiles as he draws pictures in his room, but he is interrupted by the sound of two people having a violent argument, probably his parents. (c) A drawing of Isaac's home (cf. prologue) with the words "we lived here". The past tense is intriguing. (d) A naked Isaac in a chest, now crying silently (cf. Ending #16). (e) Isaac, himself unseen, sees his mother weeping silently in front of a television (switched off) as she sits on the couch (cf. prologue). (f) Isaac is still in his chest crying, his breathing becomes heavier (cf. Ending #16).

(g) Isaac holds a polaroid picture (cf. Ending #14) of himself and his mother and father, but the father has been burned out. There is a chest full of other half-burned polaroids in the background. We see various pictures drawn by Isaac on the wall of Isaac's room: a chest, their house, a cat, Mary Magdalene (perhaps his unseen sister; cf. Ending #12), and Isaac with devil's horns, including an arrow pointing to him with the word "me" (cf. Ending #16). (h) Isaac in the chest once again, turning blue (cf. Ending #10).

(i) A wall full of polaroids and drawings. The polaroids show the following scenes: Isaac together with his mother and father, and Isaac with his mother (cf. Ending #14). The drawings are of the following things: Isaac's home; Isaac with a cat; Isaac playing with his father; Isaac witnessing a fight between his parents; Magdalene/his sister having fun; Isaac's mother with a knife looking very angry; two drawings of Isaac as a devil/vampire (cf. Ending #17), with the words "me", "bad", and "I am the devil"; a pentagram with the word "bad"; and Isaac and his mother lying dead in their own blood, with a black devil/vampire standing on Isaac's body.

(j) Isaac's skeleton lying in the chest, with cobwebs. The chest is opened by an unknown person, probably his mother (cf. Ending #17). (k) Isaac's home with a withered wanted poster on the pole (cf. Ending #15), eventually blown away by the wind. (l) After a fade-out and a fade-in, we see Isaac's silhouette in a ghoulish grey countryside (cf. Ending #17), as it walks away into the horizon.

The various endings, especially Endings #14 (pictures) and #20 (final), permit us to reconstruct Isaac's "true" story, although many uncertainties remain. Isaac lives happily with his father and mother in their "house on the hill", until Isaac's parents experience marriage problems. These family problems may be connected to the "missing" female character in the pictures, present in-game as the unlockable character Magdalena, probably Isaac's sister who seems to have vanished. Perhaps Isaac's sister died, putting an enormous strain on the relationship between her parents.

The fights between Isaac's parents intensify, until something happens that provokes Isaac's mother to force her husband/Isaac's father out of their home by wielding a kitchen knife. The father walks out of their lives, seemingly never to return again. Isaac's mother is—understandably—very sad about the separation (which may or may not have resulted in a civil divorce), and her son Isaac sees her in her sorrow, and blames himself for the situation (as happens from time to time with children of divorced parents).

Isaac, having been brought up in a Christian context, tries to find a familiar form or narrative that can help him cope with his mother's sadness, the divorce between his parents, and his self-blaming. He chooses the Biblical story from Genesis, probably because of the similarity in name: Isaac. Mixing reality and childish fantasy, Isaac comes up with a story in which he is punished by his theomanic mother who believes she is acting out God's will to purify her corrupt/sinful son.

Eventually, Isaac manages to hide permanently from his mother, whom he now regards as violent towards him. Even though his mother tries to find her lost son, she does not find him soon enough to prevent him suffocating in his toy chest. Then, Isaac walks the plains of the afterlife, leaving behind his parents in sorrow and with countless questions. We could even imagine that, while the divorce between his father and mother triggered Isaac's self-blaming, the death of their child causes them even more stress, perhaps leading them to blame themselves for the death of their child.

3. Interpretations: Constructing the Story

After examining the pre-text, the (post-)prologue, and epilogue, the game itself, and the various endings of *The Binding of Isaac*, we are now able to establish three different interpretive layers, each new layer building on the one below it.

Initially, when we look exclusively at the prologue/epilogue and the game itself, we see a narrative that is critical of religion. Borrowing from the infamous story from Genesis about a father who is prepared to sacrifice his only son "just" to prove his loyalty to his God, *The Binding of Isaac* presents a story about a theomanic mother who gives up her rationality and mother's instinct in blind obedience to an entity whose existence is probably imaginary. BoI can be read as a variation on Dawkins's point quoted above that these kinds of absurd Biblical stories stand at the source of the three monotheistic faiths, "proving" their inherent violent and intolerant nature. Fortunately enough—in the eyes of the critics—the modern-day Isaac triumphs over his mother's madness and survives the attack.

However, two points continue to puzzle in this interpretation. First, this critical interpretation ignores the actual outcome of the Biblical narrative, in which Isaac is saved too. Second, in both narratives "salvation" comes from divine intervention, in the form of a voice or of a falling Bible. The modern-day Isaac survives his crazy mother not because he uses his wits or rational thinking to combat her superstition, but because of a deus ex machina, which is exactly the kind of thinking Dawkins cum suis opposes. Following this interpretation, the intertextual relationship between the arche- and feno-texts should be qualified as a destructive one (Kristeva 1980).

However, second, this simplistic religion-critical interpretation is challenged by the post-prologue and post-epilogue in which it is substituted by the idea of religion as a coping mechanism. Isaac, confronted with an abusive mother, whose motivations are unclear for the moment, develops an imaginative story or context which he uses to successfully interpret his mother's behaviour, including a "rational" motivation. Borrowing from a familiar source, the Bible, specifically from a narrative that suits him well, the Genesis narrative about Abraham and Isaac, the child constructs an alternative reality in which he is the victim of his mother's theomania.

Isaac provides his mother with an excuse for her violence against him: she hears "voices" in her head, commanding her to do the things she does. The reality of the game itself provides a narratological context for Isaac in which he is able to actually fight against this reimagining of his mother in order to claim psychological victory over the evil that haunts him. Thus, Isaac is able to excuse his mother emotionally while securing his own survival in the process.

This interpretation renders the real ending of the story unsure, but the image of Isaac's mother standing in his doorway with a knife in her hand, the figure over whom Isaac had just triumphed with the help of divine intervention, relentlessly points to a disastrous ending for Isaac. His religiously inspired fantasy may have soothed him psychologically, but cannot prevent his mother from murdering him in the end.

The intertextual relationship between arche- and feno-text now becomes more complex, shifting from a one-dimensional destructive one to a more constructive relationship. The mother is certainly crazy, but she is no longer theomanic, just "normally" homicidal towards her son. The criticism shifts from religion to child abuse. The salvation that comes to Isaac in Genesis and in the epilogue of BoI is welcomed as positive, if ultimately unavailing.

Here, it is worth reflecting on the role of Abraham incorporated from the arche-text into the feno-text. In the video game, the main character is played by Isaac, as is common in the Jewish reception of the Genesis text. The role of Abraham is first of all played by the mother in the video game. She is the one who approaches the child with a knife, according to a voice, expressed by a Bible falling down. This shift in gender emphasizes that child abuse is not a male thing, but could be done by any adult, irrespective of his/her gender. In the arche-text, sonship is at issue: the father should have a male successor in order to continue the family tree. The Abraham of Genesis has to resolve many problems to get such a successor with his legal wife. Genesis 22:1-19 triggers this problem to focus on the male characters Abraham and Isaac. Because this family line is not an issue in the video game, the male gender is not important. To make this clear, the role of Abraham is played by the mother character. Regarding Isaac, it is important to notice that, in his form of a pink young child, he is gender-neutral. Only when his clothes are taken away, Isaac is recognizable as a boy.

However, the role of Abraham is not only played by the mother character. In the arche-text, it is Abraham who spares Isaac by not sacrificing him, but a ram instead. It is, as it were, also Abraham who has to "save" Isaac in the biblical story. In the video game, the mother can hardly be described as the one who saves her child Isaac. If a game-Abraham should be identified, it is Isaac's absent father, but he only appears on the third, not on the second narratological level. Besides, on the third level, where Isaac's father briefly appears, he does not save his son, he just leaves.

One could argue that, on the second narratological level, it is the player of the video game who has this task. By playing the video game, the player becomes Abraham. If he fails, Isaac will be dead, just as, in the Genesis narrative, Isaac would be dead if Abraham had eventually failed. If the player is successful, Isaac will be saved, even if the player does not understand all the aspects of meaning hidden in the video games, as the role of Abraham in the Genesis narrative could be interpreted as performed by someone who does entirely understand what happens. However, again, as soon as we incorporate the next interpretative level, the identification between the player and the Biblical Abraham becomes problematic.

On the third and last interpretative level, that of the game's multiple endings, especially Endings #14 and #20, the criticism of religion is minimised, and maximum emphasis is placed on (unintentional!) child abuse in the form of a violent divorce. Isaac's parents' divorce upsets his psychological balance, especially since he witnessed the physical threat his mother posed to his father, his father's desertion of him, and his mother's unbearable sadness afterwards. Isaac starts to blame himself for the divorce and the violence, seeing himself more and more as a sinner and as a devil who is destined to die, to be murdered, or to commit suicide to prevent worse.

The (unjustified) view that Isaac is possessed by a demon does not stem from the Isaac narrative, but probably from other passages in the Old and New Testament. Isaac identifies with other "sinners" in the Bible, who must on the one hand be regarded as sinners, but who must on the other hand be pitied as victims of circumstances they could not control, like Eve or Judas. The criticism of religion is mild, as the text is not extensively debated, but the dark interpretation readers of the Bible can produce, including darkening self-defamations.

The intertextual relationship changes from a destructive/constructive one to a deconstructive one, in which arche- and feno-texts mutually interpret each other. This is exactly what McMillen wanted to present with his game, especially with the multiple endings: to encourage players to have multiple interpretation of his work. Moreover, the BoI game—in all its harshness and violence—asks serious questions about uncritical receptions of Biblical narratives, and about all forms of child abuse, especially those stemming from religion itself, or from family crises like divorce and violence.

In theology, the discussions on Genesis 22:1-19 are ongoing. Our analysis has made clear that BoI as a video game could offer an important contribution to these discussions with interpreting the Binding of Isaac/Abraham's sacrifice as a model of disobedience (Boehm 2007): a protest against child abuse, religiously justified. *The Binding of Isaac* stands in the interpretative tradition of reading the story of Isaac as a protest against child sacrifices, placing the Isaac's story in a postmodern context of divorce, family troubles and (non-sexual) child abuse. Theologically, the games equates "sacrifice" with "abuse". Both actions are executed by a parent, although in both cases an external force is manipulating them, easing the moral pressure on the parents.

In Genesis, the external force is identified as God, while in BoI it is either the mother's theomania (narrartological level 1 and 2) or mental imbalance caused by a traumatic divorce and/or disappearing of unknown daughter/sister, who could have ended up living with her father, thus tearing up the family even further (level 3). In the first case, Isaac's mother is morally excused because of her mental condition. In the second case the whole "abuse" is not deliberately or actively caused by his mother, but by a very unfortunate mixture of circumstances.

The position of God in this theological interpretation is ambiguous: either He is very involved in the development of the story, as a voice from above (to the mother) or as intervener smashing the Bible on the mother's head and saving Isaac at the end (narratological level 1), or he is painfully absent, existing only in Isaac's mind while trying to psychologically cope with his troubled family problems (levels 2 and 3). God does not play a visible role in the ending narratives, nor seems there to be a "happy ending" for Isaac in anyone of them. The abuse is criticized, but not solved.

Author Contributions: Frank G. Bosman and Archibald L. H. M. van Wieringen conceived and designed the experiments; Frank G. Bosman performed the experiments; Frank G. Bosman and Archibald L.H.M. van Wieringen analyzed the data; Frank G. Bosman and Archibald L.H.M. van Wieringen wrote the paper.

Conflicts of Interest: The authors declare no conflict of interest.

References and Note

All biblical quotes are taken from the *Revised Standard Version*.

Agus, Aharon R. E. 1988. *The Binding of Isaac and Messiah: Law, Martyrdom and Deliverance in Early Rabbinic Religiosity*. Albany: State University of New York Press.

Bauer, Dieter. 2017. Ein Gott, der verlangt, dass wir unsere Kinder opfern? Die Erprobung Abrahams (Genesis 22). *Bibel Heute* 53: 16–17.

Boehm, Omri. 2007. *The Binding of Isaac: A Religious Model of Disobedience (The Library of Hebrew Bible/Old Testament Studies 468)*. New York and London: T & T Clark.

Bosman, Frank. 2016. The Word Has Become Game: Researching Religion in Digital Games. *Online. Heidelberg Journal of Religions on the Internet* 11: 28–45.

Bosman, Frank, and Marcel Poorthuis. 2015. Nephilim: The Children of Lilith. The Place of Man in the Ontological and Cosmological Dualism of the Diablo, Darksiders and Devil May Cry Game Series. *Online—Heidelberg Journal of Religions on the Internet* 7: 17–40.

Caspi, Mishael, and John Greene, eds. 2007. *Unbinding the Binding of Isaac*. Lanham: University Press of America.

Dawkins, Richard. 2006. *The God Delusion*. London: Bantam Press.

Heidbrink, Simone, Tobias Knoll, and Jan Wysocki. 2015. Venturing into the Unknown (?) Method(olog)ical Reflections on Religion and Digital Games, Gamers and Gaming. *Online. Heidelberg Journal of Religions on the Internet* 7: 68–71.

Holmes, Jonathan. 2011. How a Killer Christian Shmup Roguelike Came to Steam. *Destructoid*. July 21. Available online: https://www.destructoid.com/how-a-killer-christian-shmup-roguelike-came-to-steam-206601.phtml (accessed on 13 February 2018).

Jagielski, Rachel. 2011. The Binding of Isaac: Interview with Team Meat's Edmund McMillen. *Venturebeat*. September 2. Available online: https://venturebeat.com/community/2011/09/02/interview-with-team-meats-edmund-mcmillen (accessed on 13 February 2018).

Kristeva, Julia. 1980. *Desire in Language: A Semiotic Approach to Literature and Art*. Edited by Leon Roudiez. New York: Columbia University Press.

Lenzen, Verena. 2003. Das Opfer von Abraham, Isaak und Sara. Genesis 22 im rabbinischen Judentum. *Welt und Umwelt der Bibel* 30: 13–17.

McMillen, Edmund. 2010. *Super Meat Boy*. Asheville: Team Meat, Digital game.

McMillen, Edmund. 2011. *The Binding of Isaac*, Edmund McMillen. Digital game.

McMillen, Edmund. 2012. Postmortem: McMillen and Himsl's The Binding of Isaac. *Gamasutra*. November 28. Available online: https://www.gamasutra.com/view/feature/182380/postmortem_mcmillen_and_himsls_.php (accessed on 13 February 2018).

McMillen, Edmund. 2014. *The Binding of Isaac. Rebirth*. Santra Ana: Nicalis, Digital game.

McMillen, Edmund. 2015a. *The Binding of Isaac. Afterbirth*. Santra Ana: Nicalis, Expansion pack.

McMillen, Edmund. 2015b. *The Binding of Isaac. Afterbirth+*. Santra Ana: Nicalis, Expansion pack.

Rowley, Matthew. 2015. Irrational violence? Reconsidering the logic of obedience in Genesis 22. *Themelios* 40: 78–89.

Smith, Ewan. 2011. New Details on Team Meat Designer's New Game. *IGN*. July 12. Available online: http://www.ign.com/articles/2011/07/12/new-details-on-team-meat-designers-new-game (accessed on 13 February 2018).

Tischler, Nancy M. 2009. *Thematic Guide to Biblical Literature*. Westport and London: Greenwood Press.

Van der Toorn, Karel, Bob Becking, and Pieter W. van der Horst, eds. 1999. *Dictionary of Deities and Demons in the Bible*. Leiden: Brill.

Van Wieringen, Archibald L. H. M. 1995. The Reader in Genesis 22:1-19: Textsyntax—Textsemantics—Textpragmatics. *Estudios Bíblicos* 53: 289–304.

Westermann, Claus. 1981. *Genesis (BKAT 1/2)*. Neukirchen-Vluyn: Neukirchener Verlag.

Article

'Instant Karma'—Moral Decision Making Systems in Digital Games

Tobias Knoll

Institute of Religious Studies, Heidelberg University, 69117 Heidelberg, Germany;
tobias.knoll@zegk.uni-heidelberg.de

Received: 2 April 2018; Accepted: 11 April 2018; Published: 16 April 2018

Abstract: Moral decision making systems have long been a popular and widely discussed part of computer games; especially in—but not limited to—role-playing games and other games with strong narrative elements. In this article, an attempt will be made to draw a connection between historic and recent concepts of karma and moral decision making systems in digital games, called 'karma systems'. At the same time, a detailed analysis of one such system (that of *Mass Effect 2*) will be provided.

Keywords: digital games; game mechanics; karma; moral decision making

1. Introduction

In the recent past, research in religious studies into digital games has experienced an enormous upswing. The topic has come into the focus of academic online journals such as *Gamevironments*[1], *Online—Heidelberg Journal of Religions on the Internet*[2] and, not least through this issue of *Religions*. In addition, there has been a large increase in anthologies (cf. e.g., Cheruvallil-Contractor and Shakkour 2015; Šisler et al. 2018) and monographs (cf. e.g., Steffen 2017) dealing with religion and digital games in terms of content, theory, and methodology. Coupled with an equally growing public interest in religious (and generally cultural) aspects of games, this paints a thoroughly positive picture.

This article is intended to contribute to the growing scientific discussion about digital games. For this, an orientation was chosen which, to a certain extent, forms a unique selling point of the medium of 'games' but, on the other hand, is still rather underrepresented in the scientific debate to date.

In *Theorizing Religion in Digital Games. Perspectives and Approaches*, a framework for the identification and investigation of religious elements in digital games was presented. Besides religious influences in narratives and aesthetics, the aspect of gameplay was also highlighted (Heidbrink et al. 2014, pp. 32–35). Regarding the topic of agency and interaction, the approach closely followed Espen Aarseth's concept of "ergodic action":

> The concept of cybertext focuses on the mechanical organization of the text, by positing the intricacies of the medium as an integral part of the literary exchange. However, it also centers attention on the consumer, or user, of the text, as a more integrated figure than even reader-response theorists would claim. The performance of their reader takes place all in his head, while the user of cybertext also performs in an extranoematic sense. During the cybertextual process, the user will have effectuated a semiotic sequence, and this selective movement is a work of physical construction that the various concepts of "reading" do not account for. This phenomenon I call ergodic, using a term appropriated from physics that derives from the Greek words ergon and hodos, meaning "work" and

---

[1] http://www.gamevironments.uni-bremen.de/ (accessed on 31 March 2018).
[2] http://online.uni-hd.de (accessed on 31 March 2018).

"path". In ergodic literature, nontrivial effort is required to allow the reader to traverse the text. (Aarseth 1997, p. 1)

In order to do justice to this "ergodic" element, it is necessary to investigate those aspects of a game that make this element possible in the first place: game mechanics[3] and game rules. For this article, the choice fell on moral decision making systems which combine various differing game mechanics and rules and also usually integrate with a game's aesthetics and narrative. In particular, the focus will be on point based systems and their reception. These special forms of moral decision making systems are interesting, among other things, because in online discussions and on popular gaming websites they are often called 'karma systems' (or variations of it such as 'karma meter'[4] etc.).

The aim of this article is therefore to draw a connection between these 'karma systems' and common ideas and concepts of the religious concept of karma and to examine them for possible interactions and attributions of meaning. In addition, the detailed content analysis of a single 'karma system' (that of *Mass Effect 2*) and the associated actor perspectives are intended to illustrate the complexity of the design, reception, and negotiation processes associated with a modern computer games.

In order to achieve this, a historical analysis of the public and academic reception of the concept of karma will be carried out in the following chapter. Subsequently, an attempt will be made to create a definition of 'karma systems' in games using some examples from popular games. Finally, a detailed content analysis of the karma system of *Mass Effect 2* and a discussion of the associated design processes (intertextual and intermedial, as well as economic influences) and reception by the players will be conducted[5].

2. Public and Academic Reception of the Concept 'Karma'

2.1. History of Reception

In the following, an attempt will be made to trace the term karma and its manifold interpretations through history. For this purpose, the method of reception history analysis was chosen.

"History of reception" should be understood in the context of Hans Robert Jauß, Wolfgang Iser and—for the context of religious studies of particular importance—Michael Staußberg.

Jauß describes the concept of the history of reception (or aesthetics of reception) in his book *Die Theorie der Rezeption*, published in 1987, as follows:

> It calls for the history of literature and the arts to be understood now as a process of aesthetic communication in which the three instances of author, work and recipient [...] are equally involved. This included finally inserting the recipient as recipient and mediator, thus as carrier of all aesthetic culture, into his historical right [...]. (Jauß and Sund 1987, p. 5)

He is committed to involving the reader and not only—as had been customary in literary studies up until then—the author of a text in his or her investigation. By looking at the reader, the "recipient" of the text, the eye for the multitude of processes of communication and interpretation, which, as Wolfgang Iser puts it, constitute the "act of reading", is sharpened (Iser 1994). The focus here should no longer be on a single historically and socially universal "correct" interpretation of a text. Rather, it is about the context in which a text was and is written and read (Jauß 1994, p. 136).

---

3 For a discussion of the term "game mechanics" cf. e.g., (Sicart 2008).
4 For the sake of clearness, the term 'karma system' will be used to represent the differing terminologies for such systems. The combining factor will always be the usage of the term 'karma' as part of the description.
5 It should be noted that any kind of game content analysis for this article was based on actual playing experience by the author. All games mentioned here where played through at least once (or several times in the case of *Mass Effect 2*). In some cases, the gathered information was augmented through the usage of wikis (such as http://masseffect.wikia.com/wiki/Mass_Effect_Wiki) and other online resources. For methodological considerations on playing as research method cf. e.g., (Consalvo and Dutton 2006; Heidbrink et al. 2015).

Michael Stausberg tried to adapt and expand this methodology for religious studies in his book *Faszination Zarathustra*:

> This seemingly banal hermeneutic starting point has serious consequences—also for religious studies, since in this way, for example, the usual representation of 'the doctrine' or 'the message' of a certain religion or a certain text is undermined. The historically working religious studies would thus not so much have the task of systematizing the theology or mythology of a religion from the multitude of sources, but to present religious history as a concatenation of the productive reception and selection achievements of certain motives, themes, concepts, or texts brought about by followers of certain religions in certain historical situations, whereby the historian must take into account his own starting point, which is determined by the history of research to date, among other things[6]. (Stausberg 1998, p. 3)

He thus takes over the involvement of the "reader" demanded by Jauß and Iser. However, the term is not really accurate in the context of Stausberg's approach, since it goes beyond the purely literary or text-analytical approach and also addresses other objects of investigation. The concept of the actor or the "recipient" is probably more appropriate here (Stausberg 1998, p. 3).

The following examination of the historical reception of the concept of karma will be closely oriented to the principles presented here. For the purpose of clarity, it was necessary to make certain classifications, each of which should allow a rough allocation of certain ideas of karma. However, these should under no circumstances be understood as an immovable, 'hard' distinction between the various interpretations. Likewise, the chronological order of the individual sections should not be confused with the statement that this is a strictly linear 'evolution' of the karma term, in which one interpretation 'replaces' another. Although some developments can be observed, they are anything but linear and can also run parallel or contrary to further processes of interpretation and negotiation. Moreover, it is also quite possible that apparently separate lines of reception, which originate from the same 'origin', meet and influence each other again in the course of these processes. A 'timeline' of karma ideas is neither possible nor intended here. Rather, an attempt is made to shed light on as many lines of reception as possible, their roots, influences among themselves and through various religious and philosophical traditions, without judging by 'right' and 'wrong' interpretations.

2.2. 'Traditional Karma'?

Despite all ambiguity, in describing the term 'karma', it is appropriate to start where the concept has its origin in both the popular and the academic view: the South Asian religious traditions. In this more or less 'geographical' classification, however, the similarities between popular and scientific discussion often end.

So what is understood by the public as "traditional karma"? The Encyclopedia Britannica provides the following explanation:

> Karma, Sanskrit karman ("act"), Pali kamma, in Indian religion and philosophy, the universal causal law by which good or bad actions determine the future modes of an individual's existence. Karma represents the ethical dimension of the process of rebirth (samsara), belief in which is generally shared among the religious traditions of India. Indian soteriologies (theories of salvation) posit that future births and life situations will be conditioned by actions performed during one's present life—which itself has been conditioned by the accumulated effects of actions performed in previous lives. The doctrine of karma thus directs adherents of Indian religions toward their common goal: release (moksha) from the cycle of birth and death. Karma thus serves two main functions within Indian moral philosophy: it provides

---

[6]   All German language texts in this paper where translated into English by the author of this paper.

the major motivation to live a moral life, and it serves as the primary explanation of the existence of evil[7].

Axel Michaels sums up this idea in his review of Wilhelm Halbfass' book *Karma und Wiedergeburt im indischen Denken* (cf. Halbfass 2000):

> The ideas that are generally linked to this concept are truly radical: every act, whether culpable or meritorious, is charged for future existence, all actions appear causally in the balance of posthumous retributions. The omnipotence of the gods is limited, man has his fate in his own hands. Moreover, every action is karmically stressful and leads to a new life of suffering. In the end, only inaction and the search for salvation will help. (Michaels 2001)

He criticizes, in his view, "simplified" views of the concept of karma for drawing a "lethargic and apathetic" picture of the Indians who "can remain in their caste destiny or go into secular asceticism" (Michaels 2001). He rejects any kind of reduction of "karma" both to an inevitable "destiny", into which one has to submit powerlessly, and to complete self-determination:

> In India, man is not the plaything of a god, but also not the unrestricted master of his own life. So it is too easy to confront the omnipotence of God in Christianity with the omnipotence of self in Hinduism. Nevertheless, divergences remain. Above all these: here the requirement of a probation in life, there the desire for liberation from life. Rebirth is not a reward in most Indian liberation teachings, but punishment or a necessary evil. (Michaels 2001)

When looking at karma, Wilhelm Halbfass himself also refers to its concrete meaningful function:

> It provides a framework and guideline for moral and religious orientation by ascribing to current actions and decisions an inherent power to trigger future and punishable consequences. (Halbfass 2000, p. 210)

At the same time, however, Halbfass warns several times against talking about "the law of karma" (Halbfass 2000, pp. 31, 310). Axel Michaels joins this position:

> There are texts in which such causal relationships are established. They say, for example: He who commits adultery becomes sterile in the next life; he who eats flesh gets red limbs; he who drinks alcohol, black teeth. Nevertheless, such registers are to be seen only as rules, but not as a mechanism of the consequences of the crime, as Max Weber, who called the karmal doctrine the "most perfect solution to the problem of theodicy", still assumed. (Michaels 2001)

In his article *Reinkarnationsvorstellungen als Gegenstand der Religionswissenschaft und Theologie*, Michael Bergunder also addresses the concrete social benefits of karma concepts by, among other things, identifying them as justification for the "social norms of a society structured according to socio-religious hierarchies […] as it corresponds to the Brahman ideal" (Bergunder 2001, p. 707). Here, therefore, an authoritative and legitimatory aspect is also gaining in importance.

However, Bergunder also warns against limiting karma concepts to this aspect and also problematizes the central role attributed to them in Hindu traditions. Although at the beginning he himself refers to the close connection between "karmal doctrine" and rebirth (Bergunder 2001) he goes on in declaring that "in authoritative Hindu movements the karma rule is negated or deprived of its validity" (Bergunder 2001, p. 708). As an indication of this, he uses what he calls "popular Hinduism", for which he postulates that "concrete cases of reincarnation [are] an exceptional phenomenon" and "Karma conceptions [...] would usually have no relation to rebirth" (Bergunder 2001, p. 709). What

---

7   https://www.britannica.com/topic/karma (accessed on 11 April 2018).

exactly Bergunder understands by this "popular Hinduism", he unfortunately does not explain more precisely, but instead the use of the karma term. According to Bergunder, karma is understood here as "a kind of synecdoche for the destiny decreed by God", which "[is] used to explain accidents", but [. . .] usually resigns behind other explanations" (Bergunder 2001).

Already at this first glance at the interpretation of the karma concept, exemplarily carried out in the context of Hindu religious traditions, it becomes apparent that several views have formed on its 'true' meaning. The popular Western interpretations are in conflict with contemporary and 'classical' scientific approaches, as well as what Bergunder calls "popular Hinduism". This description is, of course, far from exhaustive, but should already show that, despite the fact that it has already been limited to a regional framework, a generally accepted definition of karma cannot be found even where its historical origin is traditionally located. Instead of continuing (in vain) to search for such a general definition, the following representations of further karma understandings will attempt to explain how this multitude of frequently contradictory interpretations and interpretations arose. It should also be made clear how past discourses, both popular and scientific, can influence current discourses.

2.3. Karma, Neo-Hinduism, and the Theosophical Society

From the second half of the 19th century onwards, the so-called Theosophical Society around Helena Blavatsky played a prominent role in the development of the karma concept prevailing. However, in order to explain their influence, it is necessary to first take a look at the image that still prevailed in Western research and mission literature at that time with regard to karma concepts. Michael Bergunder writes about this:

> Herder already states that the doctrine of reincarnation is the "opium" that enables the Indians to live in quiet passivity and in acceptance of the strict caste hierarchies. In the following period this thesis formed an independent topos both in orientalist research and in Christian missionary literature, and Max Weber still speaks of the "ingenious combination of caste legitimacy and karmal doctrine", which is "connected to the real social order through the promises of rebirth", "the fixed scheme" which legitimizes a rigid and not dynamic caste society. (Bergunder 2001, p. 711)

In the middle of the 19th century, a reform movement was created, which Bergunder calls "neo-Hinduism". The latter immediately set about presenting alternative approaches to the karma concept, which were supposed to put it in a better light:

> The beginning of this Hindu reconsideration is marked by Bankimchandra Chattopadhayay, who in his Bengali Bhagavadgita commentary, under sharp criticism of Christian concepts of the hereafter, defends the doctrine of karma and rebirth, although scientifically neither provable nor refutable, as logical and ethically reasonable. (Bergunder 2001, p. 712)

Bergunder sees here in reference to Halbfass an Indian attempt to assert oneself against the West by counteracting the image of karma as the "opium" of what Michael also calls a "lethargic and apathetic" society (Michaels 2001). Another important aspect of this "reinterpretation" is the generally positive representation of karma, which now focuses on the personal spiritual development of the individual over several lives. Bergunder also refers here to Aurobindo Ghose, for whom "the karmic process [is] an evolutionary, cosmic self-development of the mind to a higher consciousness force, which is supramental consciousness" (Bergunder 2001, p. 712).

It is no coincidence that a strong concentration on "self" and "personal development" can be seen here. These schools of thought were also significantly influenced by the criticism of institutionalized religion that emerged in the West at that time. Robert Sharf speaks here of the "nineteenth-century European Zeitgeist", which is a legacy of "anti-clericism and anti-ritualism of the Reformation, the rationalism and empiricism of the Enlightenment, the romanticism of figures such as Schleiermacher and Dilthey, and the existentialism of Nietzsche" (Sharf 1995, p. 247). Although Sharf refers specifically to the role of meditative practice and experience in Buddhist reform movements in Japan and Southeast Asia with regard to the influence of this "zeitgeist", elements of it can also be recognized in the case of the "neo-Hinduist" reform movements. An example of this would be the urge for rationalism that is evident in the Bankimchandra Chattopadhyay already mentioned above. In integrating these Western patterns of thought into one's own religion, Sharf believes he sees a typical reaction to the ongoing contact with Western culture, science, and philosophy. He attests the Buddhist reform movements a strong tendency to emphasize "private spiritual experience" in response to this contact and the subsequent "cultural relativism". According to him, this was designed transhistorically and transculturally in order to immunize against relativistic criticism (Sharf 1995, p. 268).

In the context of "neo-Hinduist" reform efforts around the concepts of karma and rebirth, overlaps can be observed. Thus, in the central role of the "self" in the "evolutionary" process of self-development, a strong reference to individual experience, detached from institutionalized religion, can also be recognized. However, the term "evolutionary" already reveals another strategy that deviates from Sharf's thesis. In addition, an attempt was made to bring karma and rebirth to a "rational", scientifically explainable level, for example by referring to "causality", i.e., the scientifically provable relationship of "cause and effect".

Although, as Bergunder also notes, the central role of karma and rebirth cannot be determined in all currents of "Neohinduism", this interpretation nevertheless exerted a strong influence, among others also in later Western interpretations. The main reason for this was the influence of the so-called Theosophical Society.

The Theosophical Society was founded in New York in 1875 by Helena Petrovna Blavatsky and Henry Steel Olcott. The society was founded on the conviction that there was a "true core" in all religions and the aim was therefore to establish a "universal brotherhood" uniting all people. At the time of its foundation, the society was marked by European "esoteric" and "mystical" traditions, which changed with the relocation of both Blavatsky and Olcott to India. The "idea" of, as Bergunder puts it, "esoterically understood unity of all religions" (Bergunder 2001, p. 714) led Blavatsky and her followers—soon also among the Indian population—to integrate elements of Indian religious traditions into their own teachings, including the karma concept. According to the doctrine of an "all-encompassing brotherhood of humanity", however, the role of the individual in determining his own destiny was reduced. Karma became a judging power, which in its influence on mankind rather fulfils "instructive" functions:

> [. . .] it is the power that controls all things, the resultant of moral action, the metaphysical Samskāra, or the moral effect of an act committed for the attainment of something which gratifies a personal desire. There is the karma of merit and the karma of demerit. Karma neither punishes nor rewards, it is simply the one Universal Law which guides unerringly, and, so to say, blindly, all other laws productive of certain effects along the grooves of their respective causations. (Blavatsky and Mead 2003, p. 161)

So the responsibility of the individual lies only in deciding whether he voluntarily accepts the "teaching" of karma without its help, or "learns" from it; he has no influence on the "law of karma" itself. At this point the theosophical doctrine strongly reminds us of certain elements of Christian moral doctrine, which put man before the decision to attempt to fathom moral values through his own experience and reflection, or to find their "clear" form in the form of God's revelation (e.g., cf. Hörmann 1969, p. 602). This similarity with Christian teachings is not surprising considering that the Western esoteric origin of theosophical teaching was also strongly influenced by concepts of Emanuel Swedenborg's "Christian theosophy" and other Christian mystical traditions (e.g., cf. Swedenborg 1880).

The concept of karma is thus expanded to include a strong moral core whose basic ethical guidelines can only be fathomed by the individual, but cannot be influenced. This view can also be found in later interpretations within theosophical circles; even after the dissolution of the Theosophical Society into numerous smaller groups after Helena Blavatsky's death in 1891, karma in the *Theosophischen Pfad* from 1912 is also called "divine law":

Karma is the law that ensures that all things serve those who love God, that is, mankind, for the best. How clearly and forcefully history teaches us that blessed work of the Law!

[…]

Karma, the lot given to us, is the will of the divine soul in us, and when we get used to looking at life with its vicissitudes and apparent contradictions from the standpoint of the law of brotherhood, then we gain another, deeper concept of good and evil and accept the judgment of the law as our own divine will. (Karma im Lichte der Geschichte 1912, pp. 304–5)

The process of this "teaching" through karma is described as "evolutionary" and continues through several incarnations, whereby the "personality" does not persist, but rather the "Ego":

Only that which is immortal in its very nature and divine in its essence, namely, the Ego, can exist forever. And as it is that Ego which chooses the personality it will inform, after each *Devachan*, and which receives through these personalities the effects of the Karmic causes produced, it is therefore the Ego, that self which is the "moral kernel" referred to and embodied karma, "which alone survives death". (Blavatsky and Mead 2003, pp. 161–62)

At this point at the latest, strong points of intersection with approaches of "neo-Hinduism" become clear. The immortal, existential "Ego" that survives the personality and is part of an evolutionary learning process strongly recalls that "evolutionary, cosmic self-development of the mind to a higher consciousness, the supramental consciousness", as Bergunder puts it with reference to Aurobindo (Bergunder 2001, p. 713). Here you can see the influence of both currents on each other, to which Bergunder also refers (Bergunder 2001, p. 712).

Another overlap with "neo-Hinduist" approaches, which survived the end of the original society, is found in the alleged "scientificness" of theosophical doctrine of karma. The Theosophical Forum of 1930 calls karma "a far-reaching application of well-known basic scientific teachings of the law of cause and effect […] and its work is therefore such of error-free justice". (Beale et al. 1930, p. 18)

The fact that the Theosophical Society and many of its daughter and subgroups lost much of their direct influence in the 20th century did not change the fact that their teachings can still be found in popular ideas of karma today. However, this wide spread was only made possible with the emergence of what is today strongly generalized as the 'New Age movement'.

2.4. Karma and the New Age Movement

Since this section deals with the role of the so-called 'New Age movement' in the spread of karma ideas, it is appropriate to briefly problematize the term 'New Age movement' itself. In fact, the term 'New Age movement' is an artificial construct trying to make a multitude of movements, single currents and groupings tangible. George Chryssides sums up the problem of such an overarching concept:

A further problem relates to the supposed constituents of the New Age. If it supposedly includes homeopathy, eastern religions, ley lines, deep ecology, angels, channeling, Tarot cards, astrology and Neuro-Linguistic Programming, what do such interests have in common? If there is no common essence, do they at least have a relationship? If they have common or related features, what is the point in conjuring up a term to refer to them collectively? (Chryssides 2007, p. 6)

It is not the intention of this paper to answer these questions. Rather, as the term continues to be used, we should be aware that it is not a single movement, but rather a makeshift umbrella term for what Chryssides calls a "counter-cultural zeitgeist" (Chryssides 2007, p. 22), which is only used in the absence of suitable alternatives.

So far, much has been written about the interpretation processes that took place within the narrow circles of the Theosophists and also within the Indian society. However, it should be noted that despite its popularity, the Theosophical Society addressed only a relatively small elite circle of scientists and intellectuals. It was not until the middle of the 20th century that the teachings of Theosophy reached a broad audience.

After Helena Blavatsky's death in 1891, the Theosophical Society fragmented into a multitude of smaller groups, which, however, were still close to the original theosophical teachings and thus kept them alive. As a result, concepts of karma, reincarnation, meditation, and many other apparently Indian religious concepts encountered the generation of "Baby Boomers" and the emerging 'New Age movement' in the mid-20th century.

At that time, after the Second World War, North America was in an economic upswing that brought the American middle class in particular a great deal of prosperity and financial security. Due to a new idealization of family life, there was an enormous increase in births in the USA.

While a similar increase in the birth rate in Europe was already over after five years, it only reached its peak in the USA in 1957 and ended in 1965: Susan Love Brown identifies the children of that time, who grew up well-protected in this prosperity and this feeling of security, in her article *Baby Boomers, American Character and the New Age* as one of the germ cells of the 'New Age movement', which at that time was rapidly gaining supporters (Brown 1992).

The influence of the "Baby Boomer Generation", as Brown calls it, on the emergence of the 'New Age movement' is explained by the social circumstances of that time. Compared to the direct predecessor generations, children of the new generation experienced much greater prosperity, were for the first time under the influence of television on a large scale and were better educated. The enormous number of births made the USA a country in which children were at the center. This general social prosperity led to a new orientation of the members of this generation away from the problems of their parents, to problems that were more oriented towards their own age group, especially because not only the parents were the only effective force for socialization, but also the mass media gained more and more importance. This in turn led to the members of this generation rebelling against their parents as they slowly grew up during the 1960s. This rebellion was based on an idealistic view of how society should be. There was no rebellion against the general values of the parents, but against the hypocrisy behind them.

Brown identifies the main characteristic of the "New Age" as a new orientation towards "self" and "experience". She explains this orientation through the wide spread of drugs in America in the 1960s. According to her, the use of drugs led many to want to explore even further the new levels of consciousness they had learned, which in turn led to interest in mysticism and Eastern religions. She uses statistics that show that "[....] 96.4 percent of those people living in communities based on eastern ideologies had used drugs before joining, compared to 56.2 percent of people joining christian communities" (Brown 1992, p. 95). In their search for "new" and "exotic" religious experiences, the followers of the "New Age" naturally also came across the teachings of Theosophy and its daughter groups. Some authors, such as Chryssides, address the influence of the Theosophical Society on the 'New Age movement' even earlier and more centrally:

> Although the Theosophical Society is not normally considered to be part of the New Age Movement, its eclectic ideas have significantly contributed to the development of the New Age phenomenon. In particular, Rudolf Steiner (1861–1925), Alice Bailey (1880–1949), Juddu Krishnamurti (1895–1986), and Dion Fortune (1890–1946), all of whose writings still feature significantly on the Mind-Body-Spirit shelves of bookshops, were at one time Theosophists, although all except Fortune abandoned the Theosophical Society. (Chryssides 2007, p. 6)

In addition, many followers of the 'New Age' began to travel to India to learn directly from Indian 'masters' and 'gurus'. Of course, they also met representatives of those Hindu reform movements that had formed under the influence of the Theosophical Society in the 19th century. They had discovered their great opportunity here to make their own concepts more widely known in the West, which was, of course, followed by commercial interests.

This influence and fascination with Far Eastern religious traditions in general ultimately led to an enormous popularization of them, including, of course, the doctrine of karma, which placed so much emphasis on individual decision-making power over personal destiny. The final impetus for the establishment of the term karma in Western society was provided by the commercialization of the 'New Age movement' from the early 1980s. Media, publishers, but also former convinced representatives of the 'New Age' itself recognized the enormous commercial potential behind its manifold theories and practices. And so bookshops soon filled shelves with works on meditation, holistic healing practices, channeling, and much more. The commercial power of karma was also discovered in this way, so it comes as no surprise that booksellers still today have an extensive range of books such as *Karma in Practice. Shaping the Future*[8] or *Karma—The Instructions for Use: . . . so That Fate Does What You Want*[9]. The concrete interpretation of the karma concept—as the titles of the books mentioned here also implies—is very 'practical'. Karma is often traced back to Far Eastern religious traditions, but the applicability of the concept is also promoted beyond religious practice, since the law of 'cause and effect' is after all a 'rational' principle.

2.5. Interim Conclusion

So what is karma? The term is widely known today, due to its popularization during the 'New Age movement' and beyond. A clear meaning cannot be determined, however, because even if a very simplified image of karma currently prevails in the general public, which is roughly associated with Indian religious traditions and at the center of which is the 'rationally' comprehensible law of 'cause and effect', this interpretation is naturally not the only one. 'Traditional' interpretations can be found as well as a multitude of interpretations that can be traced back to theosophical or 'neo-Hinduist' sources and also bring with them strong moralizing aspects—each of course again dependent on the contemporary discourse on morality and ethics. Of course, none of these interpretations should be considered 'wrong' or 'right', even if they contradict each other. Ultimately, the definition used depends on individual ideas, preferences and living conditions, the 'recipients'; and of course—and this should not be forgotten in times of mass media and the Internet—from where they get them.

The film and television industries have also discovered the concept of karma for themselves. How ambivalent the term is often used, however, can be well illustrated by a quotation from the well-known film *Ghostbusters* from 1984 by Dan Aykroyd and Harold Ramis. When at the beginning of the film the three main characters Dr. Peter Venkman, Dr. Raymond Stantz, and Dr. Egon Spengler are expelled from the university because of the dubious nature of their research, Peter Venkman (played by Bill Murray) comments as follows:

> For whatever reasons, Ray, call it fate, call it luck, call it karma. I believe everything happens for a reason. I believe that we were destined to get thrown out of this dump. (transcribed from Aykroyd and Ramis (1984))

For a religious studies view, especially in the context of the analysis of the 'karma system' of *Mass Effect 2* sought in this paper, this means that the results of the analysis carried out must not be compared with a single idea of karma—whether it be a supposedly 'present' or 'traditional'. Rather, all the ideas presented here must be taken into account, as well as the possibility that even the implementation of a 'karma system' into a game and the reception of this system by the players can again lead to new interpretations and negotiations of meaning of the concept karma.

Before a specific 'karma system', namely that of *Mass Effect 2*, is dealt with in detail in Section 4, in the following chapter a useful definition of the term itself and a basis for the comparison of different

---

[8]   German: "Karma in der Praxis. Die Zukunft gestalten" (Prophet et al. 2004).
[9]   German: "Karma—die Gebrauchsanleitung: . . . damit das Schicksal macht, was Sie wollen" (Schwarz and Schweppe 2008).

'karma systems' will be created using two popular examples: *Star Wars: Knights of the Old Republic* and *Fallout 3*.

3. Karma Systems in Games

It is difficult to describe what constitutes a 'karma system' without falling into criminal generalizations, because like so much that falls into the realm of 'new media', computer games—and with them the systems which define them—have developed rapidly over the last two decades. Moral decision making systems are not exempt from this and have been subjected to a constant process of development, which naturally always took place in the context of related games, which implemented a similar system earlier or even at the same time.

Nevertheless, in the following chapter an attempt we will be made to identify some elements that most so-called 'karma systems' have in common in order to provide a definition that can be used at least for this paper. This definition is to be worked out on the basis of two exemplary games whose moral decision making systems are called 'karma systems' by players—just like the moral decision making system of *Mass Effect 2*.

3.1. A Brief History of Karma Systems

The games with 'karma systems' presented below were selected primarily from the ranks of commercially successful games of the last 15 years. The main criteria were a verifiable connection to *Mass Effect 2*—for example via its developer studio Bioware—or a relatively close release in order to make possible demarcation processes understandable, as well as a connection with "karma systems" in relevant articles in the gaming press and/or discussions by players. The latter is particularly important, since "karma system" and related terms referring to "karma" are primarily coined by the gaming press and players themselves.

The games featured here are Bioware's *Star Wars—Knights often the Old Republic* (*KotOR*) and *Fallout 3* from Bethesda Game Studios.

KotOR was chosen because it was created by Bioware, the developer of *Mass Effect 2*, and was also under the same Game Director or Executive Producer, Casey Hudson. The moral system of *KotOR* is regarded by players and gaming press as the spiritual forefather of the "karma system" of *Mass Effect 2*.

Fallout 3, on the other hand, is the work of a development studio competing with Bioware and, like *Mass Effect 2*, is a relatively current example of the implementation of a "karma system". *Fallout 3* also has a special role to play, as it is the only game that, has a "karma system" that actually uses the term "karma" within the game. What this can mean, however, will be clarified later.

The presentation of the games will initially be largely descriptive, in order to lay the informative foundation for a more detailed analysis of the respective connections to *Mass Effect 2* in Section 4. Subsequently, an attempt will be made to find a useful definition for the "karma systems" examined here.

3.2. Star Wars: Knights of the Old Republic

Star Wars: Knights of the Old Republic was first released on 15 July 2003 for Xbox and 19 November 2003 for PC. *Knights the Old Republic* was developed by Bioware and distributed by LucasArts.

The game was a great commercial success. Four days after the release, 250,000 copies had already been sold and the international average scores amount to 93 out of 100 possible points[10].

As the title of the game suggests, it is located in the Star Wars universe based on George Lucas' films. In fact, some game elements here are based on the *Star Wars Role Playing Game*, a 'pen and paper' role-playing game by Bill Slavicsek, Andy Collins, and JD Wiker, which in turn is based on the third

---

[10] http://www.metacritic.com/game/pc/star-wars-knights-of-the-old-republic (accessed on 30 March 2018).

edition of *Advanced Dungeons and Dragons*. The technology is based on the Aurora Engine developed by Bioware itself.

The 'karma system' of Knights often the Old Republic is strongly influenced by the 'mythology' of the Star Wars universe and its pronounced conflict between the 'good' Jedi and the 'evil' Sith. The player is often faced with the choice of pursuing one of two possible solutions in quests and dialogues. A 'neutral' solution is usually not intended. For example, the player can choose to defend a village from a group of bandits or ally with them and take a share of the loot.

The decision is then evaluated by the game and is reflected in a scale that can be viewed at any time and ranges from 'Dark' to 'Light' (see Figure 1).

Figure 1. "Alignment" Bar[11].

The character shown here has reached a maximum of "dark force points", whereby it should be noted that with the collection of enough points contrary to the current attitude a "change of opinion" is still possible in the later course of the game. You can see the red fog in the background, which changes its color from red (evil) to blue (good) depending on the orientation of the character. In the player portrait in the lower right corner of the picture you can also see the physical change that the character undergoes depending on his or her orientation. The stronger this tends to the "dark side of the force", the paler the skin and the eyes get a sickly red coloration.

Additionally, depending on which side the player chooses, he has access to different special skills that are only available to either the "light" or the "dark" side of the Force. The "dark"' powers focus primarily on inflicting damage (e.g., indicated by the "+1-8 DAM" above the character portrait in Figure 1), while the "light" powers focus on healing and support.

---

[11] Source: https://staticdelivery.nexusmods.com/mods/198/images/68122_1.jpg (last access: 30 March 2018).

All these elements can be easily traced back to the Star Wars canon. The colors red and blue are found in the lightsabers wielded by Luke Skywalker, the hero of the trilogy and his teacher Obi Wan Kenobi, and Darth Vader, the villain of the films. The physical effects of the use of the "dark side" and its exclusive powers can also be found in the films and other sources belonging to the canon.

3.3. Fallout 3

Fallout 3 was first released on 28 October 2008 and was developed by Bethesda Game Studios. Bethesda Softworks and ZeniMax Media were responsible for distribution.

The two previous parts of the Fallout series had been developed by Black Isle Studios, which had supported Bioware in the development of the *Baldur's Gate* games. Initially, they were also responsible for the implementation of the third part of Fallout, but had to transfer the license rights to Bethesda after their closure by Interplay Entertainment.

This change of responsibilities brought about some radical changes. While the first two *Fallout* parts still used a 2D engine, an isometric perspective, and turn-based combat, Bethesda Game Studios used an advanced version of their modern Gamebryo engine, either 'third-person' or 'ego' perspective and an 'action-heavy' combat system with tactical elements.

This transformation paid off as *Fallout 3* proved to be a great financial success. In the first month after the release alone, more than 610,000 games were sold and the international average score was 91 out of 100 possible points[12]. Various controversies, for example in Australia, because of the possible use of drugs in the game, or in Japan, because of a mission in which it is possible to detonate a nuclear bomb, could not counteract its continued popularity.

The game itself is located in a post-apocalyptic world in 2277. 200 years after a world war between the USA and China, which culminated in a nuclear war in 2077. The player takes on the role of a "vault" resident. Before the nuclear holocaust, the "vaults", huge, self-sustaining bunkers, were built all over the United States to protect the country's elite. But humans also survived the war on the surface and when the father of the player character mysteriously disappears, the player must leave the protective "vault" and follow him into the destroyed remains of Washington D.C. Here he first encounters other survivors who have established settlements and are fighting for their survival. In search of his father, the player must perform various optional and non-optional tasks for the settlers and other groups in order to obtain new clues and information. On his way, other survivors join the player several times for a short time, but the player can never control them himself.

The "karma system" of *Fallout 3* is worth mentioning simply because the value of points awarded or deducted here for "good" and "evil" actions is explicitly called "karma". In the game, the "karma system" manifests itself through different solutions to missions, as well as generally "good" actions such as donations and assistance or "bad" actions such as theft and (unprovoked) murder.

The player starts with a fixed number of karma points, which can either be increased or reduced based on his or her own actions. The current value is then used to calculate the karma level, but cannot be viewed directly in the game. The five possible levels are "very evil" (−1000 to −750 karma points), "evil" (−749 to −250 karma points), "neutral" (−249 to +249 karma points), "good" (+250 to +749 karma points), and "very good" (+750 to +1000 karma points). Based on this level and the general level progress, the player then receives a visible title, which is composed as outlined in Table 1.

---

12   http://www.metacritic.com/game/pc/fallout-3 (accessed on 30 March 2018).

Table 1. Karma Titles in *Fallout 3*.

Level	Bad Karma	Neutral Karma	Good Karma
1	Vault Delinquent	Vault Dweller	Vault Guardian
2	Vault-Outlaw	Vault Renegade	Vault Martyr
3	Opportunist	Seeker	Sentinel
4	Plunderer	Wanderer	Defender
5	Fat Cat	Citizen	Dignitary
6	Marauder	Adventurer	Peacekeeper
7	Pirate of the Wastes	Vagabund of the Wastes	Ranger of the Wastes
8	Reaver	Mercenary	Protector
9	Urban Invader	Urban Ranger	Urban Avenger
10	Ne'er-do-well	Observer	Exemplar
11	Capital Crimelord	Capital Councilor	Capital Crusader
12	Defiler	Keeper	Paladin
13	Vault Boogeyman	Vault Descendant	Vault Legend
14	Harbinger of War	Pinnacle of Survival	Ambassador of Peace
15	Urban Superstition	Urban Myth	Urban Legend
16	Villain of the Wastes	Strider of the Wastes	Hero of the Wastes
17	Fiend	Beholder	Paragon
18	Wasteland Destroyer	Wasteland Watcher	Wasteland Savior
19	Evil Incarnate	Super-Human	Saint
20	Scourge of Humanity	Paradigm of Humanity	Last, Best Hope of Humanity

A differentiation between "very bad" and "bad" and "very good" and "good" does not take place, however.

Besides the title, the player's karma value also influences dialogues with non-player characters, the availability of special abilities ("perks") and the outcome of the main plot.

3.4. What Is a Karma System?

The purpose of this section is to formulate a working definition of karma systems and at the same time to preserve the publicly used term "karma system" and its basic meaning derived from the above examples and to distinguish it from other similar game systems. The reason for this is that, there are many games that deal with moral and ethical issues in one way or another, many of which are not associated with "karma" by players and the gaming press.

So what is to be understood here as a "karma system" and what not? To answer this question, one should first start where "karma systems" overlap with other forms of moral decisions in games: The decision between—usually two—moral absolutes.

In the case of a "karma system", this means that the player is repeatedly confronted with moral questions during the game, which usually offer a relatively clear "good" or "evil" solution, or at least cover two different moral spectra. These questions do not necessarily have to be actual "questions". They can also be problems that allow different solutions or the player's actions are constantly monitored during the game and evaluated according to fixed rules (e.g., no civilians may be killed).

Moral decisions can also occur in games that do not use a "karma system". An example of this would be games such as *Bastion* by Supergiant Games, in which at the very end of the game the player is prompted to make a single moral decision which decides the fate of the game world. The consequence of the decision is left to the player, as the game immediately ends after the decision. There are no consequences within the game.

In both cases, the decision influences the player's experience. The difference is that the decisions in the case of "externalized decision systems" like the one in *Bastion* are both unique and final. Once the player has decided, there are no further repercussions within the game. The player has to make up his or her own mind about the possible consequences—or just ignore them. The moral decisions in "karma systems", on the other hand, are part of a continuous process of moral development. The player starts in the middle of an alignment or morality chart and the final alignment as well as all consequences take place during the game and can even be undone in some cases. The "karma systems" of *Knights of the Old Republic* and *Fallout 3* are good examples of this.

Another unique selling point of "karma systems" is the evaluation of the player's decisions by the game or rather the designers of the game. This is usually done using a score scale that shifts depending on the number of "positive" or "negative" points collected, whereby every possible decision that the player can make is bound from the outset to a fixed number of points that can be gained or deducted as a result. This scale is usually directly visible to the player and the player is usually informed immediately of any change in the points account. It is also theoretically possible that the game does not give such clear feedback about the player's "karma" progress, but it is important that in this case the player's actions are still 'recorded' in the background. It is also important to note that, in the game itself, there is usually no need for a direct 'witness'—for example in the form of a non-player character (NPC)—so that the player's actions can be evaluated accordingly.

This aspect distinguishes 'karma systems' from 'consequence systems' such as CD Projekt Red's *The Witcher*. In this system the player is confronted with several—often moral—decisions, which are not evaluated with points, but only decide on the further course of the story at a later point in time. Moreover, these decisions and their consequences are usually directly integrated into the story and can thus be explained in a narrative and conclusive manner.

A final distinguishing feature results directly from the evaluation system mentioned above. A 'karma system' is always a closed system in which the moral questions the player is confronted with—whether in the form of dialogues or in the form of direct actions such as theft etc.—are always predefined. If a player carries out an action that is not intended by the designers as part of the 'karma system', this action will also not be evaluated by this system, since no corresponding 'value' was specified in advance. This can lead to paradoxical situations in which, for example, the player has to kill a larger number of enemies during a mission in order to reach a certain enemy. The game then confronts the player with the decision to spare or kill one enemy. The latter decision is part of the 'karma system' and is evaluated accordingly. However, the path to this decision is not part of the 'karma system' and thus the killing of the previous opponents is not evaluated by it either.

This closed nature of 'karma systems' distinguishes them from games that offer above-average freedom of play and movement. In so-called 'Open World Games' like the *Gothic* series by Piranha Bytes, players are often required to decide for themselves on the moral justifiability of their actions—made possible by the great freedom of play.

On the basis of the observations made here, a first compilation of criteria which constitute a so called 'karma system' can be made:

1. A 'karma system' continuously confronts the player with moral decisions and their consequences.
2. These decisions are observed by the game and—visible or invisible to the player—rewarded or punished with points, which are recorded on a scale—also visible or invisible—and influence the further gaming experience.
3. The 'karma system' is a closed and constructed system. Criteria, rules, and scenarios for the award of points are determined exclusively by the designers of the game.

These criteria should by no means be regarded as conclusive. Still they can provide some insights into the range of possible moral decision making systems present on the current game market. While Point 3 can be seen as the combining factor of all mentioned forms of moral decision making systems, both Point 1 and 2 serve in separating 'karma systems' from both 'externalized' and 'consequence' systems.

In the following chapter, a detailed analysis of the 'karma system' of *Mass Effect 2* as well as an examination of corresponding processes of reception regarding the concept of karma will be conducted.

4. Mass Effect 2

4.1. Methodology

As proposed in *Theorizing Religion in Digital Games* (Heidbrink et al. 2014, pp. 16–17), both game-immanent and actor-centered perspectives should be factored in when doing research on the topic of religion and games. The following analysis of the 'karma system' of *Mass Effect 2* is therefore conducted in three steps which each focus on at least one of these perspectives and build on each other.

The first step is the actual game (system) analysis. The aim is to clarify exactly which game mechanic and rules constitute the 'karma system' of *Mass Effect 2* and how these are connected with narratives and aesthetics of the game. The result should then be a precise picture of the system with which the players are confronted and which they call the "karma system".

In the second step, an attempt will be made to discuss the newly drawn image of the 'karma system' of *Mass Effect 2* from the 'author' or game designer's perspective. This includes a comparison with earlier forms of 'karma systems', an examination of the influences of other media such as films or television series, as well as economic considerations. This step is important in that it should prevent a certain degree of 'overinterpretation'. A separation of the perspectives of designer and player is necessary, since both sides often approach a game and its interpretation with completely different basic requirements.

The third and final step is to focus on the player's perspective. For the sake of simplicity, representatives of the gaming press will also be included in this category, as they usually take a more player-oriented perspective and are also heavily involved in the coinage and spreading of game related terms. This step is intended to clarify why the 'karma system' of *Mass Effect 2* is called as such by players in the first place. This means connections with the ideas and interpretations of karma presented in Section 3 of this paper will be drawn and an explanation will be attempted.

4.2. The Game

Mass Effect 2 is a role-playing game developed by Bioware, distributed by Electronic Arts and first released on 26 January 2010. 94 out of 100 possible points for the PC[13] and 96 points for the Xbox360 and Playstation 3[14] were awarded on average.

The game is about Commander Shepard, an officer of the "Alliance", a coalition of all nations on Earth in 2183, which is in more or less peaceful contact with numerous alien races after the discovery of extraterrestrial technology on Mars in 2148, which makes it possible to travel to distant planets. In the first part of the series, Shepard is named a "Spectre" by the Council of the Citadel, a coalition of space traveling races that have their seat on a massive space station—the Citadel. He is thus granted almost unlimited powers in the pursuit of orders entrusted to him by the Citadel Council. In one of these missions, the pursuit of a renegade Spectre, Shepard encounters evidence of the existence of an ancient race called the "Reapers", which haunts the universe every few thousand years and wipes out all intelligent life. At the end of the first part, Shepard and the people of the Citadel Council meet a first surprise attack of this threat. *Mass Effect 2* takes place two years after this first decisive battle:

> Two years after Commander Shepard repelled invading Reapers bent on the destruction of organic life, a mysterious new enemy has emerged. On the fringes of known space, something is silently abducting entire human colonies. Now Shepard must work with Cerberus, a ruthless organization devoted to human survival at any cost, to stop the most terrifying threat mankind has ever faced.

---

[13] http://www.metacritic.com/game/pc/mass-effect-2 (accessed on 30 March 2018).
[14] http://www.metacritic.com/game/xbox-360/mass-effect-2 (accessed on 30 March 2018).

To even attempt this perilous mission, Shepard must assemble the galaxy's most elite team and command the most powerful ship ever built. Even then, they say it would be suicide. Commander Shepard intends to prove them wrong[15].

4.3. The Karma System

In the following, the 'karma system' is divided into game mechanic, 'game rules' and influences on other game elements.

4.3.1. The Game Mechanics

The 'ergodic element' of the 'karma system' of *Mass Effect 2* is achieved primarily by two directly interdependent game mechanic: conducting dialogues and the so-called "interrupts".

Dialogues play a central role in the Mass Effect series and are used as the main means of continuing the story arc. A so-called "dialogue wheel" is used, in which the player can select the general tendency of the answers to be given—but not their exact wording (see Figure 2).

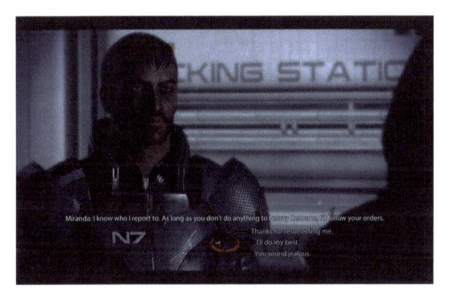

Figure 2. Dialog in *Mass Effect 2*[16].

In some situations, selecting a specific dialog option will result in the credit of either "Paragon" or "Renegade" points. However, the game does not give the player any indication as to whether the current dialogue is such a situation. Also, the game does not directly draw attention to which is the "Paragon" and which is the "Renegade" option. Whether and how many points were credited is only made clear by a message in the game after the selection. The player has no possibility to specifically choose answers based on points given.

The second central game mechanic of the "karma system" is somewhat different: the so-called "interrupts". These are directly connected to the dialogues and only occur in the course of them. During a dialog, at the bottom of the screen, one or two symbols, each representing a "Paragon" (blue

---

15 http://store.steampowered.com/app/24980/Mass_Effect_2/ (accessed on 30 March 2018).
16 All Screenshots in this chapter where taken by the author during a playthrough of *Mass Effect 2*.

wing) or a "Renegade" (red star) interrupt, appear for a few seconds at certain predefined points (see Figure 3).

Figure 3. "Interrupt" symbols[17].

The "interrupt" can then be triggered by pressing the left (Paragon) or right (Renegade) mouse button. Alternatively, the "interrupt" can also be ignored and then has no consequences. When the "interrupt" is triggered, Shepard performs a particularly nefarious or selfless act, depending on the option selected. "Renegade interrupts" usually lead to direct violent—and often spectacularly staged—actions against enemies or threats towards conversation partners and even team mates. "Paragon interrupts", on the other hand, usually result in the peaceful resolution of conflicts or the protection of the innocent. By triggering "interrupts", the player is then credited with a relatively high number of "Paragon" or "Renegade" points. Due to clear indication by coloring and symbols, the player knows exactly which decision will bring him which points. This mechanic thus differs from the dialog mechanic. Only the concrete action that Shepard performs after the "interrupt" is hidden from the player in advance.

4.3.2. The Game Rules

The rules of the "karma system" of *Mass Effect 2* determine when and how many points are to be credited through dialog options and interrupts, how these are recorded and also what effect these points have.

The concrete situations in which points can be collected were, as already mentioned above, strictly determined by the developers of the game. Outside of these predefined situations it is not possible to change the score of the player. The concrete number of points that can be collected with the respective dialogue options and "interrupts" is also firmly defined and can range from 2 points for a slightly important decision to 45 points for serious decisions throughout the story.

The points are recorded on a two-dimensional scale (see Figure 4). "Paragon" and "Renegade" points are listed separately. No points can be deducted, only new points can be gained, so "making amends" for previous actions is not directly possible; at least not in the same way as in *Knights of the Old Republic* or *Fallout 3*.

---

[17] Source: http://masseffect.wikia.com/wiki/Interrupt (accessed on 30 March 2018).

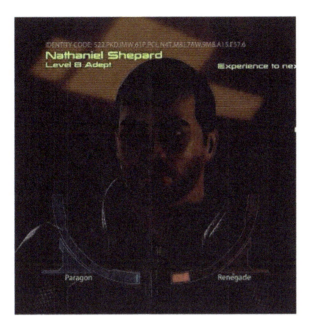

Figure 4. Character view with Paragon/Renegade bar.

The respective "Paragon" and "Renegade" values have a number of effects. The consequences for the story and the aesthetics of the game, which will be discussed in more detail in the following sections, include the change in the character's appearance as well as the general course of action and the course of individual side missions. The latter is made possible by the fact that a certain "Paragon" or "Renegade" score makes additional dialogue options available with which conversation partners can either be persuaded (Paragon) or threatened (Renegade) in order to avoid fights or to achieve discounts with traders.

The rules are based on a fixed point value that must be reached in order to trigger a consequence. Thus the appearance of the character changes only step by step with the achievement of certain "milestones" and also the additional dialogue options can only be activated from a certain, firmly defined point value. The Mass Effect Wiki points out that the availability of dialog options in *Mass Effect 2* does not depend on the total number of points currently collected, but rather on a percentage value:

> The morality system of *Mass Effect 2* works on percentages rather than the total points earned. There is a set number of morality points available in the game. Shepard's current "effective" morality score at any given point is the number of points earned out of the number of points available from the areas the Commander has explored so far. It is possible to have Shepard's Paragon/Renegade scale(s) maxed out, but still not have the percentage required for certain dialog options[18].

This can also result in a dialog option not being available for the second time when the game is played several times, although it was available with a lower score the first time.

It is also important to note that the moral decisions that the player can make can also have an impact without the respective point value having any influence here. This is especially important at

---

18   http://masseffect.wikia.com/wiki/Morality (last access 30 August 2018).

central moments during the main story. For example, the player can decide towards the end of the game, independently of his "Paragon" or "Renegade" value, whether he wants to put the wreck of a technologically very advanced spaceship into the hands of the xenophobic "Cerberus" organization (Renegade) or rather destroy it (Paragon). The player receives points according to his decision. However, the direct effect of his decision (approaching or dissociating himself from "Cerberus") is not affected by this.

4.3.3. Connections to Other Game Systems

Compared to similar systems, the "karma system" of *Mass Effect 2* is distinguished above all by its relatively strong differentiation from other "game systems". The focus of the decision effects lies in the field of the aesthetics and narratives of the game, which is probably aimed preventing the player from making "moral" decisions for "strategic" decisions in order to get special equipment or abilities instead of actually reflecting on the moral implications of his actions.

Nevertheless, there are some—albeit indirect—effects on other areas of the game. It has already been mentioned that the additional dialog options that are activated with a certain "Paragon" or "Renegade" value can also influence the course of missions and thus the narratives themselves. These dialogue options also offer the possibility to animate traders to discounts on the articles offered by them or to slightly increase financial rewards for completed missions. With the financial means released or gained in this way, the player can theoretically get to better equipment more quickly, which, above all, can reduce the difficulty of the repeated fights in the game.

In this combination of "karma system" and "battle" and "trading system" it also becomes clear that the game—despite all efforts to avoid this—prefers a way of playing in which the player chooses a single moral orientation. Such a one-sided orientation leads to a faster collection of points, which in turn makes the additional dialog options available more quickly. The concrete advantages of such a playing style are not very serious, however, since the additional financial means hardly matter and the game balance is not noticeably affected. However, depending on the skills and experience of the player, they can still have an influence on his decisions.

The second effect of the "karma system" also falls within the scope of "reduction of the degree of difficulty". For as already mentioned above, the additional "persuade" and "threaten" options also make it possible to completely avoid battles in certain situations. Here, too, a way of playing is rewarded which focusses on a single moral orientation and thus gets to the corresponding dialogue options more quickly.

4.3.4. Influences on and by the Game Narrative

The most obvious effects of the "karma system" of *Mass Effect 2* can be found in the game's narratives. Indeed, moral dilemmas play a major role in the overall plot of *Mass Effect 2*. The player has to decide again and again how closely he works together with the mysterious organization "Cerberus", which Shepard restored after his alleged death through an attack by allies of the "Reapers" at the beginning of the game. "Cerberus" is the only organization in the power network of the Citadel people that takes the threat posed by the Reapers seriously and wants to support Shepard in his fight against them. However, the organization has previously attracted particular attention for its xenophobic attitude towards all races other than humanity and for ethically dubious actions such as scientific experiments on children. Moreover, even during the course of the game, it is never quite clear which agenda the organization itself and its leader, the so-called "Illusive Man", pursues.

The major plot line of *Mass Effect 2*, the gathering of a team of specialists to free the human colonists kidnapped by the allies of the "Reapers", is also all about weighing moral issues; each of the recruited specialists representing a different moral archetype.

This becomes particularly clear in a mission in which the player must recruit one of two possible specialists, each covering opposite moral spectra. Shepard is hired by the Asari people to track down an executor of the law or "Justicar" named Samara and win her over. The "Justicar" of the Asari are notorious for their strict observance and enforcement of a strict moral code of honor. It turns out that Samara is currently looking for Morinth, her own daughter, who, due to a rare genetic effect, is able to increase her own physical and spiritual power by merging her thoughts with those of other intelligent creatures and thus killing them. Morinth has developed into a powerful being, which is at the same time enormously unscrupulous and unpredictable. At the end of the recruitment mission, the player can decide to kill either Samara or Morinth and add the survivor to his team. Samara represents the ideal image of the "Paragon" in this scenario, while Morinth could be described as "Renegade" in its most extreme form.

However, such clear moral extremes are not common in *Mass Effect 2* and other companions often turn out to be more complex and their motives usually go beyond pure hunger for power. A good example is Jack, a psychologically gifted young woman whom Shepard has to free from a prison ship and convince to join him. It turns out that Jack was a victim of the above mentioned experiments on children by the "Cerberus" organization and that she is understandably very hostile towards them. But since Shepard is initially still dependent on the support of "Cerberus", it's time to find a way to convince Jack to join him anyway, either through clear lies or the honest promise to hold the culprits at Cerberus to account. Such situations then usually lead to the so-called "loyalty missions" in the context of which Shepard must win the final loyalty of his companions by fulfilling a special mission for and with them.

These "loyalty missions" also represent another important point in the effects of the "karma system" of *Mass Effect 2*, because they usually present the player with particularly difficult moral decisions. However, if loyalty to individual team members is not established by the end of the game—for example, by denying loyalty mission or making moral decisions that the person does not support—then the possibility that this companion will be killed in the final mission of the main action also increases. As a result, this person will no longer appear in *Mass Effect 3*, the last part of the *Mass Effect* trilogy. In the most extreme case, even Shepard himself can perish in this mission—of course only after the target has been fulfilled—and can therefore not be taken over into the sequel game (the player then has to create a new "Shepard" for the game). Interestingly, this can happen especially when Shepard follows a consequent "Renegade" course, which also includes lack of personal ties to his teammates. A Shepard with a focus on "Paragon" points and decisions tends to bring more companions and above all himself through the last mission.

What may already become clear here is a slight tendency of the developers to prefer or reward the path of the "Paragon", at least in the narrative aspects of the game. Although it is also possible to save your team and yourself by focusing on "Renegade" points, it is often necessary to use "Paragon" conversation options to establish the necessary personal ties to the team members. This also illustrates the image that Bioware itself draws of the two ideal types of "Paragon" and "Renegade" and which is summarized as follows in the Mass Effect Wiki:

> Paragon points are gained for compassionate and heroic actions. […] Points are often gained when asking about feelings and motivations of characters.
>
> […]
>
> Renegade points are gained for apathetic and ruthless actions. […] Many sarcastic and joking remarks are assigned Renegade points[19].

The conversation options that lead to better understanding and thus loyalty on the part of the teammates will therefore in most cases be the "Paragon" options.

However, the "karma system" of *Mass Effect 2* influences the narrative structures of the game on another level, which is perhaps less obvious. The sheer existence of this system alone often puts action and missions—both main and sub missions—into a framework that leads to decisions between

---

[19]   http://masseffect.wikia.com/wiki/Morality (last access 30 August 2018).

two options from which the player must choose. However, the "karma system" of *Mass Effect 2* only knows two values, namely "Paragon" and "Renegade", which, simply through their presentation in dialogues, the presentation in the character view, as well as through aesthetic aspects, almost impose the image of two moral spectra to be understood as contradictory. Accordingly, each such decision must be assigned a moral value, which contradicts the principle of moral dilemmas actually pursued by the developers.

A good example of how the "karma system" can also superimpose narrative structures and principles is provided by Daniel Floyd, owner of the Youtube Channel Extra Credits[20]. He refers to a situation in *Mass Effect 2* where the player has to decide whether he should wipe out or reprogram a species of artificial intelligences that are hostile to humans and have developed their own consciousness. In the game, the wiping is rewarded with "Renegade" and the reprogramming with "Paragon" points. Floyd comments on this:

> This moment in the game really only falls short in one way: Not embedding the question into the game mechanics.

> As our medium evolves, designers are learning to embed and reference these dilemmas with all the tools that games provide. *Mass Effect 2* does a brilliant job of making you live the dilemma of choosing between what may well be genocide and the utter subversion of an entire race's free will.

> Unfortunately the designers missed a great opportunity to reinforce this dilemma at its conclusion. If both choices had resulted in renegade points instead of one being labelled the "Renegade" choice, and the other being the good "Paragon" choice, this would have been a fully realized attempt at using the medium of gaming to provide the player with a moment of introspection.

> Here alone, the designers fell short, looking at the question and the game as separate entities[21].

Here the limits of a purely narrative-based game analysis become clear, because before the moral intention of the developers can be examined here, it should be considered that in this case "game system" and narratives were actually treated separately in order to keep the possibility open for the player to finish the game without collecting "Renegade" points.

This view of course opens up new perspectives on the moral intentionality of the developers. However, this should always be taken with caution without appropriately documented statements by the developers themselves.

4.3.5. Influences on the Game Aesthetics

The (visually) most obvious effect of the "karma system" of *Mass Effect 2* is in its aesthetics and above all in the aesthetic development of the player character. As already mentioned, Shepard is fatally injured at the beginning of the game by an attack of allies of the "Reapers" and then recovered and restored by "Cerberus". As a result of this process, slight scars appear on his face after the treatment (see Figure 5). These scars correspond to Shepard's "Paragon" and "Renegade" value. In the game itself, this is explained in a message that the player receives: "Negative attitudes and aggressive acts create adverse reactions with your cybernetic implants, while peaceful thoughts and compassionate actions promote healing. If you maintain a positive outlook, I believe your facial scarring will heal on its own".

---

[20] https://www.youtube.com/channel/UCCODfTcd5M1JavPCOr_Uydg (last access 30 August 2018).
[21] Transcribed from https://www.youtube.com/watch?v=_2Tp8Jopdlc (last access 30 August 2018).

If the "Renegade" value is high, the appearance of the player character can change drastically and give Shepard a very gloomy, perhaps even "inhuman" look, with the change taking place gradually and not fluently (see Figure 5).

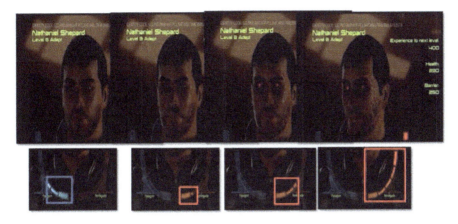

Figure 5. Scar development in relation to the "Renegade" value.

The "Paragon" value itself does not create any additional change in appearance. A high score in this area only causes Shepard to keep his "normal" face—free of scars; a corresponding visualization of a high "Paragon" value does not exist. At this point there is also the only possibility of making up for "evil" decisions made earlier, because at least the optical effects of the "Renegade" way can be compensated with a sufficient number of "Paragon" points.

Another form of visualization of the "karma system" is found in the coloring of individual game elements; blue stands for the "Paragon" and red for the "Renegade". This color coding runs through the entire game, such as the respective bars in the character view and the color of the "Renegade Scars" (see Figures 4 and 5) and the respective symbols during the "Interrupts".

This coding becomes very clear again at the end of *Mass Effect 2*. During the game, Shepard must keep in touch with the "Illusive Man", the leader of "Cerberus". In such moments he is always shown sitting on a chair in front of a red and blue shining sun. Depending on whether the player decides at the end of the game to surrender (Renegade) or destroy (Paragon) the alien ship, the sun is colored either red or blue in the background during the last dialog between Shepard and the "Illusive Man" (see Figure 6).

Due to the lack of direct comments by developers on the coloring and aesthetic effects of the "Paragon" and "Renegade" values, it makes little sense to attempt to attribute an intention or interpretation to the respective design decisions. However, the influences that may have played a role here will be discussed in more detail in the following sections.

Figure 6. "Illusive Man".

4.3.6. Preliminary Conclusion

In the previous sections, an attempt was made to draw as precise an image as possible of the 'karma system' of *Mass Effect 2*. Among other things, one aspect stands out here above all that runs through the entire system; whether it is the technical implementation of the point system, the concrete design of moral questions or the 'visualization' of the system: 'duality'.

Despite all the efforts of the game developers, it creates the overall impression of a clear juxtaposition of two moral spectra, which are not mutually exclusive from a game rules point of view, but achieve the greatest in-game effect in each extreme. A system of moral grey areas and dilemmas can thus develop into a system of 'black and white', of 'good and evil'. Mind you: 'can', but not 'must'. How the system is ultimately received is always in the player's view and will therefore also be examined in more detail in the following sections.

But first the view of the game's developers and designers, Bioware, will be taken to get a better insight into the design process and the influences it is subject to.

4.4. The Game Designer Perspective

It has already been pointed out that attributing certain intentions of game developers when creating a game is an extremely critical process. The main reason for this is that a multitude of factors play a role in the process of game development which are not immediately apparent when looking at the actual game and thus lead to the attribution of meanings which—at least by the developers of the game—were not intended at all.

But how do design decisions come about and what are the factors that can play a role here? Ulf Hagen addressed this question in his article "Where do Game Design Ideas Come From?" He conducted exemplary surveys at four development studios and compiled the "sources of inspiration" in a ranking sorted by importance. First, however, he notes that in most computer games both "new" and "reprocessed" ideas can be found:

My study shows that a game concept generally consists of two parts:

1. The recycled part consists of ideas that has been used before in earlier games, in a movie, a book etc. Usually they can be bundled together under labels—e.g., a genre name ("This is a First Person Shooter game") or a brand ("This is a new game in the Battlefield series") or with reference to a film ("The game is based on a film with the same title").

2. The inventive part consists of game ideas that have not been used in the same way in games before. It is hard to make an unambiguous definition of what an inventive idea is, since newness is a relative concept. (Hagen 2009, p. 4)

He then divides the actual design ideas into the following areas:

1. The game domain

   (a) The game's (dominant) genre
   (b) Another game genre
   (c) Another game (or game brand)

2. Narratives and visual art

   (a) Cinematography and the film domain
   (b) Books
   (c) Other narratives

3. Human activities

   (a) Sports
   (b) Playful activities

(c)   War and warfare

4.   Human technology and artifactss

(a)   Historical or contemporary technology and artifacts

(b)   Future technology and artifacts (Hagen 2009, p. 10)

For the context of the study of the 'karma system' of *Mass Effect 2*, above all points 1 and 2—which are to be dealt with under the umbrella term "intertextual and intermedial influences" are of importance, since neither sporting, playful or warlike activities play a direct role here and the recourse to possible future technology can also be neglected.

Another important point that Hagen only touches on briefly is the economic factor (Hagen 2009, p. 3). This includes above all considerations regarding the feasibility and 'sellability' of design decisions, because after all, a computer game today is primarily a product that should sell as well as possible.

4.4.1. Intertextual and Intermedial Influences

When looking at intertextual influences—i.e., influences from the field of computer games—it is noticeable that a clear separation between intertextual and intermedial factors is often not possible. An example of this is the observation made by Hagen that the dominant game genre has a great influence on design decisions. In the case of *Mass Effect 2*, this is the genre of 'role playing games'. Apperley points out, however, that the genre of "role-playing games" is a "remediation"—perhaps inaccurately translated as "processing" or "adoption"—of concepts of classical "pen and paper role-playing games", such as the well-known *Dungeons and Dragons* from 1974 onto the computer (Apperley 2006, p. 17). Here, as in computer-based "role-playing", the progress of the character, or—as he calls it with reference to David Myers—the "character transformation" is the defining criterion of the genre (cf. Myers 2003, p. 19).

If we now look at *Mass Effect 2* in this light, we notice that although character progression also plays an important role here, direct references to "classic" role-playing games such as *Dungeons and Dragons* can hardly be found. This connection only becomes clear again through an intertextual view of the development of the genre. This can be illustrated by the "karma systems" of *Mass Effect 2* and *Star Wars—Knights often the Old Republic* and the moral decision making system of another game from Bioware, namely *Baldur's Gate 2* from 2000.

Baldur's Gate 2 is set in the fantasy world of *Dungeons and Dragons* (specifically in the "Forgotten Realms" setting) and its moral system is, like many other aspects of the game, closely linked to the *Advanced Dungeons and Dragons* ruleset. When creating a character at the beginning of the game, as in the 'pen and paper' template, the player is asked to select the "alignment" of his main character. The selection of the available "alignments" are based on the two-axis "Good to Evil" and "Lawful to Chaotic" systems specified by the rules.

The combination of "Good", "Evil", "Lawful", "Chaotic", and the "Neutral" in the middle of the axis results in nine possible (see Table 2).

Table 2. Alignment Matrix in Dungeons and Dragons.

Lawful Good	Neutral Good	Chaotic Good
Lawful Neutral	True Neutral	Chaotic Neutral
Lawful Evil	Neutral Evil	Chaotic Evil

The player—true to the principle of a 'role playing game'—is now required to fit in with the role he has chosen and to make appropriate decisions during the game.

Baldur's Gate 2 was a great financial success for Bioware at that time, which was mainly due to the different experiences of the player playing through the game several times, based on the moral orientation. So it comes as no surprise that this principle was essentially adhered to when the next major project was launched—*Star Wars: Knights of the Old Republic*.

Here too, Bioware took the moral principles provided by the original—in this case the *Star Wars* films by George Lucas—and processed them in the 'karma system' of the game. The film template provided a strongly dualistic moral system at the core of which the possibility was reserved to change from one moral spectrum to the other; from the "dark side of Force" to the "light side" and back again. Implementing this principle in the game again guaranteed an increased replay value and allowed Bioware to tell a multi-layered story with different perspectives at the same time, just as *Baldurs Gate 2* had already done. However, the multidimensional moral system of *Dungeons and Dragons* and *Baldur's Gate 2* was reduced to the simple two-dimensional conflict between 'good' and 'evil'; most likely due to the lack of compatibility with the clear dualism between 'light' and 'dark' firmly anchored in the *Star Wars* saga.

Although *Mass Effect 2*, in contrast to *Baldur's Gate 2* and *Knights of the Old Republic*, is a game whose complete scenario was created by Bioware itself, when looking at the 'karma system' of *Mass Effect 2* and above all the comparison between the two, it quickly becomes clear that the same principles were applied here and that in many places it is a direct adoption or further development of elements of the predecessor systems.

For example, it is very likely that the typical color scheme, which has elements of both "Paragon" and "Renegade", is directly inspired by the classic "red equals evil" and "blue equals good" classification of the Star Wars universe. The aesthetic development of the player character is similar in both *Mass Effect 2* and *Knights of the Old Republic*. Because in the latter it belongs firmly to the rules of the fictional world that a permanent turn towards the "dark side" brings about a rapid deterioration of the physical appearance. The same process is found in *Mass Effect 2*, only here—true to the highly technological universe of Mass Effect—it is rationally explained with Shepard's medical restoration at the beginning of the game.

Interestingly, the element of 'ugly evil' can also be found in other games with 'karma systems' such as the *Fable* series or the *Black and White* games by Peter Molyneux. Usually the 'ugly', sometimes even almost 'devil-like' appearance of characters with evil orientation is opposed by a corresponding 'angelic' appearance of characters with particularly good orientation, which is neither the case with *Mass Effect 2* or *Knights of the Old Republic*, nor with any other game from Bioware. It is therefore reasonable to assume that the 'moral aesthetics' of *Knights of the Old Republic* and *Mass Effect 2* are not inspired by the latent Christian aesthetics of these other games, but rather refer directly to the Star Wars canon and its own aesthetics.

This could be further reinforced by another game created by Bioware in 2003 (so after *Knights of the Old Republic* but prior the first *Mass Effect*): *Jade Empire*. Here, the 'karma system' (represented by the "Way of the Open Palm" and the "Way of the Closed Fist" works very much like the "light side/dark side" system of *Knights of the Old Republic* and both alignments are represented by the colors blue (open palm) and red (closed fist) as well as visual representations on the player character. The fan-made wiki of *Jade Empire* even draws a direct comparison between both systems[22].

An important point in which the 'karma system' of *Mass Effect 2* clearly differs from that of *Knights of the Old Republic* is the way in which the collected points are 'recorded'. While the points collected in *Knights of the Old Republic* move a marker back and forth on a 'light to dark' scale (see Figure 1) and thus—true to the Star Wars model—allow switching between the 'light' and the 'dark' side, the 'Paragon' and 'Renegade' points in *Mass Effect 2* are listed separately. This is probably best explained by Bioware's own Mass Effect Universe, in which clear 'good' and 'evil' attributions do not occur frequently and 'moral grey areas' are more prevalent.

---

[22] http://jadeempire.wikia.com/wiki/Way_of_the_Open_Palmandhttp://jadeempire.wikia.com/wiki/Way_of_the_Closed_Fist (accessed on 11 April 2018).

Furthermore, Bioware also tried to separate the 'karma system' of *Mass Effect 2* from other systems of the game where possible, which differentiates it in another point from the 'karma system' of *Knights of the Old Republic*. The reason for this was probably the attempt to integrate the moral decisions in the game 'more sensibly' into the narrative structures and thus not force the player to make certain decisions if he wants to receive certain rewards or abilities that cannot otherwise be obtained. This decision can also be regarded as an economic decision, but this will be examined in more detail in the next section.

For the later investigation of the reception of the 'karma system' of *Mass Effect 2* by the players, the observations made here are important in such a way that they naturally do not remain hidden from the average player himself and even more so from the gaming press. A game is never received in a 'vacuum', but is always perceived in the context of related games, the respective genre and above all narrative influences. Especially systems that are technically and aesthetically very similar can be and are easily compared by the players and received in the same context.

4.4.2. Economical Factors

Ulf Hagen also briefly addresses the question of economic factors in the design process:

When producing expensive AAA-titles, the phases of the production process are substantially influenced by the financing situation of the game. The first stage, often called the concept phase, is about designing a game concept to be presented to a potential sponsor (often an external publisher or the internal financial department). The pitch could be presented in a (pitch) document, but it could also take the form of an oral presentation, maybe supported by a Powerpoint presentation, or so called concept art. In this stage the design team is very small, since there is yet no money provided for the game. (Hagen 2009, p. 3)

However, he does not go into the exact factors that can influence the decisions of the funders, nor into the fact that the contact between the publisher and the game developer does not end with the initial financing. Rather, the publisher of a game—depending on the respective company philosophy and the reputation of the developer studio—sometimes exerts more or sometimes less influence on the entire process, for example by setting deadlines and checking the progress and quality of the game product. This task often falls to the so-called 'game producer', who among other things acts as a liaison between publisher and developer (Jobs in der Spielebranche 2008). It goes without saying that the economic success of the end product is in the interest of the investor and ultimately—in most cases—also of the development studio.

The internet video series *Extra Credits*, written by James Portnow and narrated and illustrated by Daniel Floyd, explains how relevant this factor can be for the analysis carried out here. In the episode *Video Games and Choice* he defines the process of creating a computer game as 'designing decisions':

As a game designer, you are crafting a series of decisions for a player to make. And that chain of decisions makes up the gameplay experience. This is the core of game design and it's one of the first things they teach you as a game designer.

He divides these 'decisions' into 'problems', i.e., problems with a clear 'best' solution, and 'choices', i.e., decision possibilities for which there is no clear best solution.

In addition, *Extra Credits* notes that problems occur far more often in computer games than real decisions. He even goes so far as to postulate that many apparent decisions in current games are merely problems disguised as such and explains this using a practical example:

Problems are really at the heart of what we consider gaming today and there's nothing wrong with that. But it's important that we distinguish them from choices. [...] Because without distinguishing between the two it's very easy to reduce choices to just being simple problems to solve. How many times has a game presented you with something that should be a choice but instead was just a simple problem with a clear right answer.

[...]

Say you have to decide between and apple and an orange, which we would normally consider a choice. But say you know that an apple is worth five bucks and an orange is worth ten and the goal of the game is to get the most money. Deciding between those two is no longer a choice, it's basic problem solving[23].

Extra Credits attributes this tendency to problems and away from "real" decisions to what he considers to be a predominant preference among players for the "tentiable benefit of solving problems over the more nebulous and work intensive satisfaction of making a choice", even if such a statement is difficult to prove without appropriate data.

Nevertheless, this observation is important for the context of this examination, because it implies that in the process of game design not always a 'deeper' or 'more significant' background of decisions is sought, but also the very practical aspect of the 'entertainment' of a game or 'game system' should be considered. In the case of the moral decisions of a 'karma system', this may mean that the developers' preference for a certain moral orientation does not necessarily have to be understood 'pedagogically'. Of course, this possibility cannot be ruled out and ultimately also depends strongly on the 'game experience' that the designers of the game want to convey, but from a purely economic perspective—far from any possible 'instructive' intention—factors such as 'fun', 'game flow', and 'accessibility' are of course also important. Questions such as 'What has proven itself?' or 'What could possibly overtax or frustrate the player?' take center stage and influence the design decisions.

How central these factors ultimately turn out in the design process strongly depends on the success and design philosophy of the respective development studio as well as the degree of "interference" by the publisher. On the one hand, a high degree of independence can be assumed in the case of Bioware, which can be explained by the enormous financial success of earlier titles of this developer. In a comparison of the 'karma systems' *Mass Effect 2* and *Star Wars: Knights of the Old Republic*, however, it can be assumed that the publisher and license holder LucasArts, founded by George Lucas, had far more influence on the development process—especially to ensure the game's loyalty to the Star Wars 'franchise'—than Electronic Arts did with the former. Thus, with *Mass Effect 2* Bioware had more creative scope, especially in the design of the "karma system" and could shift its design more towards "real" decisions, even if, as explained above, this did not succeed 100 percent.

In another episode called *Video Games and Moral Choices*, *Extra Credits* then comes directly to a conclusion that is of enormous importance for the understanding of the design and reception of 'karma systems'. He deals here with the question why such systems are often so simple and two-dimensional and do not offer a broader selection of moral spectra and comes to a simple but extremely accurate result:

A lot of people may lay the blame on bad writing, but I don't think the writers are to blame for this one. I think it comes down to something much simpler: money.

When most people think of deep moral choices they think about a breadth of options, but a broad set of options for a story line decision usually means a very divergent story and a divergent story means more content and more content is going to cost more development dollars. And those dollars are almost never there[24].

The development of a complex, multidimensional moral system within a game, which should then also have a noticeable effect on the narratives, costs money. A two-dimensional moral system is therefore practicable because, on the one hand, it makes different decisions possible, but, on the other hand, it is manageable enough to actually 'count' the decisions made. If we look at this in the

---

[23]   Transcribed from https://www.youtube.com/watch?v=jlOXAtPvMDk (last access 30 August 2018).
[24]   Transcribed from https://www.youtube.com/watch?v=6_KU3IUx3u0 (last access 30 August 2018).

context of *Mass Effect 2*, it may explain why, despite the developers' attempt to move away from a pure 'good/evil' dichotomy, a clearly oriented moral attitude has stronger effects and is therefore more desirable for the player than a 'balanced' way of playing. This could then be understood as a 'balancing act' between 'more realistic' moral questions based on 'real' decisions and at the same time recognizable and motivating consequences for the player. Of course, a multidimensional version of the 'karma system' of *Mass Effect 2* would have been conceivable, for example by adding another bar for 'neutral' points. Due to the strong connection of the 'karma system' to the narrative structures of the game, however, this would have meant an increased production effort, which would probably not have been worthwhile in the eyes of the developers and sponsors.

To strengthen this observation, it is perhaps useful take a look at another game with a 'karma system' which arguably does not fit this description: *Planescape: Torment* by Black Isle Studios[25]. Without going into too much detail on the story of this very complex and deep role playing game, *Planescape: Torment*'s 'karma system' can be seen as a mixture of dynamic moral systems like that of *Mass Effect 2* and static systems like those of *Baldur's Gate* and *Dungeons and Dragons*. The player starts on a *Dungeons and Dragons*-like alignment matrix as "true neutral". From there, his alignment is dynamically changed due to decisions made during the course of the game[26]. In contrast to *Mass Effect 2* and many other 'karma systems', this is a multidimensional system, where every possible alignment offers unique consequences and effects, both in the story of the game (e.g., availability of factions) and in the form of items that can only be used with a certain alignment.

This is made possible by the fact that *Planescape: Torment* is a primarily text-based game. Although there are graphical representations of environment and characters in the game (the game uses the Infinity engine created by Bioware), the story is usually driven forward in the form of (mostly non-voice acted) dialogues. The production effort is thus significantly lower than with more elaborately produced games such as *Mass Effect 2*, where complex animations, the work of voice actors and possibly cut scenes have to be considered for each new element.

It should not be implied here at all that these economic factors alone decide on the design of game elements. Especially a developer studio like Bioware which traditionally attaches great importance to sophisticated narratives and emotional involvement of the player would be wronged by such a statement. However, it cannot be denied—and must not be ignored in any way when analyzing such a game element—that the development of a game in our time is a business in the millions and sponsors, as in the film industry, take a high financial risk when financing a new game. Accordingly, the influence of the industry on the conception, design and not least the resulting reception by the players must also be assessed.

4.5. The Player Perspective

If you take a look at the results obtained so far regarding the processing of the karma concept in 'karma systems', then these initially seem rather sobering, as karma is not mentioned at any point by the game designers. Although intertextual, intermedia, and economic influences can plausibly trace how the design of a 'karma system' can come about, they do not provide an indicator as to why the term karma was used at all for these systems.

However, in the preceding chapters, it was already mentioned that the term 'karma system' or 'karma meter' or 'karma scale' is not an invention of the game designers, but a term used by players and the gaming press to summarize and compare these systems.

Using the discourse history of the karma concept presented in Section 2 and the detailed description of the 'karma system' of *Mass Effect 2* given in this chapter, an exemplary attempt will

---

[25]   Interestingly, Black Isle Studies are also known for doing contract work for Bioware (including for *Baldur's Gate I* and *II*).
[26]   http://torment.wikia.com/wiki/Alignment (accessed on 11 April 2018).

now be made to clarify how such a game system can come to be associated with karma and what this means for recent receptions of the concept.

4.5.1. Where Does the 'Karma' in Karma Systems Come From?

Before dealing with the question of the contextual connection between 'karma systems' and karma concepts, it is important to point out that at a significant point in their connection, the player's perspective and the designer's perspective meet. Even if the adoption of the karma term to certain forms of moral decision making systems is indeed the work of players and the gaming press, the term itself was associated with them for the first time in a game.

This game is *Fallout 3*, already presented in Section 3, because only here—and in no other game—is the 'moral value', which is credited to the player for good and bad deeds explicitly called karma. Due to the strong reception of the game and its direct successor *Fallout: New Vegas*, the responsible developers, Bethesda Softworks, can certainly be identified as 'initiators' of the term karma in the game landscape.

But moral systems, which players currently call 'karma systems', existed before *Fallout 3*, so the use of the term alone does not explain why it has become a generic term for other moral systems, such as that of *Mass Effect 2*—which differs from that of *Fallout 3* in crucial points.

Nevertheless, the adoption of the term says a lot from the point of its introduction to the world of games—namely, that certain types of moral systems combine elements that seem to be so compatible with the ideas of the players of karma that it can serve as an umbrella term for a number of comparable systems. If we now look at the 'karma system' of *Mass Effect 2* depicted in the preceding sections, the question then arises as to which elements make it so compatible with the player's understanding of karma and whether traces of the discourse history of the karma term can be found here.

4.5.2. How Much 'Karma' Is in Karma Systems?

In order to attempt to examine the acceptance of the karma concept by players with regard to certain moral systems, it is necessary to refer again to the definition of 'karma systems' presented in Section 3.4. However, this definition is mainly based on observations from exemplary games—which are also associated with 'karma systems' by players and the gaming press—and mainly serves the purpose of providing a technically precise delimitation of the research object. For this reason, we want to check again what players and game journalists actually associate with 'karma systems' in their own words and compare the two definitions with each other.

An example of player side definitions can be found on the *Tvtropes.org* website, a Wikipedia-like Web 2.0 platform, where users of the site can mainly describe so-called 'tropes'—i.e., elements and topics that occur repeatedly in films and TV series but also in computer games. On this page an entry with the name "karma meter" can be found:

> Some games employ a type of morality in their gameplay. Actions taken within the game affect the player, and sometimes how the player is treated by the plot and NPC. This happens even if there were no witnesses to the action and no circumstances that point to you. Some games will make it impossible for one to continue if their karma Meter is too low, or give a bad ending. Others will simply result in the character having an "evil alignment" and playing this way[27].

A similar description can be found on the online platform *Gamasutra.com* in an article by Christopher Aaby called *Mass Effect 2* and game storytelling with karma systems, which takes a somewhat more critical approach:

---

[27] http://tvtropes.org/pmwiki/pmwiki.php/Main/KarmaMeter (accessed on 30 March 2018).

There have been countless takes on the same theme—from the arbitrary "dark side/light side" sliders, over reputation meters (general or spread over factions), personal morality, or even styles of play that are very specific to the game at hand [. . .].

It's hard to generalize about these systems, but safe to say that these systems measure something which relates to your character, and that character's relationship with the surrounding world. Interestingly, these systems are generally in place whether or not others are around to witness your actions. In other words, it would appear that these systems measure a sort of internal dialogue for your character. It's really like the identity of your character, as seen by the character itself.

Either that, or Big Brother is watching, and news travel really fast. This can feel like the case in, say, *Fallout 3*, where you might steal something completely unnoticed, or butcher a group of innocents out in the middle of nowhere, and it will still come back to haunt you. (Aaby 2011)

If we now refer again to the somewhat more technical definition in Section 3.4, we can actually find similarities here, even if the weighting of the various criteria shifts.

Firstly, there is the moral aspect. As in the definition previously formulated, this seems to be a decisive factor; whereby Christopher Aaby's description also makes it clear that the "simple" categories "evil" and "good" are not always assumed. He cites an example of this:

Overlord 1 & 2 for instance had a corruption meter which was not a measure of how evil you are, but rather just what kind of evil you are, alluding of course to the fact that you play an evil character, like it or not. (Aaby 2011)

This explains why the 'karma system' of *Mass Effect 2* can also be counted as such, although here too there is no clear distinction between "good" and "evil", but as Aaby puts it "something like idealism versus cynicism".

This statement is also made on *Tvtropes.net*:

Mass Effect included a clever reconstruction on the karma meter with the Paragon/Renegade system. Rather than good and evil, the meter represents idealism and cynicism[28].

However, as already explained earlier in this chapter, this new approach is diluted in some places by certain design decisions made by Bioware and replaced by a more classic impression of "good" and "evil".

A second aspect that can be found in players and the gaming press as well as in the definition formulated for this work is what could perhaps be described as 'cause and effect'. In concrete terms, this means that the actions carried out by the player—within the framework of the rules defined for the 'karma system'—can have consequences for the further course of the game, be it an "evil alignment" or a "bad ending" as described by *Tvtropes.org*, or an influence on the appearance and relationship with fellow players as in *Mass Effect 2*, the tenor here is that actions can have consequences that the player must consider.

The third aspect is how these actions are registered by the game. Both *Tvtropes.org* and Christopher Abbey find that, in a 'karma system', the player actions are evaluated "whether or not others are around to witness your action". The 'karma system' presents itself to players as an invisible force of judgement or, as Aaby puts it, as an "internal dialogue". This is also the case in *Mass Effect 2*, where at least part of an attempt is made to explain the consequences of the player's actions on the player himself 'rationally'; for example with the 'scientific' explanation of scar formation based on Shepard's physical restoration at the beginning of the game and the effects of aggressive and compassionate

---

28 http://tvtropes.org/pmwiki/pmwiki.php/Main/KarmaMeter (accessed on 30 March 2018).

actions. This 'rational' approach is not consistently maintained even in *Mass Effect 2*; for example, the survival of teammates dependent on Shepard's "Paragon" or "Renegade" value at the end of the game may just as well be explained by their loyalty and thus increased performance, other factors such as Shepard's own survival at the end of the mission or other aesthetic aspects such as the discoloration of the sun in the final dialogue can hardly be explained.

It is these three aspects of a 'karma system' such as that of *Mass Effect 2*—morality, "cause and effect" and the "invisible judgement instance"—on the basis of which a possible connection to the discourse history of the karma concept can be recognized. For example, it is quite conceivable that for the recipients, the players of 'karma systems', the connection of karma and moral questions does not seem to be problematic because they are not the first ones who have connected karma and morality. Rather, this understanding can be explained by processes of interpretation and reinterpretation that began almost 150 years ago with the Theosophical Society and have continued through various channels such as the 'New Age movement' and the mass media into modern times. But it is also important to note that although the category of morality is included in the term karma here, the concrete meaning of 'morality' is again the result of complementary factors. These include not only current discourses on morality and ethics, which are reflected in the "cynic versus idealist" system of *Mass Effect 2*. Christopher Aaby writes:

> The first thing this makes me think is that it is a very believable system within the Mass Effect narrative. I often have a problem believing when my wickedly evil character decides to earn a couple of gamebucks rescuing kittens, or my virtuous hero agrees to do a little assassinating... all in the name of good of course. Mass Effect has a narrative to stick to—as Commander Shephard, you are out to save the galaxy, no discussion. And to have any kind of integrity, that character has to be pretty damn virtuous in some way or other. The system lives within those limitations, without feeling stifled or meaningless. (Aaby 2011)

Aaby speaks of "limitations", which result from the story that the game is supposed to tell. Depending on the focus of the respective developers on high-quality and thus credible narratives—and especially Bioware has a reputation to lose here—the notions of morality in 'karma systems' are often also to be sought in these limitations and explained with them.

It can also be assumed that the reference to morality and moral questions alone does not legitimize the use of the karma concept. This is only achieved through the combination with the 'cause and effect' principle, which can be traced back to the rationalization efforts of the neo-Hinduist reform movements; as well as the frequent feeling of an omnipresent, invisible authority of judgement, which certainly bears similarities with theosophical ideas of karma as an infallible law and as 'instructive power'. Even if the instructive effects of 'karma systems' can vary greatly from game to game, based on the above-mentioned 'limitations'.

Of course, it should never be assumed that the adoption of the karma term into computer game jargon—both on the part of the players and on the part of some designers—is a direct and also deliberate adoption of neo-Hinduist or theosophical ideas. In fact, it is much more probable that here a very ambivalent concept of karma comes to the surface, which in its most fundamental form may be influenced by theosophical thoughts; however, in the course of the spread of the term during the 'New Age movement' and later mass media such as films, series and books and the resulting adaptation to the understanding of a broader audience, its meaning was greatly simplified and broken down to that basic understanding which is also reflected in the reception of the 'karma system' of *Mass Effect 2*: An invisible moral authority that acts in accordance with the law of cause and effect.

The concrete meaning and weighting of individual elements of this idea of karma depends on how a game presents itself and how the respective 'karma system' is implemented, which in turn depends among other things on the influencing factors presented earlier.

But not all elements of a 'karma system' show traces of past discourses around the karma concept. There is one topic in particular which can be found time and again—especially in forum discussions: that of karma 'points'. This particular case will be discussed in the next section.

4.5.3. How Much 'Karma System' Is in Karma?

Already in the definition formulated in Section 3.4 it was pointed out that 'karma systems' use a point system, which evaluates the actions of the player to different degrees and then tracks this value on a clear scale. In the above mentioned descriptions of Christopher Aaby this is not directly reflected, but on *Tvtropes.org*:

> *Mass Effect 2* does away with non-combat skills and makes your ability to intimidate or charm people based entirely on your Renegade and Paragon points, respectively. This has the unfortunate side effect of penalizing you heavily for not always picking the same thing, or even taking a more neutral approach[29].

In other places too, in connection with "karma systems", "karma points", or "karma values" are repeatedly spoken of. For example, on the *Mass Effect 2* website *The Foxhole*:

> The real change when it comes to the conversation system regards the Paragon (good) and Renegade (Evil—or rather "pragmatic") status of the character and diplomatic choices related. Strictly speaking, the karma system of *Mass Effect 2* is about the same than the first game with however one novelty that I'd call "Instant karma Actions". When such an action is possible, a mouse icon appears for a limited time either in blue and to the bottom right of the screen for paragon karma actions or in red and at the bottom left for renegade ones. Clicking the corresponding mouse button when the icon is displayed triggers a cinematic in which Shepard performs either a bold or nice move with interesting results and which automatically grants the corresponding karma points. (Starfox 2010)

Further references to karma points or a karma value interestingly enough can be found especially when players talk about problems in the game in web forums. For example, forum user *R1c3* on the forum of the website *Computerbase.de* reacts to a question about a situation in *Mass Effect 2* in which the player has to settle a dispute between two companions with the following comment:

> There is also a dialogue option with which you don't lose loyalty to either of them, at least with me all squad members were loyal, without exception, but you might need a high karma value to get this dialogue option.

In the same discussion, the user *Andianer* also speaks out:

> During the fight between Tali and Legion you need a lot of good/bad karma. In case of need you can have another 4 eyes conversation with everyone afterwards—if I remember correctly. But it's also in the wiki[30].

Karma points or karma values are discussed especially when there are concrete problems within the game. This is particularly interesting because such questions are only possible due to the special nature of a game and, above all, its dependence on fixed game rules, as already explained above. It is therefore also possible that 'karma systems' are associated with points and fixed values precisely because the corresponding rules in a game require such a system to function. Players who consider playing—as *Extra Credits* noted earlier—above all as the solving of problems, will try to figure out how the specific point system works in order to achieve the best possible result. As can be seen from the quotes above, this results in a public discussion about the respective system and an association of the 'karma system' with corresponding 'karma points', which—as in the case of *Mass Effect 2*—can be collected. But this discussion is also dependent on the "effectiveness" of the karma points, because if they have no real and clearly noticeable influence on the further gaming experience, then they soon

---

[29]   http://tvtropes.org/pmwiki/pmwiki.php/Main/KarmaMeter (accessed on 30 March 2018).
[30]   https://www.computerbase.de/forum/showthread.php?t=807957 (accessed on 30 March 2018).

lose their meaning for the player, or as the forum user *snakeeater420* puts it regarding the 'karma system' of *Fallout: New Vegas* on the website *IGN.com*: "so, what does karma do? I'm going to not care unless it affects something"[31].

While in strong need for more solid data, these observations are still important in that they at least imply the possibility of a contribution to the discourse on the karma concept based on the peculiarities of the medium of games, namely its problem-oriented structure and dependence on fixed rules and mechanics. An indication that karma is now also associated with points and fixed point values outside games—even if not far away from them—can at least be found in the fact that various web forums and community portals such as the website *Reddit.com* have a rating system in which users of the site can rate other users with—explicitly so-called—"karma points"[32]. Based on this value, each user can see how much he or she has already contributed the respective community and how much other users liked the content. Before a direct connection between karma points in online communities, karma points in games and the religious concept of karma is established, however, further research is needed.

5. Conclusions

In this article, an attempt was made to draw a connection between historic and recent concepts of karma and certain moral decision making systems in digital games, called 'karma systems'. At the same time, a detailed analysis of one such system (that of *Mass Effect 2*) was provided. It can be concluded, that even though the game designers behind *Mass Effect 2* never refer to the term "karma" directly, the moral decision making system of the game (similar to other such systems) features strong elements of moral duality (tracked via a points based rules system), invisible judgement, as well as a strong notion of 'cause and effect'. While none of these elements necessitate a direct connection to the concept of karma by the players, they are also seen as non-contradictory up to a point, where the term is commonly used in referring to such systems.

There seems to be a general consensus—at least among players who have expressed themselves in the internet forums and online articles examined—about what can and cannot be called a 'karma system' (and in extension 'karma'). Because one must also remember that there are moral decision making systems that are not called 'karma systems' (or a variation thereof), such as the above described 'externalized' and 'consequence' moral systems. This understanding of the term is difficult to pin down without further research and particularly personal statements by players, and so the observations made here on morality, 'cause and effect' and 'invisible judgement" as well as on the relationship between karma and scores can of course only be made with caution. Nevertheless, the similarities of these elements, which indisputably occur in 'karma systems' and are specifically named by players and game journalists, with earlier understandings of the karma concept are at least an indication that both are connected by the players; even if this happens largely unconsciously and by several detours.

Conflicts of Interest: The author declares no conflict of interest.

References

Aaby, Christopher. 2011. *Mass Effect 2* and Game Storytelling with Karma Systems. Available online: http://www.gamasutra.com/blogs/ChristopherAaby/20110418/7451/Mass_Effect_2_and_game_storytelling_with_karma_systems.php (accessed on 30 March 2018).

Aarseth, Espen J. 1997. *Cybertext: Perspectives on Ergodic Literature*. Baltimore: Johns Hopkins University Press.

Apperley, Thomas H. 2006. Genre and game studies: Toward a critical approach to video game genres. *Simulation & Gaming* 37: 6–23.

Aykroyd, Dan, and Harold Ramis. 1984. *Ghostbusters*. Directed by Ivan Reitman. Los Angeles: Columbia Pictures.

---

[31] http://boards.ign.com/fallout/b5729/201522995/p1/ (accessed on 30 March 2018).
[32] https://www.reddit.com/ (accessed on 30 March 2018).

Beale, A. A., H. T. Edge, and M. M. T. 1930. Fragen und Antworten: Was versteht man unter der Lehre von karman? Paper presented at Das Theosophische Forum, 1: pp. 17–18. Available online: http://www.theosophie.de/images/stories/pdf/Theos_For_1930_I_03.pdf (accessed on 14 April 2018).

Bergunder, Michael. 2001. Reinkarnationsvorstellungen als Gegenstand von Religionswissenschaft und Theologie. *Theologische Literaturzeitung* 126: 701–20.

Blavatsky, Helena Petrovna, and George R. S. Mead. 2003. *Theosophical Glossary*. Whitefish: Kessinger Publishing.

Brown, Susan L. 1992. Baby Boomers, American Character and the New Age: A Synthesis. In *Perspectives on the New Age*. Edited by James R. Lewis and J. Gordon Melton. Albany: State University of New York Press, pp. 87–97.

Cheruvallil-Contractor, Sariya, and Suha Shakkour, eds. 2015. *Digital Methodologies in the Sociology of Religion*. London: Bloomsbury Publishing.

Chryssides, George D. 2007. Defining the New Age. In *The New Age Movement and Western Esotericism*. Edited by James R. Lewis. Boston: Brill, pp. 5–24.

Consalvo, Mia, and Nathan Dutton. 2006. Game analysis: Developing a methodological toolkit for the qualitative study of games. *Game Studies* 6: 1–17.

Hagen, Uulf. 2009. Where Do Game Design Ideas Come From? Invention and Recycling in Games Developed in Sweden. In *Breaking New Ground: Innovation in Games, Play, Practice and Theory: Proceedings of the 2009 Digital Games Research Association Conference*. London: Brunel University.

Halbfass, Wilhelm. 2000. *Karma und Wiedergeburt im Indischen Denken*. München: Hugendubel.

Heidbrink, Simone, Tobias Knoll, and Jan Wysocki. 2014. Theorizing Religion in Digital Games. Perspectives and Approaches. *Online—Heidelberg Journal of Religions on the Internet* 5: 5–50.

Heidbrink, Simone, Tobias Knoll, and Jan Wysocki. 2015. Venturing into the Unknown(?) Method(olog)ical Reflections on Religion and Digital Games, Gamers and Gaming. *Online—Heidelberg Journal of Religions on the Internet* 7: 61–84.

Hörmann, Karl. 1969. *Lexikon der Christlichen Moral*. Innsbruck: Tyrolia-Verlag.

Iser, Wilhelm. 1994. *Der Akt des Lesens: Theorie Ästhetischer Wirkung*. München: Fink.

Jauß, Hans R. 1994. Literaturgeschichte als Provokation der Literaturwissenschaft. In *Rezeptionsästhetik: Theorie und Praxis*. Edited by Rainer Warning. München: W. Fink.

Jauß, Hans R., and Horst Sund. 1987. *Die Theorie der Rezeption—Rückschau Auf Ihre Unerkannte Vorgeschichte*. Konstanz: Univ.-Verl.

Jobs in der Spielebranche. 2008. Producer. Available online: http://www.pcwelt.de/ratgeber/Producer-Jobs-in-der-Spielebranche-248285.html (accessed on 30 March 2018).

Karma im Lichte der Geschichte. 1912. *Der Theosophische Pfad X(11)*. Pasadena: Hauptstelle, pp. 303–8. Available online: http://www.theosophie.de/index.php?option=com_content&view=category&id=430&Itemid=495 (accessed on 31 March 2018).

Michaels, Axel. 2001. Des Lebens ewiger Stachel. In *Frankfurter Allgemeine Zeitung 18.06.2001*. Frankfurt: Frankfurter Allgemeine Zeitung GmbH, p. 56.

Myers, David. 2003. *The Nature of Computer Games: Play as Semiosis*. Pieterlen: P. Lang.

Prophet, Elizabeth Clare, Patricia R. Spadaro, and Andrea Fischer. 2004. *Karma in der Praxis: Die Zukunft Gestalten*. Güllesheim: Silberschnur.

Schwarz, Aljoscha, and Ronald Schweppe. 2008. *Karma-Die Gebrauchsanleitung:... Damit das Schicksal Macht, Was Sie Wollen*. München: Lotos.

Sharf, Robert H. 1995. Buddhist Modernism and the Rhetoric of Meditative Experience. *Numen* 42: 228–83. [CrossRef]

Sicart, Miguel. 2008. Defining Game Mechanics. *Game Studies* 8: 1–14.

Šisler, Vit, Radde-Antweiler Kerstin, and Xenia Zeiler. 2018. *Methods for Studying Video Games and Religion*. New York: Routledge.

Starfox. 2010. *Mass Effect 2—Good and Evil*. Available online: http://foxhole.starfoxweb.com/reviews/review-tp/289-mass-effect-2?start=6 (accessed on 30 March 2018).

Stausberg, Michael. 1998. *Faszination Zarathushtra: Zoroaster und die Europäische Religionsgeschichte der Frühen Neuzeit*. Berlin: Walter de Gruyter.

Steffen, Oliver. 2017. *Level up Religion. Einführung in Die Religionswissenschaftliche Digitalspielforschung*. Stuttgart: Kohlhammer.

Swedenborg, Emanuel. 1880. *Leben und Lehre: Eine Sammlung Authentischer Urkunden Über Swedenborgs Persönlichkeit, und ein Inbegriff Seiner Theologie in Wörtlichen Auszügen aus Seinen Schriften.* Frankfurt am Main: J. G. Mittnacht.

Article

The Dark of the Covenant: Christian Imagery, Fundamentalism, and the Relationship between Science and Religion in the Halo Video Game Series

P.C.J.M. (Jarell) Paulissen

Tilburg School of Catholic Theology, P.O. Box 90153, 5000 LE Tilburg, The Netherlands;
p.c.j.m.paulissen@tilburguniversity.edu

Received: 20 March 2018; Accepted: 10 April 2018; Published: 12 April 2018

Abstract: What do a bionic supersoldier, space stations and religious fanaticism have in common? They are all vital elements of the plot in Halo, a series of first-person shooter games developed by Bungie and published by Microsoft Games. One of the interesting things about Halo is that the developers made use of quite a number of religious images and themes, especially from the Christian tradition. In modern Western society, science and religion are often portrayed as polar opposites, and Halo appears to reaffirm this narrative. Yet it might still be interesting to look at how exactly this animosity is portrayed, and to see whether there is more to it. This paper is an inquiry into the significance of religious imagery and themes in Halo, as well as an attempt to place the game in the broader context of the geopolitical situation of its time. In short, this article is going to be a case study of how the relationship between science and religion can be explored through the medium of video games. For an overview of the current debate on how science and religion relate to one another in academia, I am going to look at the works of American physicist and scholar of religion Ian Barbour, American paleontologist and historian of science Stephen Gould, and British ethologist and evolutionary biologist Richard Dawkins. To justify the academic study of videogames I will be drawing from the writings of Dutch cultural theologian Frank Bosman. The analysis itself will consist of a summary of the game's main story, its portrayal of religion on the one hand and its depiction of science on the other, and its representation of how these two fields relate to one another. In the conclusion, finally, I will connect the dots between the different parts of the analysis and provide an answer to the main question.

Keywords: religion; science; science fiction; fundamentalism; religious violence

---

"There was only one ship."

"One? Are you sure?"

A warrior in golden armour is being questioned by three creatures in floating seats.

"Yes," he replies "They called it, *Pillar of Autumn.*"

"Why was it not destroyed with the rest of their fleet?!" another demands.

"It fled as we set fire to their planet," says the warrior on trial

"But I followed with all the ships at my command."

"When you first saw Halo," one of the interrogators started "Were you blinded by its majesty?"

"Blinded?" the warrior asks.

"Paralysed? Dumbstruck?"

"No!"

"Yet the humans were able to evade your ships, land on the sacred ring, and desecrate it with their filthy footsteps!" said another of the seated creatures.

"Noble hierarchs," says the warrior "Surely you understand that once the parasite attacked ... "

The audience becomes disgruntled and there is unrest in the stands.

"There will be order in this council!" the second interrogator shouts. The third now comes forward

"You were right to focus your attention on the Flood," he says "But this demon, this 'Master Chief' ... "

"By the time I learned the demon's intent, there was nothing I could do." the warrior sighs. The first creature leans over to the third.

"Prophet of Truth," he whispers

"This has gone on long enough. Make an example of this bungler! The council demands it." The Prophet of Truth raises his hand.

"You are one of our most treasured instruments. Long have you led your fleet with honour and distinction. But your inability to safeguard Halo was a colossal failure."

"Nay!" yells someone from the stands "It was heresy!" The crowd starts jeering at the warrior.

"I will continue my campaign against the humans!" he objects.

"No!" says the Prophet of Truth "You will not. Soon the Great Journey will begin. But when it does, the weight of your heresy will stay your feet, and you shall be left behind."

Thus concludes the opening cinematic of *Halo 2* (2004), the second instalment in the *Halo* video game series. Like its predecessor, *Halo: Combat Evolved* (2001), the game is of the so-called first-person shooter (FPS) genre, and was developed by Bungie and published by Microsoft Games. The main series continued with *Halo 3* (2007), *Halo 4* (2012) and *Halo 5: Guardians* (2015). Other storylines were explored in *Halo 3: ODST* (2009) and *Halo: Reach* (2010). All of these titles belong to the FPS genre, while *Halo Wars* (2009) and *Halo Wars 2* (2017) are real-time strategy (RTS) games.

One of the interesting things about Halo is that the developers of the game made use of quite a number of religious images and themes, especially from the Christian tradition. This immediately becomes apparent upon reading the 'thick description' (Heidbrink et al. 2014) of the opening scene described above. Words like 'sacred', 'desecrate', and 'heresy' have very strong religious connotations, which might seem rather strange in the context of classic science fiction tropes like aliens and spaceships. However, established franchises like *Star Wars* and *Star Trek* are readily associated with these themes, and modern science fiction continues to build on this tradition (McGrath 2011). In modern Western society, science and religion are often portrayed as polar opposites, and at first glance Halo appears to reaffirm that these two areas are mutually exclusive. It is, however, interesting to look at how exactly this animosity is portrayed, and to see whether there is more to it.

This paper is an inquiry into the significance of religious imagery and science in Halo, as well as an attempt to place the game in the broader context of the geopolitical situation during its development. The main question that I will be trying to answer is as follows:

How do science and religion relate to each other in the Halo video game series?

To answer this question, I will list and analyse a wide range of in-game references to and imagery taken from Christianity through a close reading of the game (Grieve and Campbell 2014). I will then do the same with the way science is presented in the game. The focus of my analysis will be on *Halo: Combat Evolved*, *Halo 2*, and *Halo: Reach*, as these put together provide the backdrop for the rest of the franchise. The information one needs to fully grasp the story and its scale become apparent over the course of these three games.

Before this can be done however, it will be necessary to present a theoretical framework on the relationship between science and religion, which I am going to base on the works of Ian Barbour,

Stephen Gould, and Richard Dawkins. To support the academic study of video games I will be drawing from the writings of Dutch cultural theologian Frank Bosman.

The main body of this article will consist of a few different elements. In the first part I will give a short summary of the background story of the game world, as well as the context of the time in which the game was developed. Then I will present a thorough overview of the religious imagery and themes, based on an already existing analysis of the game made by Wisecrack (a group of dedicated pop culture enthusiasts that makes YouTube videos mainly about the philosophical implications, symbolism and social commentary in motion pictures, television series and video games). This will be followed by a similar account of the science in Halo, partially based on an already existing analysis made by planetary physicist Kevin Grazier. After that I am going to connect the two partial analyses, enriched with my own observations, and the theoretical framework, in order to reach my conclusion.

An important note I would like to make here is that although not all of the interpretations are mine alone, I adopted from others only those I can also see for myself. Some of the points made by Wisecrack in their video, for example, have been left out of this article because I could not discern them.

1. Theoretical Framework

In his book *Religion in an age of science*, Barbour argues that there are four different ways in which science and religion can relate to each other: conflict, independence, dialogue, and integration (Barbour 1989). According to Gould, science and religion are 'non-overlapping magisteria', by which he means that both realms have their own distinctive fields and that neither is suitable to study the subject matter of the other. The main principle of this model is that science should be concerned with the physical world and can be used to explain natural phenomena, while religion ought to be focused on the human experience and moral values. Moreover, if religion is no longer capable of explaining the natural world, then science can no longer claim any moral truth (Gould 2002).

Dawkins criticises the notion of non-overlapping magisteria. The division proposed by Gould, he says, is not maintainable. For Dawkins, the idea that religious doctrine can provide an absolute basis for morality is wishful thinking, because people choose to adopt the parts of scripture they like, while rejecting those they do not. Since scripture is subjected to this process of selection, it follows that there must be some source of morality outside of religion. Alternatively "it is completely unrealistic to claim, as Gould and many others do, that religion keeps itself away from science's turf, restricting itself to morals and values. A universe with a supernatural presence would be a fundamentally and qualitatively different kind of universe from one without. The difference is, inescapably, a scientific difference. Religions make existence claims, and this means scientific claims" ((Dawkins 1998, para. 15) "Religion on Science's Turf").

Bosman defines video games as "digital (interactive), playable (narrative) texts. As a text, a video game is an object of interpretation. As a narrative, it communicates meaning. As a game, it is playable. And as a digital medium, it is interactive" (Bosman 2016, p. 33). He also proposes a four-step methodology for close reading games, namely internal and external reading plus internal and external research.

2. The Background Story of Halo

The year is 2552. Humanity is at war with an alliance of different alien species known as the Covenant. The different species that make up the Covenant are bound together by the belief that they have been chosen as the instrument of the gods. Under the leadership of the Hierarchs, three self-proclaimed prophets named Truth, Mercy, and Regret, these aliens are driven to cleanse the universe of humanity in pursuit of some type of salvation that involves reaching a higher state of being. For the Covenant, ascension is reserved only for those who have been chosen. Because humans have not been promised salvation, they are seen as inferior and sinful creatures that are standing in the way of the aliens' divine destiny.

The object of their worship is an ancient space-faring civilisation known as the Forerunners, who have left behind a number of mysterious buildings and space stations throughout the galaxy. The Covenant sees itself as the successor to the Forerunners, and they believe these structures were made for them specifically. The most significant of these are the massive ring-shaped installations with simulated natural environments on the inside referred to as Halos. The Covenant seeks to activate these Halos because they wrongfully believe this will send them on 'the Great Journey' towards salvation. In truth, the Halo installations were built by the Forerunners to get rid of a parasitic alien species called the Flood. Since the only way to achieve that goal was to wipe out all sentient life in the galaxy in order to starve the Flood, the Halos were designed to do just that.

The United Nations Space Command (UNSC) is mankind's last and only line of defence against the aliens. At the start of the series, the war is not going well for humanity. The technologically superior Covenant is able to keep up a relentless onslaught, spurred on by the promise of eternal salvation and under threat of exclusion from the Great Journey, and every rare human victory is a very costly one.

3. Halo Game Synopsis

After suffering a crushing defeat on the planet Reach, the crew of a human ship called the *UNSC Pillar of Autumn* uses navigation data from the Forerunners to escape. The data turns out to be coordinates to a Halo installation. Moments later, a Covenant ship follows, and another battle ensues. In an attempt to keep the ship's artificial intelligence, Cortana, out of enemy hands, an elite soldier codenamed John-117, also known as the Master Chief, is woken up from cryogenic stasis to fight off the Covenant and give the crew a chance to evacuate before boarding the last available escape pod himself.

Master Chief and Cortana must then work to reunite the scattered groups of human survivors on the surface, and save the ship's captain, Jacob Keyes, who is being held by the Covenant aboard their cruiser. After saving the captain and learning the installation is called Halo by the Covenant, Cortana hacks into the alien's communications and finds out that the aliens believe the installation is sacred, and that it is an immensely powerful weapon. It falls to Master Chief and Cortana to keep the Covenant from using Halo to wipe out the human race. It does not take long for them to find the control room, but when they get there, Cortana picks up new Covenant communications that reveal something is very wrong. While exploring the Halo installation, the Covenant found something they should not have, and the captain is about to make the situation far worse. Master Chief then goes to find Keyes, while Cortana stays behind to find out what she can about Halo. Upon arrival at the captain's last known location, Master Chief discovers that Keyes accidentally released the Flood, which was sealed away underground. This allows the parasite to consume UNSC personnel and Covenant forces alike, and turn them into mindless husks that are hostile to both sides. As he returns to the surface, Master Chief is suddenly drafted by the installation's artificial intelligence (AI) monitor, nicknamed 343 "Guilty Spark", to retrieve a key so that they can activate Halo's defences and get rid of the parasite.

After retrieving the key, Master Chief is transported back to the control room. Just as he is about to turn the key, Cortana stops him and tells him the truth. Instead of destroying the Flood, Halo will wipe out their food; sentient life, i.e., humans and aliens. Master Chief and Cortana eventually manage to destroy Halo, escape, and return to Earth to tell UNSC high command of their discovery. As Master Chief is being awarded a medal for his service, a small Covenant fleet suddenly arrives and begins to invade earth. UNSC forces are able to fend off the aliens, and when the Covenant tries to retreat, Master Chief decides to follow them. When they arrive at their destination, it turns out the aliens have found another Halo. As Master Chief and Cortana again try to stop both the Covenant and the installation's own AI from activating this Halo, they discover it is only one of seven such devices and that they can all be activated at once using another Forerunner station called the Ark. It now becomes a race against time to keep them from activating the Ark and wipe out all sentient life in the galaxy.

As the series is still ongoing, it is not possible to provide a much more satisfying conclusion to this overview of the game's narrative than this rather tense cliffhanger. However, it is my hope that it instead encourages readers to play the game for themselves.

4. False Prophets and the Galactic Apocalypse: Religious Imagery in the Halo Series

Some of the references to religion in Halo are quite obvious. Others require a more thorough analysis. In what follows, I will present a non-exhaustive overview of the most important references to Christianity.

4.1. Musical Score

The name of the game itself is of course taken from the Aureole, the golden disc used in medieval Christian art to represent Jesus, angels, or saints, which in English is often also called a Halo or Nimbus (Schiller 1971). Upon loading the game, there is another quite clear-cut reference: the musical score. It starts with Gregorian chanting, which lasts for about thirty seconds before switching to techno beats or electric guitars, depending on which game in the series one is playing. This juxtaposition of medieval devotional singing and contemporary music could be interpreted as either a confirmation of the religion-versus-science narrative or, since the two genres actually go surprisingly well together, as a musical counterargument.

4.2. The Covenant

Perhaps a less obvious reference, but still quite easy to see, is the alien Covenant. In both the Jewish and Christian traditions, the Covenant (Mendenhall and Herion 1992) is the sacred agreement between the people of Israel and God. Only the Noahic Covenant applied to all mankind (Gen. 9:8–10, 14–16), whereas later ones were only made with the Israelites (Gen. 15:18, 17:21; Ex. 2:24; Josh. 1:2–3, 21:43). It is possible the developers of Halo used this word not only to indicate the religious nature of the alien alliance, but also to highlight the way the aliens see themselves as superior over humans. The Covenant believes the Halo installations were built for them by the Forerunners, and only by activating the rings can they fulfil their destiny (Wisecrack Join 2015). As a science fiction game, Halo of course features space ships, and those used by the Covenant are often named after Christian concepts, such as Truth and Reconciliation. The same goes for Covenant vehicles available in the game. Seraph fighters, for instance, are named after the angelic beings (Mettinger 1999) that are supposed to accompany God in Heaven (Isa. 6:2–3; Rev. 4:8).

4.3. The Ark

Another piece of evidence found on the surface is the Ark. In the game, the Ark is the central control hub for the Halo installations, capable of activating all of them at once. There are two possible interpretations. Firstly, it could be a reference to Noah's Ark (Bailey 1992). After all, the Halos were built to eradicate the Flood by wiping out all life to starve the parasites to death. As strange as it may sound, this will ultimately save the galaxy because it gets a chance to start over. This mirrors the story in Genesis, in which God decides to destroy all life on earth to rid it of sin and begin anew (Gen. 6:13, 17, 7:10–12, 17–24; 8:1–2). Only the chosen may survive, and the ark saves them from the flood. The second possibility is that it is in fact a reference to the Ark of the Covenant (Seow 1992), which contained the Ten Commandments. On top of that it was also a powerful weapon, since it was used by the Israelites to bring down the walls of Jericho after making seven laps around the city (Josh. 6–8, 11, 14–16, 20). Similar to the Ark of the Covenant being regarded as holy, the alien Covenant reveres all Forerunner technology as sacred.

4.4. Christ Figures: Master Chief, Captain Keyes and Thel'Vadam

There are many direct allusions to scripture as well. The first clue comes from Master Chief's codename, John-117. In the New King James translation of the Bible, John 1:17 reads "For the law was given through Moses, but grace and truth came through Jesus Christ". Similar to Jesus enacting this law through grace and truth, Master Chief enforces it with guns. What's more is that he is symbolically resurrected multiple times throughout the series. For instance, at the beginning of the first game, he is awoken from cryostasis; he was artificially kept in a frozen state to be 'thawed' in a time of need. This is a figurative resurrection. Another more literal example is when Master Chief appears to drown in a lake and is transported to some sort of underworld before being revived. This matter will be analysed more thorough in a while.

In light of this analogy between Jesus and Master Chief, Captain Keyes may be compared to another important character in the stories about Christ: John the Baptist. The evidence here is that Keyes gives Master Chief his pistol after being woken up from cryogenic stasis, or resurrected, in the first game. In other words, he hands out the tool with which Master Chief enforces the law (Matt. 3:12–17; Mark 1:9–11; Luke 3:21). Moreover, when the captain becomes consumed by the Flood halfway through the first game, Master Chief ends his suffering by punching through his skull to retrieve an important bionic device from his brain. This is perhaps similar to the beheading of John the Baptist (Matt. 14:10; Mark 6:27), since Keyes also loses his head (Wisecrack Join 2015).

Yet there is more than one character that shows a resemblance to Jesus. After his failure to protect Halo, the commander of the Covenant fleet, Thel'Vadam, is punished for his so-called 'heresy' by being stripped of his rank and forced into the role of the Arbiter to atone for his quote-on-quote 'sins'. The Arbiter is a special kind of warrior who is only deployed in highly dangerous situations where it is almost certain he won't survive. Dying in battle is the only way for Thel'Vadam to make amends. The ritual that marks his transition to Arbiter is visually evocative of Jesus' crucifixion. Similar to Christ hanging on the cross, Thel'Vadam has his arms spread out as his golden armour is forcefully torn off, and the ritual culminates with him being branded with a mark to signify his shamed status. The way in which Tartarus applies this brand evokes the image of Jesus being stabbed with a lance by the Roman soldiers (John 19:34). With his old self figuratively dead, Thel'Vadam is resurrected as the Arbiter. Moreover, his passing through the lair of the Gravemind, the 'brain' behind the Flood, later on in the game is similar to when Jesus descended into the underworld (Eph. 4–9; 1 Pet. 3:18–19). Having learned the truth about Halo, the Arbiter returns from this journey with a new message, so that he may save his fellow Elites and stop the false Prophets. This is reminiscent of how Christ brought a new religious truth to mankind (John 8:31–32, 14:6).

The journey through the Gravemind's lair is interesting for other reasons as well. On the one hand it is a significant event because it not only happens to the Arbiter, but also to Master Chief. It is where the two first meet; this figurative underworld is where both characters with a resemblance to Jesus are together in one place. What should also be mentioned here is the fact that, similar to Master Chief and his pistol, the word arbiter refers to law enforcement, albeit with a stronger emphasis on the judge rather than the executioner. This in turn is another reference to Jesus, who is also sometimes described as judge (2 Cor. 5:10; John 5:22, 27, 30, 9:39; Rom. 2:16).

4.5. Satan

The parallel between the Gravemind's lair and the underworld also allows for a comparison between the Gravemind himself and Satan. In the Christian tradition, Satan is often portrayed as a trickster who seduces people with false knowledge (Breytenbach and Day 1999). He is the primary antagonist of Jesus, who represents the Truth, and the Church represents him on earth, but with the Gravemind it is the other way around: he is in fact speaking the truth, whereas the Prophets are peddling lies. It should be noted, however, that the Gravemind, being the Flood, is also serving himself, similar to the devil (Riley 1999). After all, if the Halos were to be activated, he would die as well.

4.6. The Monitor

One more character that should be mentioned here is the AI monitor of the first Halo, 343—"Guilty Spark". The number is taken from the equation 7^3 (each of the Halo monitors is numbered seven to one less the power of their respective installation and this one is in charge of the fourth). The numbers seven and three are, perhaps unsurprisingly by now, also significant in the Judeo-Christian tradition. The number seven appears over 400 times in the Bible and symbolises the rhythm of time, while the number three refers to the vertical and hierarchical structure of the cosmos (Labuschagne 2000). No official explanation is provided for the nickname "Guilty Spark", but fans have theorised that it refers to what transpired approximately 100,000 years before the events of the game. When the Forerunners had to use the Halos and wipe themselves out in order to keep the Flood from spreading, it just so happened that the one under 343's supervision was activated first. Thus he is fully aware of their destructive power and might feel guilty about what happened.

Although he initially comes across as a benign custodian of ancient technology, it turns out that his intentions are far more sinister. The Forerunners programmed him to make sure the Flood does not leave the installation if it ever breaks out of containment, but his first response is to resort to the most drastic option: activating Halo and wiping out all nearby sentient life. Since 343 has the same goal as the Covenant, it appears that he is aligned with the false Prophets. Moreover, the fact that he tries to trick Master Chief into activating the installation can be compared to the snake who tricks Eve into eating from the Tree of Knowledge (Gen. 3:3–6), which adds to his seemingly villainous nature. However, the monitor consistently refers to Master Chief as the 'Reclaimer', which is evocative of the epithet 'Redeemer' that is sometimes given to Christ (Gal. 3:13; 1 Pet. 1:17–19). This makes it sound more plausible that the AI is, in fact, also misguided in believing he is carrying out the will of the Forerunners.

4.7. How to Destroy a Planet

Another important theme in the game is the end times. The main motif of the whole series is the threat of total annihilation via the Halos, of which there are seven. This may refer to the seven seals of the apocalypse and the seven trumpet blasts signalling the beginning of the end times (Wisecrack Join 2015).

According to the Book of Revelation, the site of the final battle against Satan and the Antichrist is a place called Armageddon (Rev. 16:16). This, although it is a symbolic location, can be translated as "Mountain of Megiddo", and the opening and closing cinematics of *Halo: Reach* feature a broken mountain range. Christian apocalyptic literature also mentions that "fire came down from God out of heaven" (Rev. 20:9), and this be connected to the destruction of a different human colony on the planet Harvest. This invasion was the start of the conflict between the Covenant and humans, and ends with the Covenant unleashing the full might of their fleet to 'glass' the planet: they burn everything with laser beams that are so hot they turn everything into glass. The glassing of Harvest is reminiscent of the fire from God mentioned in Revelation, because from the Covenant's perspective, they are destroying the unworthy. It could also be argued that the Covenant represents the Antichrist instead, because he also has the power to call down fire (Rev. 13:13).

4.8. The Covenant and Manifest Destiny

The Covenant wrongfully believes that activating the Halos will send them on the 'Great Journey' towards salvation, and that whoever stands in their way must be annihilated. In conjunction with the name Harvest, the Great Journey suddenly sounds a lot like Manifest Destiny. This was the idea that the United States was destined to spread its influence across the whole continent, and that, as Christians, they had the right to take it from the native 'heathens' by force. These so-called 'civilising missions' were justified by stating that Native Americans were savages, and thus were inferior to white colonists. Projected onto Halo, the alien Covenant's extermination of humans can be seen as a form of Manifest Destiny: the Covenant sees humans as primitive and therefore unable to go on the Great Journey, so their eradication is justified (Wisecrack Join 2015).

4.9. Corruption and (High) Charity

One more reference is the alien capital of High Charity. In the Christian tradition, charity is held to be the most important virtue. According to the Catechism of the Catholic Church, charity is "the theological virtue by which we love God above all things for His own sake, and our neighbour as ourselves for the love of God" (The Holy See 1993). In St. Paul's first letter to the Corinthians it says: "And now abide faith, hope, love, these three; but the greatest of these is love" (1 Cor. 13:13). The fact that the alien capital in Halo is named after the Christian notion of charity is quite ironic, since the Covenant is everything but charitable. What is more is that High Charity is eventually consumed by the Flood after the Gravemind manages to infect the human spacecraft *In Amber Clad* and crash it into the mobile city. Not only could this be interpreted as symbolic for the ultimate corruption of the Christian virtue, but it could also be seen as an inverse of the story of Sodom and Gomorrah (Gen. 19:24–25; Deut. 29:23; Luke 17:29). Rather than God destroying the corrupted cities of the sinful (2 Pet. 2:6), the Gravemind destroys the corrupted city of the faithful.

5. "AI Constructs and Cyborgs First!": Science in the Halo Series

The word halo is not reserved for the golden discs used to represent Jesus and saints in works of art. It is also used in the realm of natural science.

5.1. The Science behind the Fiction

Astronomers use the term galactic halo to indicate a round and 'flat' galaxy with relatively large distances between stars, such as the Milky Way (Naab and Ostriker 2012). In the game, a Halo is a vast, circular structure orbiting in space. Because of its size, a Halo appears to be what is known as a megastructure. A megastructure is an artificial structure with one of its three dimensions equal to or exceeding one hundred kilometres. The concept of a circular megastructure first appeared in a sci-fi novel by Larry Niven, called *Ringworld* (Niven 1971). Niven's design of the Ringworld is best explained as an intermediate stage between planets and Dyson spheres. In *Search for artificial stellar sources of infra-red radiation*, Freeman Dyson posed the hypothesis that it would be possible to build a megastructure around a star to capture most or all of its radiation energy (Dyson 1960).

Planetary physicist Kevin Grazier has attempted to analyse the science behind Halo. He begins by stating that although the installations are based on Niven's concept of a Ringworld, the Halos are in fact more similar in size to a Bishop Ring, an actual hypothetical space habitat that rotates to create its own gravity, named after its inventor Forrest Bishop (Yeffeth and Thomason). The megastructure in the video game has a metallic exterior, but its interior has the features of a habitable planet, with an atmosphere and water, as well as unique flora and fauna (Hiatt 1999). The exterior of a Halo is littered with what seem to be docking ports and even windows, which might indicate that the megastructure is partially hollow on the inside. This hollow space might be used for maintenance and power generation, or even as living quarters. Another problem is the fact that the Halos are exposed to high levels of radiation. Since earth has a magnetic field to protect it from this kind of radiation, Grazier hypothesises that the entire circumference of the rings may be lined with conductive cables. Running an electric current through these cables would create a safe atmosphere on the installations, allowing them to sustain life (Yeffeth and Thomason).

5.2. Mjolnir Kombat

Returning briefly to Master Chief, it should be noted that his armour is a highly advanced piece of technology. The Mjolnir Powered Assault Armor, named after the legendary hammer wielded by the Norse god of thunder, is a combat exoskeleton designed to enhance the strength, agility, and durability of the wearer. The armour is made of a multilayer alloy, augmented with a special coating that can negate a limited amount of energy projectiles, and comes with a number of clips, belts, and magnetic holsters to carry additional weapons and ammunition. One of the layers in the armour is made from reactive metal crystal that allows an AI normally reserved for spacecraft to accompany a SPARTAN-II supersoldier. The SPARTAN project was set up by a scientist named Dr. Catherine Halsey, who also designed the Mjolnir armour, and was intended to create an elite class of soldiers capable of going toe-to-toe with the Covenant's strongest warriors, such as the Elites. These supersoldiers played a pivotal role during the defence of Reach, and Master Chief is the last remaining SPARTAN-II. Because of their prowess in battle and the illusion that they were invincible, the Covenant began to refer to them as Demons.

5.3. Cortana

A final scientific element of the game that needs to be addressed is Master Chief's AI companion: Cortana. Cortana was created from the cloned brain of Dr. Halsey by using her synaptic networks as a template for Cortana's processors, which is why she also sounds like her. Unlike the monitor of a Halo such as 343 "Guilty Spark", Cortana is a so-called smart AI, which means that she can learn new things and is not limited by basic pre-programmed parameters. The downside of this limitless ability to adapt is that smart AI's have a relatively short lifespan of only seven years. This is because they eventually slip into rampancy, which is a permanent state of being where the AI starts thinking it has godlike powers, as well as developing contempt for its makers. Cortana has no physical form, but she can speak via existing communication systems and even project a holographic image of herself onto certain interfaces (Nylund 2001). Since the game was developed by Microsoft's video game division, the software company decided to name its voice-activated computer assistant after Cortana as a tribute to the character.

6. Halo and Its Geopolitical Context

It is important to view Halo in its historical context. Since the first game was released in November of 2001, it seems very likely that the terror attacks of 9/11 influenced at least some parts of its development. The ideological politics surrounding terrorism are interwoven with certain elements of the storyline. For instance, the Covenant sees itself as the successors of the Forerunners, by which they elevate themselves over everybody else. In their view, they are the only ones able to attain salvation. Humans, on the contrary, are seen as unworthy of being saved. Moreover, with humanity they are confronted by other claims to divinity, and this leaves the aliens with two options; they can either accept there are multiple truths, or they can exterminate the heretics to protect theirs. Needless to say they chose the latter (Wisecrack Join 2015).

6.1. The Covenant and Religious Violence

In the context of a post 9/11 world, it becomes difficult to deny that the alien Covenant is a metaphor for religious violence. American scholar of religion Mark Juergensmeyer (2017) states that although religion is often used as an after the fact moral justification for this type of violence, it is not the cause of it. The blame usually falls on a variety of political and social issues. Religion can, however, provide a symbolic dimension to acts of terrorism.

Moreover, religious violence is not reserved for one single tradition. Nearly every major religion has the potential for religious violence, and even secular movements can inspire it. Still, it is important to note that acts of terrorism committed in the name of religion are different from those motivated by secular aspirations. Some differences are easy to see, such as the transcendent moral justification and the almost ritualistic manner in which attacks are carried out, while others go deeper: "familiar images of struggle and transformation—concepts of cosmic war—have been employed in this-worldly social struggles. When these cosmic battles are conceived as occurring on the human plane, they result in real acts of violence" (Juergensmeyer 2017, p. 9). Similar to the way the Covenant justifies their extermination of humans by referring to themselves as successors to the Forerunners and thereby interpreting their conflict as part of the legacy of ancient and powerful species, so too do the perpetrators of religious violence (from here on referred to as religious fanatics) justify their actions by interpreting their struggle in terms of cosmic war. Both the aliens in Halo and those who commit religiously motivated acts of terrorism in the real world believe they are chosen by a higher power, both believe they are guided by divine will, and both believe they are therefore justified in the killing of innocents.

Religious violence is also often spoken about in terms of purification. Those who do not conform are seen as a danger to the status quo and must therefore be eliminated. Once they have been removed from society, such individuals or groups can then be framed as either having fallen victim to their own evil, which allows their removal to be viewed as cleansing, or as having sacrificed themselves for the greater good (Ellens 2007). This is another thing the Covenant and religious fanatics have in common: the idea that violence is necessary to root out heresy. The only way to begin the Great Journey is by destroying those who stand in the way, and to perish while fighting for this cause means to be guaranteed salvation. This mirrors the promises made to those who carry out acts of terrorism in the name of religion, because both the Covenant and religious fanatics believe that dying in the name of their faith will absolve them of their sins.

6.2. The UNSC and the U.S. Military

Terrorism motivated by religion is often linked to religious fundamentalism, which is in turn seen as threatening to 'our way of life', whatever that may be. So-called Islamic fundamentalism in particular is seen as the most urgent threat to Western civilisation. In this discourse, the secular West is spearheaded by the United States of America, placing this nation at the forefront of the perceived fight against Islamic fundamentalism (Larsson 2017). In the fiction of Halo, the United Nations Space Command fights to protect humanity from the Covenant. It might be possible then to compare the UNSC to the U.S. Military, which is currently often presented as defending Western values from religious fundamentalism in and out of the Middle East. Yet if I take my theoretical framework into account this leaves me with a new question, namely: does the UNSC then represent science?

In the fiction of the Halo universe, humanity in the 26th century has unlocked the secrets of long-distance space travel, can build advanced power armour capable of withstanding energy projectiles, and is able to construct smart AI from people's brains. Thus science is clearly an important part of human society. Yet if the comparison to the US military is supposed to hold up to scrutiny, I would argue that the rival claim to divinity is equally important. After all, the United States is still quite a religious nation, which means their ideology has to have at least some religious elements. In the context of American civil religion, the military has a very important symbolic function (Baker et al. 2014). Those who serve in the U.S. military are seen as the defenders of not only American values like freedom and democracy, but also Christianity; there is a double religious dimension. What is then interesting about Halo is that a rather dark part of the role Christianity has played in U.S. history, the civilising missions that resulted in the displacement of Native Americans, can be connected to the Covenant, which serves as the main antagonist to UNSC. Perhaps this could be interpreted as an attempt to present an antithesis between 'good' Christianity and 'bad' Christianity.

The problem with this interpretation, however, is that the UNSC is not solely intended to protect humanity from outside threats. Before the conflict with the aliens, extremely poor socio-economic conditions in some of the outer colonies led to uprisings, and the UNSC used military action to suppress them. Moreover, the training methods they use on new recruits are harsh, almost to the point of being inhumane, especially when it comes to the SPARTAN program. This second theme in particular is explored in some of the short (animated) films set in the Halo universe, such as *Halo: The Fall of Reach* (2015). Drawing a comparison between the UNSC and the U.S. military might still be possible, but it is very important to take these factors into consideration as well.

7. Conclusions

However, does Halo say anything about the relationship between science and religion? On the one hand there is the apparent dichotomy between humans portrayed as rational thinkers and the aliens that are presented as religious fanatics. Yet on the other hand the fact that the Covenant is technologically superior shows they are also engaged in science. Take for example the weapons used by the aliens. Whereas the UNSC still equips its soldiers with weapons that require 'old-fashioned' bullets, such as pistols and assault rifles, the Covenant issues armaments like plasma rifles and energy swords to its warriors. What is more is that the aliens see the Forerunners as gods, and fancy themselves to be their successors. Since the Forerunners were able to build the Halo installations, it is safe to assume they were a highly advanced species. The fact that the Covenant holds the technology left behind by this ancient civilisation to be sacred might mean that it is in fact technology itself they are worshipping. A final thing to add here is that human religion plays a role in why the aliens see humanity as an inferior race of heretics.

In short, the theory I put forward in the introduction that Halo appears to reinforce the idea that science and religion are polar opposites, and appears to be too short-sighted. Especially from the perspective of the Covenant, the relationship between science and religion presented here is, as Barbour would have put it, dialogue. There is overlap between the two domains, but the idea that they complement each other is rejected as well. Although the Covenant is quite technologically advanced and worships Forerunner technology, they still refuse to accept the truth about the Halo installations and do not cease their pursuit of the Great Journey and their crusade against the unworthy humans. This fits into the narrative that although we have an open society and value dialogue over conflict, science and religion are ultimately at odds with one another. We are able to co-exist peacefully, at least most of the time, but we find it difficult to fully reconcile the two domains. Perhaps the developers of Halo wanted to remind us that science and religion have a more complicated relationship than we like to think.

Comparing the UNSC and the US military to each other is more difficult, and I think additional research is in order here. This question thus has to remain unanswered for now. What I can say is that humanity does not adhere to pure science, nor does the Covenant represent pure religion. This means that the Halo series seemingly rejects the theory put forward by Gould that science and religion are separate magisteria, and instead appears to affirm the objection to that theory given by Dawkins that religion cannot avoid stepping on science's turf.

In conclusion, the relationship between science and religion presented in Halo is dialogue; there is overlap between the two domains, but there is no interconnection. Even though the Covenant does not represent pure religion, its claim to religious truth is the main reason behind the conflict with humanity. Moreover, the Covenant's fundamentalist rhetoric also means there is no room for hesitation when it comes to destroying the unworthy, and that failure is tantamount to heresy.

This comparison is exemplified in the case of the Arbiter. Because he was unable to prevent the destruction of Halo and defeat the humans, Thel'Vadam is stripped of his rank, shamed, and branded as a heretic. To atone for his failure, he is then sent on a suicide mission, and if he dies, all his past sins will be forgiven. If not, he will not be eligible for salvation: "Soon the Great Journey will begin, but when it does, the weight of your heresy will stay your feet, and you shall be left behind."

Conflicts of Interest: The author declares no conflict of interest.

References

Bailey, Lloyd R. 1992. Noah's Ark. In *The Anchor Bible Dictionary*. Edited by David Noel Freedman. New Haven: Yale University Press, p. 1131.

Baker, Joseph O., Christopher D. Bader, and Kittye Hirsch. 2014. Desecration, moral boundaries, and movement of law: The case of Westboro Baptist Church. *Deviant Behavior* 36: 42–67. [CrossRef]

Barbour, Ian G. 1989. *Religion in an Age of Science*. London: SCM.

Bosman, Frank G. 2016. The Word has become game: Researching religion in digital games. *Online: Heidelberg Journal of Religions on the Internet* 11: 28–45.

Breytenbach, Cilliers, and Peggy L. Day. 1999. Satan. In *Dictionary of Deities and Demons in the Bible*. Edited by Karel van der Toorn, Bob Becking and Pieter W. van der Horst. Leiden: Brill, pp. 726–32.

Dawkins, Richard. 1998. When Religion Steps on Science's Turf. *Free Inquiry* 18: 18–19. Available online: http://pds4.egloos.com/pds/200709/04/59/Richard_Dawkins_-_When_Religion_Steps_On_Sciences_Turf.pdf (accessed on 5 January 2018).

Dyson, Freeman J. 1960. Search for artificial stellar sources of infra-red radiation. *Science* 131: 1667–68. [CrossRef] [PubMed]

Ellens, J. Harold. 2007. The destructive power of religion. In *The Destructive Power of Religion: Violence in Judaism, Christianity, and Islam*. Edited by J. Harold Ellens. Westport: Praeger.

Gould, Stephen Jay. 2002. *Rocks of Ages: Science and Religion in the Fullness of Life*. New York: Ballantine Pub.

Grazier, Kevin 2006. Halo science 101. In *Halo Effect: An Unauthorized Look at the Most Successful Video Game of All Time*. Yeffeth, Glenn, and Jennifer Thomason, eds. Dallas: BenBella, pp. 37–56.

Grieve, Gregory Price, and Heidi A. Campbell. 2014. Studying religion in digital gaming: A critical review of an emerging field. *Online: Heidelberg Journal for Religion on the Internet* 5: 51–67.

Heidbrink, Simone, Tobias Knoll, and Jan Wysocki. 2014. Theorizing religion in digital games: Perspectives and approaches. *Online: Heidelberg Journal for Religion on the Internet* 5: 5–50.

Hiatt, Jesse. 1999. Halo: The closest thing to the real thing. *Computer Gaming World* 184: 94–96.

Juergensmeyer, Mark. 2017. *Terror in the Mind of God: The Global Rise of Religious Violence*. Berkeley: University of California Press.

Labuschagne, Casper J. 2000. *Numerical Secrets of the Bible: Recovering the Bible Codes*. North Richland Hills: BIBAL.

Larsson, Johan P. 2017. *Understanding Religious Violence: Thinking Outside the Box on Terrorism*. Abingdon: Routledge.

McGrath, James F., ed. 2011. *Religion and Science Fiction*. Eugene: Wipf and Stock Publishers, pp. 1–8.

Mendenhall, George E., and Gary A. Herion. 1992. Covenant. In *The Anchor Bible Dictionary*. Edited by David Noel Freedman. New Haven: Yale University Press, pp. 1179–202.

Mettinger, Tryggve N. D. 1999. Devil. In *Dictionary of Deities and Demons in the Bible*. Edited by Karel van der Toorn, Bob Becking and Pieter W. van der Horst. Leiden: Brill, pp. 742–44.

Naab, Thorsten, and Jeremiah P. Ostriker. 2012. Theoretical challenges in understanding galaxy evolution. *Physics Today* 65: 43.

Niven, Larry. 1971. *Ringworld*. New York: Ballantine.

Nylund, Eric. 2001. *Halo: The Fall of Reach*. New York: Ballantine.

Riley, Greg J. 1999. Devil. In *Dictionary of Deities and Demons in the Bible*. Edited by Karel van der Toorn, Bob Becking and Pieter W. van der Horst. Leiden: Brill, pp. 244–49.

Schiller, Gertrud. 1971. *Iconography of Christian Art*. London: Lund Humpries, vol. 1.

Seow, Choon-Leong. 1992. Ark of the Covenant. In *The Anchor Bible Dictionary*. Edited by David Noel Freedman. New Haven: Yale University Press, pp. 386–93.

The Holy See. 1993. *Catechism of the Catholic Church*. New York: Doubleday.

Wisecrack Join. 2015. The Philosophy of Halo—Wisecrack Edition. November 3. Video File. Available online: https://www.youtube.com/watch?v=c3r03STeHCA (accessed on 12 January 2018).

MDPI

St. Alban-Anlage 66

4052 Basel

Switzerland

Tel. +41 61 683 77 34

Fax +41 61 302 89 18

www.mdpi.com

Religions Editorial Office

E-mail: religions@mdpi.com

www.mdpi.com/journal/religions